Korean Immigrants in America

Korean Immigrants in America

A Structural Analysis of Ethnic Confinement and Adhesive Adaptation

Won Moo Hurh and Kwang Chung Kim

Rutherford • Madison • Teaneck
Fairleigh Dickinson University Press
London and Toronto: Associated University Presses

© 1984 by Associated University Presses, Inc.

Associated University Presses
440 Forsgate Drive
Cranbury, NJ 08512

Associated University Presses
25 Sicilian Avenue
London WC1A 2QH, England

Associated University Presses
2133 Royal Windsor Drive
Unit 1
Mississauga, Ontario
Canada L5J 1K5

Library of Congress Cataloging in Publication Data

Hurh, Won Moo.
  Korean immigrants in America.

  Includes bibliographies and index.
  1. Korean Americans—Social conditions. 2. Korean Americans—Ethnic identity. 3. Adaptability (Psychology)
4. Korean Americans—Psychology. I. Kim, Kwang Chung, 1937- . II. Title.
E184.K6H88 1983   305.8'957073   82-48466
ISBN 0-8386-3145-2

Printed in the United States of America

*To our fellow Korean immigrants
and their posterity*

Contents

List of Figures	9
List of Tables	11
Foreword	15
Acknowledgments	19
Introduction: Theoretical Framework and Methodology	21
Chapter 1 A Historical Overview of Korean Immigration to the United States	39
2 New Korean Immigrants: Demographic Characteristics	53
3 Settlement Patterns: Residential Distribution and Mobility (Siyoung Park)	61
4 Acculturation: Adhesive Adaptation to American Culture	73
5 Social Relations: Ethnic Segregation and Confinement	87
6 Occupational Career: Containment in the Segregated Labor Market	101
7 Family Role Adjustment: Persistence and Change in the Traditional Role	122
8 Religious Participation: Ethnic Roles of the Korean Church	129
9 Life Satisfaction: Shrinking Aspirations and Contentment	138
Conclusion: Structural Roots of Ethnic Confinement and Adhesive Adaptation	157
Theoretical Propositions	171
Appendices: A. Qualitative Analysis of Interviewers' Comments	175
B. Methodological Problems in the Study of Korean Immigrants	184
C. Interview Schedule	201
D. Tables	209

References	241
Selected Bibliography on Korean-Americans	259
Name Index	273
Subject Index	277

List of Figures

Figure		Page
1.	Links between Limited Assimilation and Related Variables	26
2.	Major Variables Related to Immigrants' Adaptation	28
3.	Los Angeles Districts by Zip Codes	69
4.	Korean Households in Los Angeles 1972	70
5.	Korean Households in Los Angeles 1975	71
6.	Korean Households in Los Angeles 1979	72
7.	The Social Structure of Job Information Transmissions	108
8.	Length of Residence and Life Satisfaction: A Hypothetical Model	140
9.	Degree of Life Satisfaction in Relation to Length of Residence (Male, Female, and Male Professional)	145
10.	Relationships among Variables Related to Korean Immigrants' Life Satisfaction	153
11.	Types of Korean Immigrants Based on Adaptation Dimensions and Degrees	178

List of Tables

Table		Page
0.1	Adhesive Adaptation in Comparison to Other Modes of Ethnic Adaptation	210
1.1	Korean Immigration to the United States, 1903–1978	210
2.1	East Asian Immigrants by Country of Birth, 1965–1977	211
2.2	Socioeconomic Characteristics of Asian Americans, 1970	212
2.3	Respondents' Ages by Sex	213
2.4	Length of Residence in the United States	213
3.1	Rank Order of Korean-Concentrated Neighborhoods by Zip Code	214
3.2	Distribution of Korean Households in Southern California	214
4.1	Proficiency in English	215
4.2	Length of Residence in the United States, Current Age, Age at Immigration and Current Occupation of Respondents Classified by Levels of Education	215
4.3	English Proficiency by Length of Residence in the United States and Level of Education	216
4.4	Cultural Assimilation and Length of Residence in the United States	216
4.5	Ethnic Attachment and Length of Residence in the United States	217
4.6	Response to Statements on Ethnic Attachment by Length of Residence in the United States and Level of Education	217
4.7	Cultural Assimilation and Ethnic Attachment by Level of Education	218
4.8	Relationship Between Cultural Assimilation and Ethnic Attachment (I)	219
4.9	Relationship Between Cultural Assimilation and Ethnic Attachment (II)	219
4.10	English Proficiency by Three Items of Ethnic Attachment	220
5.1	Korean Friends	220
5.2	Non-Korean Friends	221

5.3	Association with White Friends and Participation in American Voluntary Association Among Three Groups of Respondents	221
5.4	Length of Residence in the United States and Association with White Friends and Participation in American Voluntary Associations	222
5.5	Length of Residence in the United States and Social Assimilation Among Three Groups of Respondents	223
5.6	Association with Korean Friends, Kin, and Participation in Korean Voluntary Associations Among Three Groups of Respondents	223
5.7	Length of Residence in the United States and Association with Korean Intimate Groups Among Male Respondents	224
5.8	Length of Residence in the United States and Association with Korean Intimate Groups Among Female Respondents	224
5.9	Presence of Kin in the Los Angeles Area, Association with Korean Friends, and Participation in Korean Voluntary Association	225
5.10	Social Assimilation in Relation to Association with Korean Friends, Kin, and Participation in Korean Voluntary Association	225
5.11	Distribution of the Persons with Whom Respondents Discuss Their Personal Problems	226
5.12	Types of Voluntary Association Participated	226
6.1	Current Occupations of Respondents	226
6.2	Methods of Job Information Transmission in Relation to Quality of Job Introduced	227
6.3	Distribution of Respondents by Occupation and Ethnicity of Major Work Colleagues or Customers	228
6.4	Distribution of Respondents by Occupation and Proportion of Those Who Work on Saturday or for More Than Eight Hours a Day	229
6.5	Distribution of Respondents by Their Annual Individual and Family Incomes	229
6.6	Distribution of Respondents by Occupation and Annual Individual Income	230
6.7	Multiple Classification Analysis of Annual Individual Income by Education, Ethnicity, Occupation, and Length of Residence in the United States (Employed Non-small Business Males)	230
6.8	Multiple Classification Analysis of Annual Individual Income by Ethnicity, Education, and Length of Residence in the United States (Men in Small Business)	231
6.9	Multiple Classification Analysis of Annual Individual Income by Occupation and Ethnicity (Employed Females)	231

List of Tables

6.10	Subjective Work Experience of Respondents	232
6.11	Occupation of Respondents and Their Subjective Work Experiences	232
6.12	Subjective Work Experiences Among Three Groups of Respondents	233
7.1	Distribution of Married Respondents' Families by Six Categories of Task Performance	233
7.2	Discrepancy Between Role Behavior and Role Expectation Among Family Members (Percentage)	234
7.3	Distribution of Respondents' Families with Children by Three Categories of Actual Performance (Role Behavior)	234
7.4	Distribution of Respondents' Families with Children by Three Categories of Expected Performance (Role Expectation)	235
8.1	Foremost Reasons for Attending Church	235
8.2	Ranked Reasons for Attending Church by Sex	236
8.3	Advantages and Disadvantages in Attending Church	236
8.4	Foremost Reasons for and Foremost Advantage in Attending Church (A Cross-Tabulation)	236
9.1	Economic Adaptation and Choice of Comparative Reference Group in Relation to Length of Residence in the United States	237
9.2	Factor Analysis of Six Life-Experience Items by Varimax Rotation	237
9.3	Degree of Job Satisfaction and Score of Life Satisfaction	237
9.4	Life Satisfaction Scores of Respondents in Relation to Length of Residence	238
9.5	Life Satisfaction Scores of Male Professionals and Semi-professionals in Relation to Length of Residence	238
9.6	Differential Effects of Dominant Group as Reference Group on Minority's Life Satisfaction	239
9.7	Variables Related to Relatively High Degree of Life Satisfaction of Respondents	239

Foreword

The Korean immigrants are among the "new" peoples of Asia to grace American society. New to America—about two-thirds of the present Korean population of the United States arrived after 1970—the Koreans are an ancient people with a long history and a highly developed culture. Yet, Korea itself has been propelled into the twentieth century, first by the long and largely oppressive Japanese occupation, then by the war that brought thousands of American troops to fight in the peninsular civil war, and presently by its "economic miracle" of rapid industrialization. As a result, Korea has emerged from its nineteenth-century status as a "hermit kingdom" to become an important, if politically divided, industrial and military power in Northeast Asia. Emigration to the United States from Korea reflects these changes. Korea is no longer an isolated peninsular pawn, standing between Russia, China, and Japan, exporting a surplus population of unskilled and agricultural labor. The new Korean immigrants are of the middle classes—owners of small businesses, managers, white-collar workers, or semi-professionals. As Professors Hurh and Kim, the authors of this book, so carefully point out, one-fourth of the current number of Koreans in the United States are semiskilled or unskilled workers. But even these can be readily differentiated from the first boatload of 101 Koreans who arrived in Honolulu on January 13, 1903, to work the sugar and pineapple plantations. The Koreans who have come to the United States in the past three decades are modern men and women, whose fate is inextricably intertwined with that of the polyglot peoples of America in the coming years.

The authors emphasize the "adhesion" that characterizes the acculturative process among these Koreans who are able to graft elements of the mainstream American way of life onto their own transplanted customs and manners without suffering from either debilitating cognitive dissonance or painful loss of familiar folkways. The relative ease with which the Korean immigrants have carried this "adhesion" off has been facilitated in part by the subtle but widespread forms of social distancing practiced in America. Although a considerable number of Koreans work in racially mixed settings, or, if in small business, have regular commercial contact with Caucasian and black, as well as Chinese- and Japanese-American customers, the relationships thus established are confined to the workplace and remain largely secondary, if not formal. At home, among family, friends, recreational colleagues, and religious congregants, the Korean ethnic circle is drawn tightly. In the United States both integration and congregation are practiced by the same people at different times of the day and night. The line separating these two social forms tends to be drawn at the institutions of intimate contact. Under such a condition a new people like the Koreans, a great many of whom enjoy a modest membership in the lower echelons of the middle class, can still maintain their traditional language and reinforce their homeland domestic practices.

Visitors to New York in recent years have commented on the proliferation of retail fruit and vegetable shops owned and operated by Koreans. Some have also noticed the Korean wigseller, his racks of carefully coiffed women's hairpieces displayed along Fourteenth Street from Broadway to the Avenue of the Americas. Although most are pleased by the neat rows of highly polished apples, oranges, peaches, plums, nectarines, grapes, and melons displayed in the Korean-owned markets, or by the concern shown in wig design to meet current American (and especially black American) female styles, few realize that these retail outlets are represented by Korean American marketing associations that, in the case of the fruit sellers, protect their members against independent upstarts, and, in the case of the wigsellers, organize the entire business from the original sale of Korean farm women's hair in the homeland, through the cleaning and styling process, the trans-Pacific marketing, and ultimately to the sale to the retailer. Modern business methods have become part and parcel of this new immigration.

Koreans have been spared a specially demeaning pejorative term of reference such as has been applied to Chinese ("Chink," "Chinaman"), Japanese ("Jap"), Jews ("Kike," "Sheeny"), Irish ("Mick"), Italians ("Wop"), Hungarians ("Hunky"), Germans ("Kraut"), or Blacks ("Nigger"). Apparently, because they are few in number and tend to be confused by many Americans with Japanese and Chinese the Koreans have thus far failed to elicit a unique ethnophaulism. The more recent racist epithet "Gook" appears to have been applied by American GIs to Koreans, Chinese, and Vietnamese without distinction, and the World War II term, "Slopey," seems to have been confined to Chinese. The absence of a particular racist designation, however, does not indicate the absence of prejudice against Koreans. Rather, it reflects the status of the Koreans and the fact that among educated, middle-class Caucasian Americans prejudices are generally expressed more subtly and without terms of abuse. The authors point to the information and communication barriers that, *inter alia*, keep Koreans from finding out about better job opportunities, and to the general practice of intraethnic commensalism as evidences of these more subtle practices. The American Dilemma has not been resolved; for the Korean immigrants it has taken on more sophisticated styles and mannerisms.

What is the future of the Koreans in the United States? Professors Hurh and Kim rightly are cautious about making definite predictions. In part, the future of the Koreans is governed by relations between Korea and the United States. Despite acculturation, other immigrant peoples the Jews, Irish, Germans, Italians, Chinese, and—most disastrously—Japanese, have discovered that their real or imagined identification with a country of origin has its effects in the United States, especially in times of national crisis. It is doubtful that the Koreans or any other people will experience wholesale incarceration as happened to the Japanese-Americans during World War II—despite the fact that 65 percent of the latter were American-born citizens of the United States. Nevertheless, that event cannot help but loom large in the minds of any Asian people in America. Perhaps, more realistically, we should wonder about the second and third generations of the current Korean immigrants. Unlike the first eight decades of Chinese immigration to America, the recent Korean arrivals include women, making possible the birth and rearing of Korean-Americans and, perhaps in two generations, American-Koreans. Will these future Americans continue the "adhesive" process, or will they, as seems more likely, sort out their heritages in new and yet-to-be-conceptually formulated ways? Professors Hurh and Kim have made some tantalizing suggestions about this matter. These issues, however, are the proper subject of future sociological studies. For the present, and for these future studies, this comprehensive survey and interpretation provides the basic foundation.

Kyoto, Japan
September 1981

Stanford M. Lyman
Fulbright Lecturer
Doshisha University
Ryukoku University

Department of Sociology
Graduate Faculty
New School for Social Research
New York City

Acknowledgments

When in Rome, learn the Roman's ways but keep your roots. Is this a new universal maxim? It seems it is—at least for the new Korean immigrants in the United States. This book is about their adaptation patterns as epitomized in this maxim. In this nation of immigrants, more than one-third of a million Koreans are striving toward the creation of the Korean-American ethnicity—a community and identity that is new to both Koreans and Americans.

This new immigrant group from Korea is struggling to become another chapter of the history of American pluralism. As Korean immigrants ourselves, we are privileged to partake in their historical endeavor through this research. In this sense, we have been participant observers of the group, although most of our empirical data for this study are derived from interviews with the immigrants.

In many ways, this book is a product of collective effort. Most of all, we would like to express our special gratitude to the U.S. Department of Health and Human Services (formerly Health, Education and Welfare) for the grant (1 R01 MH 30475-01 and 5 R01 MH 30475-02) without which this research would have been impossible.

We also wish to thank our respondents and interviewers, especially in the Los Angeles area, for their time, effort, and cooperation. We would like to recognize our interviewers individually; Sylvia Y. Byun, Chunghi Cho, Chunghee Choe, Soonie Choe, Ae Mun Kim, Dong Chul Kim, Insook C. Kim, Joo Young Kim, Mikyung Kim, Myung Soon Kim, Young Mee Kim, Henry La, Kyung Soon Lim, Chanho Park, Young Sun Park, Suck Zin Rhee, Myoung Ok Roh, and Jim-Young Son. Especially, we would like to express our deep appreciation to Mr. Dong Chul Kim who worked as the field supervisor of our interviewers.

Our sincere thanks are due to the members of the site-visit team, National Institute of Mental Health, Drs. Rodney M. Coe, Herbert H. Coburn, William T. Liu, and Russell G. Thornton, for their valuable suggestions at the early stage of our research proposal. Dr. Coburn's most efficient and cordial help as the chief of the Social Problem Section in the Applied Research Branch of NIMH is particularly deeply appreciated.

We are also deeply indebted to Dr. Eui-Young Yu, chairman and professor of Sociology at the California State University in Los Angeles, and Dr. Hwasoo Lee, the former director of the Korean Mental Health Service Center in Los Angeles, for their most efficient consultation and help throughout our research project in the Los Angeles area. We are also grateful to Dr. Siyoung Park, assistant professor of Geography at Western Illinois University, who contributed a chapter on residential mobility of Korean immigrants to this book.

The generous assistance from Mr. Myron P. Mustaine and Mrs. Shirley J. Myers of the Research Office, Mrs. Ava Nell Hawkins of the Business Office, and Mrs. Nina D. Houlton of Printing Services, Western Illinois University, made the efficient management of our grant possible.

Our cordial thanks are due to Drs. Igolima T. D. Amachree and Richard T. Schaefer, who have always encouraged our research and helped us in various ways as chairmen of the Sociology and Anthropology Department, Western Illinois University. We also thank Miss Carol A. Skiles for her most efficient typing of our final manuscript. Often we forget those persons who are close to us and did editorial corrections and proofreading. We thank Gloria Hurh and Shin Kim for their help and patience.

The late Dr. Hei Chu Kim was also involved in our project as a co-investigator at the initial stage of research. We are perpetually indebted to his valuable contribution to this study. We also acknowledge support for this book from the Research Training Program on Institutional Racism at the University of Illinois in which Kwang Chung Kim has been a participant.

Macomb, Illinois
January 1982
The centennial year of
the Korean-American Treaty

Won Moo Hurh
Kwang Chung Kim

Introduction: Theoretical Framework and Methodology

Koreans are one of the most rapidly increasing immigrant groups in the United States. The 1970 Census found about 70,000 Korean residents in the United States, but since then the number has risen very rapidly, with approximately 30,000 Koreans being admitted into the country annually. A Korean demographer estimated the total number of Koreans in the United States in 1976 as about 290,000 (Yu, 1977:123). According to the 1980 U.S. Census, 354,529 Koreans were living in the United States (U.S. Department of Commerce, 1981). This dramatic population increase is mainly a result of the revised U.S. immigration law (P.L. 89-236 of 1965), which has had similar results among other Asians.

These new immigrants from Korea are geographically more dispersed than other recent Asian immigrants, but a substantial majority of them are concentrated in metropolitan areas, such as Los Angeles, New York, Chicago, San Francisco, and Washington, D.C. The heaviest concentration of Koreans has occurred in the Los Angeles area where the estimates of the Korean population vary between 65,000 and 150,000.[1] Until the early 1970s, the Koreans were thus an "invisible minority" in the United States; however, the rapidly increasing number of the new Korean immigrants and their socioeconomic and geographic mobilities have already affected the fabric of interethnic relations in the major metropolitan areas in the United States. For instance, the emergence of "Koreatowns" in Los Angeles (Olympic Bouleavard and the 8th Street), New York (Lower Manhattan and Flushing), and in Chicago (North Clark and Lawrence streets) seem to represent a new pattern of ecological succession and also possibly a new case of "middle-man minority."

In sharp contrast to the early Korean immigrants (mostly single males) who reached the Hawaiian shores during the period

1903–1905 and intended to stay to provide temporary labor, the new Korean immigrants arrive at American airports with their families and relatives for permanent settlement. Unlike their uneducated predecessors, the new immigrants from Korea are highly educated; they are the most highly educated immigrant group in the American immigrant history. Approximately two-thirds of the Korean adult immigrants have received four years of college education or more, and most of them held white-collar occupations in Korea prior to their emigration.

Unfortunately, very little sociological research has been done on the Koreans in America, although the first wave of Korean immigrants arrived in Honolulu in 1903. A number of empirical studies recently have been carried out on the new Korean immigrants,[2] but these studies are still in the exploratory stage in comparison with the extensive studies already available on the Chinese- and Japanese-Americans. This lack of research on Korean-Americans is mainly the result of their small number, but it may also derive from the Americans' general ignorance about Koreans as a distinct ethnic group differing significantly from the Chinese and Japanese (Hurh and Kim, 1982).

American diplomatic and trade relations with Korea began as early as 1882 with the Korean-American Treaty of Chemulpo. In 1945, the American armed forces liberated Korea from Japanese colonial rule, and subsequently more than thirty-three thousand American soldiers died on Korean soil during the Korean War (1950–53). American troops remain in Korea even to this day. Despite this close contact with Korea during the past thirty-five years, many Americans seem to know very little about the Korean people and their culture; some Americans even confuse Koreans with Vietnamese. Among those Americans who have some knowledge about Korea, this knowledge is often either partial or negative, such as the hardships of the Korean War, the problems of underdevelopment, the struggle with communism, and the corruption of Koreagate (Jo and Nahm, 1979). Given the fact that the American people rank the Koreans lowest or very close to the lowest among all ethnic groups in the United States in the social distance scale over the past fifty years, the Koreans must have certainly been either least known or most disliked by the Americans (Bogardus, 1968; cf. Hurh, 1977a). Ignorance or unfamiliarity between Americans and Koreans seems to be, in a way, mutual. The Korean immigrants are more handicapped than some other Asian immigrants from the Philippines, Hong Kong, India, and Pakistan in terms of their unfamiliarity with the Western culture in general and in the use of English in particular, largely because Korea's contact with the Western countries has been relatively recent.

Introduction: Theoretical Framework and Methodology   23

In light of this situation, one may wonder about adaptation patterns and problems of this new immigrant group in comparison to those of other immigrant groups, especially of the Chinese and Japanese. According to Lyman (1977:119-30), Chinese immigrants in the United States have shown stronger ethnic attachment to Old World values,[3] and they are thus more socially isolated from the host society than their Japanese counterparts. Lyman explicates his observations by identifying factors that may constitute such differences: political conditions of sending countries, the immigrants' marital and job statuses, ecological settlement patterns, and modes of ethnic organizations. Would the new immigrants from Korea follow more or less the adaptation pattern of Chinese-Americans or that of Japanese-Americans? Or neither?

For the purpose of our study, the following research inquiries are formulated: (1) What are the general patterns of cultural and socioeconomic adaptation of Korean immigrants in comparison with those of other immigrants in the United States?[4] (2) What are the major problems the Korean immigrants face in their adaptation process? (3) What are the possible sources and consequences of such adaptation patterns and problems? (4) Derived from the answers to these inquiries, would any new theoretical paradigm and practical implications emerge toward solving ethnic community problems in the United States?

The main purpose of this books is to answer these questions based on our empirical and theoretical research on the Korean immigrants that we have carried out during the past several years. Since 1975, we have conducted four major field studies on the Korean immigrants in the United States. Our first pilot study which dealt with the cultural and social adjustment patterns of Korean immigrants in the Chicago area, was funded by a small grant from the National Institute of Mental Health, U.S. Department of Health, Education and Welfare in 1975-76 (Hurh, Kim, and Kim, 1978). As an exploratory research, the study described and analyzed the general patterns of sociocultural adjustment of the immigrants in relation to their demographic and socioeconomic variables. A series of hypotheses were also tested for generating theoretical implications.

Our second and third studies, supported by the Research Council, Western Illinois University in 1977-79, were also conducted in the Chicago area but on more specific dimensions of the immigrant's adaptation—their occupational career, family role adjustment, and religious involvement (Kim, Kim, and Hurh, 1978, 1979, and 1981; Kim, Hurh, and Kim, 1978; Kim and Hurh, 1980c).

Our most recent research examined various patterns and

problems of Korean immigrants' adaptation in the Los Angeles area and was funded by a two-year grant from the NIMH, U.S. Department of Health, Education and Welfare. This study was our largest and most intensive research project and probably the first comprehensive *sociological* study on the Korean immigrants in the United States. The Los Angeles project was, in a way, the culminating point of our Korean immigrant studies since it covered almost all major aspects of the immigrants' adaptation, such as demographic characteristics, cultural adaptation and ethnic attachment, social networks and interpersonal relations, occupational and career adjustment, family role adjustment, religious participation, life satisfaction, and problem areas (Hurh and Kim, 1979b; 1980a). More importantly, the study tested several new hypotheses derived from the findings of our previous studies in the Chicago area and cross-analyzed major significant variables for theoretical, methodological, and practical implications.

This book draws heavily upon the findings from our last project. After discussing the theoretical framework and methodology, we begin by a historical overview of the Korean immigrants in the United States in order to understand the new immigrants from a historical perspective. Next, the new immigrants' demographic and socioeconomic backgrounds are analyzed in comparison with their predecessors and also with their Filipino, Chinese, and Japanese counterparts. In the third chapter, the immigrants' settlement patterns are examined in terms of their residential mobility in the Los Angeles area. The residential distribution of Korean households for 1972, 1975, and 1979 is compared in order to describe the changes in the residential mobility of Koreans and to analyze their geographic adaptation patterns, such as concentration, streaming, and scattering ecological processes. The fourth and fifth chapters examine the immigrants' general patterns of cultural and social adaptation in the United States. Their particular mode of adaptation—adhesive adaptation[5]—receives a highly intrusive theoretical analysis. Closely related to these areas of investigation, the occupational career of the immigrants is investigated in light of the job information deprivation, labor market segmentation, and human capital theories in the sixth chapter. Our pivotal concern is the effect of ethnic confinement and adhesive adaptation on the economic life of the immigrants. In addition to sociocultural and economic adaptation, two other adaptation dimensions—family role adjustment and religious participation—are examined in the seventh and eighth chapters. Chapter 7 focuses particularly on the division of household tasks in the immigrant families as they reflect the changing and per-

Introduction: Theoretical Framework and Methodology 25

sisting aspects of the traditional family role. Chapter 8 describes and analyzes the behavioral and motivational patterns of the immigrants' church participation in order to examine major functions of the Korean ethnic church, particularly in the context of adhesive adaptation. The last chapter explores the subjective dimension of the immigrants' adaptation; that is, their perception of general life satisfaction. All major variables related to the degree of life satisfaction are cross-analyzed for possible inferences. To conclude the book, the structural roots of ethnic confinement of the Korean immigrants are delienated and relevant theoretical propositions are advanced for the future study of nonwhite immigrants in the United States in general.

Theoretical Framework

Because of the lack of a comprehensive theory dealing particularly with the Korean immigrants' adaptation in the United States, this book draws its theoretical framework mainly on the general theory of assimilation advanced by Gordon (1964); the classic work on adaptation of immigrants in Israel by Eisenstadt (1951, 1954b); and recent empirical and theoretical studies on the American pluralism by Glazer and Moynihan (1963), Greeley (1971), and Newman (1973). In addition, Doeringer and Piore's (1971) seminal work on the labor market segmentation is the basis for our occupational analyses of the immigrants. For a comparative perspective, references are also made to other Asian minority studies (e.g., Petersen, 1971; Lyman, 1974; Kitano, 1976; Bok-Lim Kim, 1978c; cf. Hurh, 1977a).

The mainspring of our theoretical framework is the distinction between acculturation and social assimilation, noted by Park and Burgess as early as in 1924 and explicated by Gordon in 1964. According to Gordon, acculturation ("cultural assimilation" in Gordon's terms) refers to the change of immigrants' cultural patterns to those of the host society, whereas social assimilation ("structural assimilation") refers to the large-scale entrance into cliques, clubs, and institutions of the host society on the primary group level (1964:71). Unlike acculturation, social assimilation thus requires acceptance of the immigrant group by the dominant group (cf. Spiro, 1955; Teske and Nelson, 1974). Gordon also argues that whereas acculturation of racial and ethnic minorities has taken place to a considerable degree in the United States, their social assimilation has not been extensive (cf. Rosenthal, 1960). This has been true for all ethnic minorities including the Jewish-Americans, but more so for the nonwhite minorities (cf.

Kitano, 1976). The persisting pattern of racial endogamy and social distance on the primary group level attests to this fact (cf. Simpson and Yinger, 1972; Bogardus, 1968; Hurh, 1977a).

Gordon and others suggest a proposition that acculturation is a necessary but not sufficient condition for social assimilation. Even high socioeconomic status of immigrants is not necessarily related to social assimilation (Weinstock, 1963; Hurh, Kim, and Kim, 1978). The following diagram illustrates the links between the limited assimilation (acculturation without assimilation) and related variables.

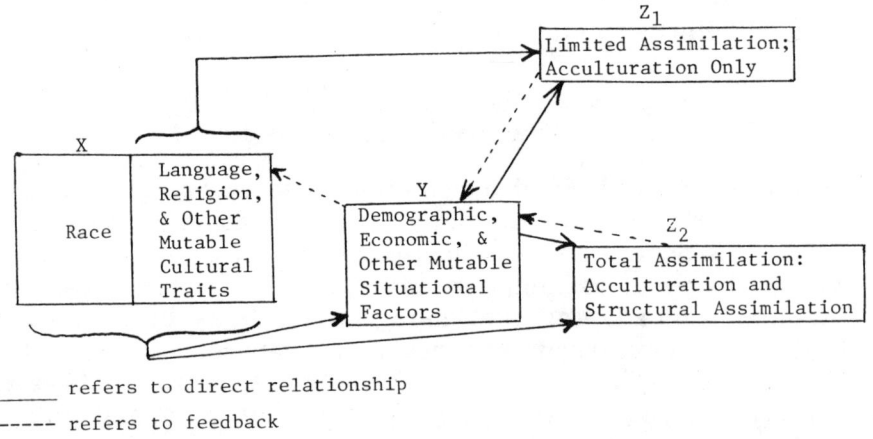

Figure 1. Links Between Limited Assimilation and Related Variables

In Figure 1, it is apparent that as long as the block of independent variables (X) contains an immutable factor, "race," there emerge two different patterns of dependent variables (Z_1 and Z_2), which are mediated by a common block of intervening variables (Y). When "race" becomes mutable through extensive miscegenation or loses its symbolic significance by cognitive change, the "culture-only" type of adaptation (Z_1) may also disappear. Then, the degree of acculturation *and* social assimilation (Z_2) will entirely be determined by the socioeconomic system and situational contingencies. In short, such mutable factors as demographic, economic, political, and other related variables may effect the degree of acculturation of nonwhite immigrants, but exert little influence on social assimilation (Hurh, 1977a).

These theoretical considerations suggest that the Korean immigrants would be structurally separated or ethnically confined from the larger society, regardless of their acculturation, socioeconomic status, and length of stay in the United States. The immigrants' perception of such structural limitations would also

Introduction: Theoretical Framework and Methodology

limit their aspirations for social acceptance by the dominant group, and as a defense, the immigrants may feel they must maintain or even enhance their ethnic attachment for sustaining their sense of security, primary-group satisfaction, social recognition, and identity. In other words, the immigrants' strong and persisting ethnic attachment may largely be a function of involuntary factors, such as ethnic segregation inherent in the American social structure, limited adaptive capacities of the immigrants, and economic and ecological conditions of the host society at a particular time. Yuan's study (1963) on the involuntary factors involved in voluntary segregation of the Chinese community in New York is a good example.

In light of this conjecture, the mode of Korean immigrants' adaptation would be generally adhesive; that is, they would be Americanized both culturally and socially, but to a limited extent (especially in social dimension), and such Americanization would not replace or weaken any significant aspect of Korean traditional culture and social networks. If this is true, the Korean immigrants' adhesive mode of adaptation would be far from a zero-sum model of assimilation (ethnic detachment and Anglo-conformity) but a variant of pluralistic mode of ethnic adaptation. An "ideal" pluralistic mode of adaptation would have to include a full acceptance of cultural and social dimensions of their native and new countries. As a particular form of pluralism, adhesive adaptation is thus different from other types of intergroup adaptation, such as assimilation, separatism, and pluralism. Table 0.1 shows the difference in terms of ethnic attachment and Americanization patterns.

As a variant of pluralism, one may consider that adhesive adaptation would be a transitory stage toward the ideal pluralism or a kind of temporary accommodation. The term "accommodative pluralism" was coined by Kurokawa to mean a particular mode of minority response that occurs "when minority members who are discriminated against accept their segregated role while attempting to integrate whenever possible" (Kurokawa, 1970:133). Kurokawa cites the pattern of Japanese-Americans' adaptation as an example of such accommodative pluralism. Regardless of its modal transiency and conceptual ambiguity, adhesive adaptation remains as a distinctive analytical category so long as the immigrants maintain strong ethnic attachment and achieve only a limited degree of Americanization.

Our theoretical contention and analytical framework may thus be illustrated by the relationships among major variables (structural, situational, and psychological) related to the mode of immigrants' adaptation (see Figure 2).

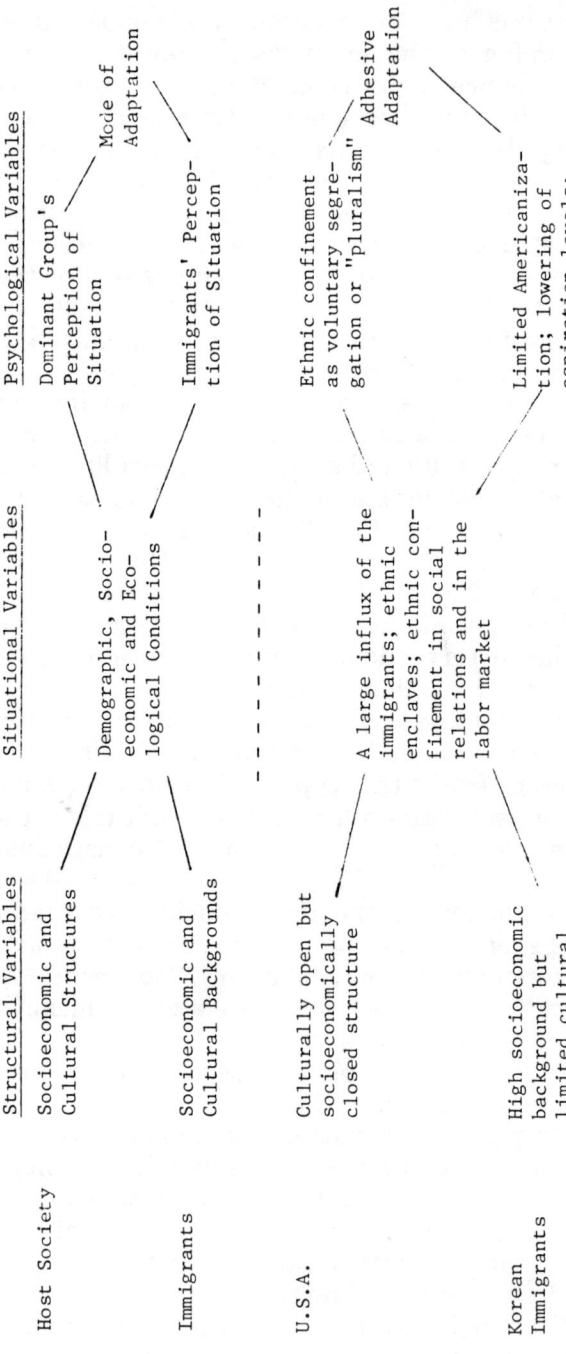

Figure 2. Major Variables Related to Immigrants' Adaptation

Introduction: Theoretical Framework and Methodology   29

As indicated in the upper portion of Figure 2, mode of adaptation depends on the following variables in general (cf. Eisenstadt, 1951; Wagley and Harris, 1958:264; Yancey, Ericksen, and Juliani, 1976):
1. Structural Variables
   (a) Socioeconomic Structure and Value Systems of the Host Society—the degree of openness in the socioeconomic structure and value systems of the host society for absorbing immigrants into its mainstream.
   (b) Socioeconomic and Cultural Backgrounds of Immigrants—the extent of immigrants' educational, occupational, and linguistic capacities including their cultural heritage for competing effectively with the dominant group.
2. Situational Variables
   Demographic, socioeconomic, and ecological conditions of the immigrant community in relation to those of the dominant group and other minorities at a particular time.
3. Psychological Variables
   (a) The extent of the dominant group's perception of the immigrants' intergroup relations (e.g., economic competition, political expediency, humanitarian concerns, etc.).
   (b) The extent of immigrants' perception of the host society's structural conditions, their own adaptive capacities, social acceptance by the dominant group, and willingness to participate in the mainstream of the host culture and society.

The relationship between variables particularly related to the Korean immigrants' adhesive adaptation are illustrated in the lower portion of Figure 2, which does not require further explication. In light of this analytical framework—ethnic confinement and adhesive adaptation—we examine not only various patterns and sources of Korean immigrants' adaptation in the United States but also some of their possible consequences.

Methodology

In an attempt to go beyond the testing of hypotheses and to advance new theoretical propositions, the method employed in this book is both deductive and inductive. In other words, this book is a cumulated result of a series of reciprocal interactions between theories and empirical findings through "probative research" (Merton, 1964:100). Except for the first pilot study in

Chicago, all of our subsequent studies did not follow the unidirectional standard research procedure—from theory to hypotheses, to observation, and to verification of hypotheses. For recasting or refocusing of existing theories, our research sequence was often reversed or rather traversed whenever serendipitous empirical findings emerged (Merton, 1964:103–117).

Our methodology is thus oriented toward developing what Merton calls "theories of the middle range"—intermediate theories applicable to limited ranges of data between minor working hypotheses and all-embracing grandiose theories (Merton, 1964:5–10). For instance, our theoretical conceptualization of adhesive adaptation applies generally to nonwhite immigrants in the United States, and is intermediate to working hypotheses focused on Korean immigrants' adjustment problems and Gordon's general theory of assimilation.

To this end, constant dialogues between theoretical and empirical inquiries were facilitated by analyzing each dimension of the Korean immigrants' adaptation in light of existing theories (review of literature), secondary data (documents), and primary data (interviews). Because of the paucity of literature and secondary data on Korean immigrants, as noted earlier, we rely heavily upon our primary data collected mainly through intensive interviews with the immigrants. The data for our first pilot study were obtained by interviewing 283 persons randomly selected from the first-generation Korean immigrants in the Chicago area in 1975–76 (Hurh, Kim, and Kim, 1978). For our second study, we interviewed a sample of 140 Korean immigrants who were affiliated with four different Korean ethnic churches in the Chicago area (Kim, Kim, and Hurh, 1979; Kim, Hurh, and Kim, 1978; Kim, Kim, and Hurh, 1981). The third study was also based on interviews—a sample of 116 Korean blue-collar workers in various plants in the Chicago area (Kim and Hurh, 1980c). Our most recent study in the Los Angeles area, upon which this books is primarily based, again employed the interview method. We discuss in detail the method used for the collection of data in the Los Angeles study as a typical example of our research procedure and methodological problems.

Our original plan was to draw a sample of 500 persons from the first-generation Korean immigrants in the Los Angeles area and an additional sample of 100 Korean immigrants in the same category but who have resided in the United States more than ten years. The sampling of the second group was designed to ensure inclusion of a sufficient number of "old settlers" in our research. However, we changed our original plan and decided to select 600 persons from the universe of the first-generation adult Korean

Introduction: Theoretical Framework and Methodology 31

immigrants without regard to the length of their sojourn in the United States.[6] Eventually, we interviewed 622 persons, including a sufficient number of old settlers (98).

Our sampling was based on *The Korean Directory of Southern California, 1979*, which lists names, addresses, and telephone numbers of 25,112 Korean residents in southern California. From this directory, we selected our target population, who reside in Los Angeles and Orange counties; we identified them by the zip code numbers of their addresses. The directory often included more than one person for each household, and we sorted out one person for each household (or family) by identifying the same telephone numbers in the directory. Although this was not a perfect method, it served the purpose of generally identifying households well with only a few exceptional cases. By these procedures, we eventually obtained the names, addresses, and telephone numbers of 8,732 persons.[7]

In February 1979, we made an announcement of our research project through two major Korean newspapers in the Los Angeles area, *Joong-ang Ilbo* and *Hankuk Ilbo*. In March and April, letters were sent out to 1,100 persons who were randomly selected from the 8,732 persons. The letter sent to these individuals explained the purpose of our research, the position of the investigators, the sponsoring organization, assurance of anonymity, and proposed payment of ten dollars to the respondents. Enclosed were a photocopy of a newspaper announcement of our research project (*Joong-Ang Ilbo*, February 9, 1979) and a postcard with a return address stamped on it. Our prospective respondents were requested to indicate the names, ages, and sex of their adult family members (20 years old or more) on the postcard and to return the completed postcard to our research office in Los Angeles.

The overdrawing of the sample was done in expectation of a high rate of refusal and unreachable respondents. As expected, a small number of persons returned the filled-out postcards (161 persons). Through telephone calls, we made contact with 306 cooperative persons who had received our letter, but failed to return the postcard. Subsequently, we interviewed either these two categories of persons or their adult family members selected by the procedure that is explained later. Among others who had received our letter, 293 persons refused to be interviewed either from the beginning of our telephone contact or later when they were contacted again by our interviewers. Because of incorrect addresses or telephone numbers, 340 persons could not be reached.

Because of our failure to interview 600 adult Koreans by this method, we randomly selected an additional 375 persons from the directory and attempted to make direct telephone calls without mailing letters. Through this contact, we found 155 cooperative persons and we interviewed either them or their adult family members.

The Korean Directory of Southern California, 1979 did not provide complete information on all adult members in each immigrant family. Individual immigrants were, however, our target sample population. In order to select individual immigrants randomly from such an incomplete listing, we used Leslie Kish's table for selecting one adult from each dwelling (1965:398–401). Kish's table allows a proper fractional representation of each adult on the basis of number of adult members in each family or dwelling, their sex, and their ages. As already mentioned, we obtained the necessary information of adult members of immigrant families from the returned postcards or our telephone conversations with prospective respondents.

As Kish observed, we noticed that a majority of families (394, 64%) in our sample had two adult members who were usually husband and wife. From such families, the selection of a prospective respondent was, therefore, usually a matter of choosing either the husband or the wife. About one-fourth of the families had either only one adult (10%) or three adult members (14%).

A total of 622 persons were finally interviewed, but 7 of them were inadequately included and hence dropped from our data analysis. The total sample population for the Los Angeles study was, therefore, 615—281 males (45.7%) and 334 females (54.3%). The sex ratio of our sample roughly corresponded to the actual sex ratio of the Korean adult residents in the Los Angeles area (Yu, 1979a).

Prior to the main interviews, forty Korean immigrants were interviewed by six trained interviewers during the last two weeks of February, 1979 for pretesting. After meeting with our pretest interviewers, we analyzed the pretest results with our consultants, and the interview schedule was finalized and printed in Korean.

Our interview schedule consisted of sixty-two structured questionnaire items including ten open-ended questions. The questionnaire items were designed to collect both quantitative and qualitative data in order to (1) describe various patterns of Korean immigrants' adaptation, and (2) test specific hypotheses for theoretical implications of our findings (see Appendix C for the interview schedule).

The main interviews were conducted by eighteen interviewers from April to June 1979. Most of the interviewers were graduate or undergraduate students of universities in the Los Angeles area.

Introduction: Theoretical Framework and Methodology 33

Five staff members of the Korean American Mental Health Service Center were also included in the interview team. Interviewers' training sessions were held in March and two additional discussion sessions took place—an interim check of interviewers and a postinterview meeting.

Each interviewer was given the names, addresses, and telephone numbers of the persons who had been selected by Kish's method. It was the responsibility of the interviewer to make appointments with prospective respondents for interviews. Our field coordinator and interviewers, however, found that telephone numbers of our prospective respondents obtained from *The Korean Directory of Southern California, 1979* were often incorrect. There were additional problems. Some prospective respondents changed their mind after setting appointments and refused to be interviewed or became evasive and uncooperative. Interviewing such respondents required a considerable amount of skill and patience on the part of our interviewers.

The preceding discussion shows that our sampling procedure failed to include the following types of prospective respondents: (1) those who were not listed in *The Korean Directory of Southern California, 1979*, (2) those who were included in our original sample, but could not be reached because of incorrect addresses, and (3) those who refused our interview requests.

We have already discussed the types of persons who would not likely be listed in the Directory (see note 7). The immigrants with incorrect addresses appeared to be those who were struggling hard under unstable life conditions or were in certain mobile status categories such as students or young singles.

It is difficult to classify those who refused our interview requests into definitive categories. Generally, the highest refusal rates were found among young males, the lowest rates among older females, and others in between. It is even more difficult to speculate on the motivation of those who refused our interview requests. Some indirect clues, however, came from twenty-two respondents who had originally refused our interview request, but reversed their mind by repeated telephone calls of our interviewers. They indicated the following three major reasons for their initial refusal: suspicion of the investigators' status or motives, physical exhaustion, and irregular work schedules. Some suspected that the investigators might be Communist spies or sympathizers conducting research under a disguised identity. Others indicated that they were too tired after they had worked for long hours and did not want to be bothered by an interview. A few of them mentioned that they had irregular daily schedules since they worked at night. Under these circumstances, they were reluctant to be interviewed.

In sum, the following types of Korean immigrants appear to have been excluded from our sample: (1) those who have lost contact with the Korean community because of their unusual status (e.g., war brides, children adopted by American families), (2) those who were under unstable life conditions in the United States, (3) those who had irregular work schedules and physical exhaustion, and (4) those who were so self-defensive that they were highly reluctant to disclose some aspects of their lives to others. These probable exclusions set the limitation for our study.

To conclude our methodology section, a few words about the setting of the actual interview are in order, such as place, time, and length of the interview. Most of our respondents were interviewed at their homes (443, 75%). More female respondents (257, 79%) are found to be interviewed at home than male respondents (186, 67%). One-tenth (86, 14%) were interviewed at their workplace—office, store, and the like. Others were interviewed at various places such as a coffee shop or restaurant (24, 4%), church (13, 2%), school (10, 2%), office of the interviewer (usually the Korean American Mental Health Service Center—12, 2%), and so on. Nearly half of the female respondents (138, 43%) were interviewed in the afternoon, whereas the same proportion of the male respondents (116, 43%) were interviewed in the evening. As a whole, three-fourths of the respondents (452, 76%) were interviewed either in the afternoon or in the evening. Nearly one-fifth of the respondents (104, 17%) were interviewed in the morning, and a small proportion (39, 7%) were interviewed during the lunch hour.

On the average, our interviews took one-and-one-half hours. Some extreme cases ranged from under an hour to over three hours. When the interview was exceptionally long, it was because of one of the following reasons: the interviewer's explanation of the interview questions to the respondents who did not understand them, or the interviewer's listening to the respondents talk on his or her personal experiences beyond the formal interview. It was not uncommon that our interviewers were invited by their respondents to a dinner or lunch either at the respondents' homes or a restaurant after the interview. Interviewing of fellow immigrants, therefore, often opened a channel of emotional catharsis for both the interviewer and the respondent.

More details on the interview setting, the latent functions of interviewing, and other methodological problems in the study of non-Western minorities in general and the recent Korean immigrants in particular are discussed in Appendices A and B.

Notes

1. The lower side of the estimation is from demographic estimates (Yu, 1979a and Lee and Wagatsuma, 1979) and the higher side is from a local newspaper account (*The Joongang Daily News*, January 1, 1980).
2. See selected bibliography on Korean-Americans at the end of this book.
3. *Ethnic attachment* refers here to the individual immigrant's subjective identification with a particular ethnic group and maintenance of intimate social ties with members of his or her ethnic group (cf. Greenstone, 1975).
4. For the purpose of our study, *adaptation* is defined as the process in which immigrants modify their attitudinal and behavioral patterns in order to maintain and improve their life conditions compatible with the new environment (cf. Eisenstadt, 1952:225; Honigmann, 1964; Cohen, 1974:3).
5. The term *adhesive adaptation* used in this book refers to a particular mode of adaptation in which certain aspects of the new culture and social relations with members of the host society are added on to the immigrants' traditional culture and social networks, without replacing or modifying any significant part of the old. The term has very little to do (if any) with Tylor's concept of "adhesion," which refers to "the tendency for traits to be associated in diffusion, so that where one trait of a complex is present, the other trait would able be present" (Winick, 1964:5; Tylor, 1889). Details on the theoretical conceptualization of adhesive adaptation are elaborated later.
6. Dr. Eui Young Yu, our demographic consultant, advised us that such a separate sampling strategy was not necessary since a sufficient number of "old-timers" would be included by random procedure. We are thankful for his advice.
7. Limitations of using *The Korean Directory of Southern California, 1979* as a sample base should be recognized. It is compiled by a commercial firm, and "many have systematically omitted those Koreans who are not exposed to the activities of the Korean community, Korean brides married to Americans, Koreans adopted by American families, the early immigrants who have no connection with the recent immigrants. Without alternative sources, this directory may be the only and the best sampling frame available." This information was provided by Dr. Eui-Young Yu, our demographic consultant.

Korean Immigrants in America

1
A Historical Overview of Korean Immigration to the United States

Korea, "the Hermit Kingdom," was the last nation in Northeast Asia to open her doors to the United States by signing the Korean-American Treaty in 1882. The treaty, also known as the Chemulpo Treaty or more correctly the Treaty of Amity and Commerce, contained the following provision that has proven to be particularly relevant to Korean immigration to the United States:

> Subjects of Chosen (Korea) who may visit the United States shall be permitted to reside and to rent premises, purchase land, or to construct residences or warehouses, in all parts of the country. They shall be freely permitted to pursue their various callings and avocations, and traffic in all merchandise, raw and manufactured, that is not declared contraband by law. (Article VI; Choy 1979:46-47)

Soon after the ratification of the treaty, a team of Korean diplomatic envoys visited the United States during 1883 and 1884 on a goodwill mission and the first Korean legation was eventually established in Washington, D.C. In 1888, a small number of Korean students, political exiles, *insam* (ginseng) merchants, and migrant laborers began to arrive on American shores (Warren Kim, 1971:1-4; Choy, 1979:69-72).[1] The total number of Koreans in the United States was estimated at less than fifty before the first large wave of Korean immigrants reached the Hawaiian shores during the period 1903-1905.

The history of Korean immigration to America thus began in 1903. On January 13, 1903, 101 Korean immigrants (55 men, 21 women, and 25 children) aboard the S.S. *Gaelic*, a U.S. merchant ship, arrived in Honolulu, Hawaii. By 1905 a total of 7,226 Korean immigrants (6,048 men, 637 women, 541 children) had reached

39

Hawaiian shores by 65 different ships (Warren Kim, 1971:10). Such a relatively large influx of Korean immigrants within a short period of time was not to take place again until the late 1960s.

A combination of three factors may account for this cessation of immigration. The first factor was the Japanese protectorate treaty with Korea in 1905 and the subsequent Japanese annexation of Korea in 1910. Under the thirty-six years of Japanese colonial rule (1910–1945), no Koreans were allowed to emigrate to the United States except approximately 1,100 "picture brides" to join their prospective husbands in Hawaii (951) and in mainland United States (115) between 1910 and 1924 (Warren Kim, 1971:22–23). Political refugees and students, however, continued to come to the United States from Korea, but the total number of these nonimmigrants did not exceed 900 during the period (Yu, 1977:118).

Second, the Korean government prohibited the further emigration of Korean laborers because of the concern over the hardships that were being encountered by Korean emigrants, especially those who were sent to Mexico (Kim and Patterson, 1974:87–89). An extreme example occurred in 1905, when 1,031 Koreans (802 men, 207 women, and 22 children) were illegally recruited by a British merchant named John G. Meyers of the Continental Settlement Company and were sent to Merida, Yucatan, to work under a four-year labor contract without the Korean government's authorization. "At the time of recruitment, the immigrants were lured into slave labor by a false promise that they could earn a fortune in just four years in Mexico" (Warren Kim, 1971:17; cf. Yun, 1977). Of these unfortunate migrants, 288 laborers emigrated further to Cuba in 1921 (Warren Kim, 1971:21).

The third factor was the American immigration quota levied against non-Europeans, especially Asians during the period 1924–1965. Under the Immigration Act of 1924, which grew out of the Quota Act of 1921 and was slightly revised later in 1929, the total number of immigrants to be admitted into the United States annually was 150,000, and the quota for each country would be based on the proportionate number of the particular nationality already residing in the United States as of 1920 in relation to the total U.S. population for that year.[2] A minimum quota of 100 for each country was also established (Berry and Tischler, 1978:181–82). For example, according to this formula, Great Britain was assigned a quota of 65,361, whereas China would be entitled to a quota of only 105. Ironically, however, no quota was allowed for Asian countries until around the end of World War II because of the discriminating clause included in the Act—"no alien ineligible for citizenship shall be admitted to the United States."

All Asians were generally forbidden to become naturalized citizens until the passage of Walter-McCarran Act in 1952. "Even the alien wives of citizens of Oriental ancestry were barred by the clause" (Simpson and Yinger, 1972:117). No wonder the inflow of picture brides completely ceased in 1924. The Immigration Act of 1924 has thus been known as the Oriental Exclusion Law. In 1943, China was assigned an annual quota of 105, and after World War II other Asian countries, including Korea, received their quotas. In most cases, the minimum number of 100 per year was assigned; Korea received 100; the Philippines, 100; India, 100; and Japan, 185 (Simpson and Yiner, 1972: 122; Berry and Tishler, 1978:182; Lyman, 1977:134). Korean immigration to the United States started to resume slowly in the 1950s. A crude statistical overview on the Korean immigration to the United States during the past seventy-five years is shown in Table 1.1.

As indicated in Table 1.1, the history of Korean immigration to the United States can be studied in three parts; (1) the early labor immigration of predominantly male laborers to Hawaiian islands (1903–1905) and their picture brides (1910–1924); (2) the interim or post-Korean War immigration of predominantly young women and children during the period 1951–1964, when "war brides" of American servicemen, war orphans through intercountry adoption, and a small number of professional workers arrived in the United States; and (3) the new wave of "family immigration" since 1965. In this chapter, we discuss the first and second periods and include students and political exiles who become permanent residents. The rest of this book is devoted to the last period, the new immigration.

The Early Immigrants

To begin with, the following classic questions ubiquitous to any human migration should be asked. What was the general background of the immigrants? Why did they come? How did they adapt themselves to the new country?

Scholars seem to be divided into two camps concerning the socioeconomic origin of the early Korean immigrants. One contends that the majority of the immigrants were farmers (Choy, 1979:77; Hyung-chan Kim, 1974:25), whereas the other claims that they came from urban areas, predominantly from port cities (Patterson, 1979; Bernice B. H. Kim, 1934; Yun, 1977). For example, the following two quotations characterize the contrast:

The classification of the immigrants by sex, age, education, and occupational background was roughly as follows: 90 percent were males, 10 percent were females; 93 percent were adults, 7 percent were minors; about 35 percent were literate, 65 per cent illiterate. Their previous occupations varied. As expected, farmers comprised the majority, followed by manual laborers, soldiers, Christian church workers, and a small number of students and highly educated Confucian scholars. About 40 percent were Christians, and gradually most of the Koreans became church-goers. (Choy, 1979:77)

Heterogeneity characterized the Korean immigrant group. There were people from every province of Korea, from all walks of life. Very few came from the rural districts, so that the farming class made up less than one-seventh of the entire group. The largest proportion was common laborers or coolies who worked periodically in port cities and towns, next, ex-soldiers of the Korean army (who had sensed Japanese encroachment), then manual laborers, household servants, policemen, woodcutters, and miners. Over 6,000 of them were young men between the ages of twenty and thirty and the remaining few were young married couples. (Bernice B. H. Kim, 1934:410–11)

Through painstaking analyses of extensive data collected by several scholars from interviews with surviving immigrants over the years, Patterson (1979) convincingly argues that the majority of the early immigrants were common laborers who had lived in cities prior to their emigration, although many of them might have been uprooted from the rural areas by war, famine, and oppressive taxes and forced to seek employment in various cities.

A careful examination of the available data enables us to portray the general socioeconomic background of the early immigrants who arrived at the Hawaiian sugar plantations during the period 1903–1905: The majority of the immigrants were young bachelors between the ages of twenty and thirty, who came from the port cities throughout Korea, were largely uneducated, were engaged in semiskilled or unskilled occupations, and had some exposure to Christian missionaries. A few were relatively well educated and already converted to Christianity prior to their emigration from Korea.

Because of the unbalanced sex ratio (10 males to every 1 female), the exchange of photographs between prospective grooms in Hawaii and brides in Korea took place for arranged marriages. As mentioned earlier, 1,100 picture brides arrived during the period 1910–1924. The picture brides were generally very young (17 on the average) and from rural villages in the southeastern (Kyongsang) province of Korea (Lyu, 1977:29; Sunoo and Sunoo,

1977). The number of females who arrived as picture brides still fell short of balancing the sex ratio.

According to Yu (1977:119), a noted Korean demographer, about 3,000 male Korean immigrants had to spend the rest of their lives as bachelors. Only 104 Korean males married outside their own race, predominantly Hawaiian women, during the period 1912-1924 (Adams, 1937:336-37).

Having described the general socioeconomic background of the early Korean immigrants, we now turn to the push-pull factors involved in their migration. Both factors were closely related to the political economy of international relations. For several centuries Korea closed its doors to the outside world except for China with whom tributary relations were maintained. However, in the last half of the nineteenth century, Korea found herself at the crossroads of a power struggle among her neighbor nations—Japan, China, and Russia. To make the situation worse, the Western powers began to force Korea to open her ports for trade and commerce. Similar to the fate of China, Korea had little alternative but to sign treaties with the big powers starting with Japan in 1876, the United States in 1882, and followed by Great Britain, Russia, Germany, France, and Italy. Eventually, Korea became an international competition ground for economic and political hegemony. Choy describes the situation well:

> After Korea opened its doors to foreign powers, the peninsula became a semi-colony of Japan and the West. The country was divided into zones of influence of the various foreign powers. The United States obtained mining concessions and communication and transportation franchises. Japanese merchants began to monopolize Korean import and export businesses. Russians were interested in timber concessions. The native handicraft industries and the primitive agricultural economy faced bankruptcy and the national treasury become empty. (1979:73)

Finally, Japan emerged as the victor of the power struggle after winning two wars (Sino-Japanese War of 1894-1895 and Russo-Japanese War of 1904-1905), and Korea became the victim who lost her political autonomy in 1905 and was completely annexed to the Japanese empire in 1910. Interestingly, Japan's dominance over Korea was endorsed by the United States and Great Britain through the Taft-Katsura Secret Agreement and the Anglo-Japanese Alliance (cf. Choy, 1979:63-64; Warren Kim, 1971:2-3).

In addition to the political and economic turmoils that resulted from these international power struggles, there were also other push factors, such as famine, cholera epidemics, heavy taxes, and institutionalized governmental corruption accompanied by extortion and graft. In sum, push factors involved in the Korean immigration were politico-economical calamities derived from both foreign encroachment and domestic failure to meet the crisis. Under these circumstances, the exodus of Korean peasants and laborers was an expected phenomenon. For example, already more than one million Korean emigrants were residing in Manchuria and about nine thousand in Russia prior to 1884 (Hyung-chan Kim, 1974:23).

What were the pull factors to America? The most important was the U.S. demand for inexpensive labor in sugar plantations in Hawaii toward the end of the nineteenth century. There were several reasons for the increasing labor demand: (1) the decline of the native Hawaiian population that used to be a main source of cheap labor; (2) the increasing demand for sugar in the world market in general; (3) the Chinese Exclusion Act of 1882 which terminated the labor supply from China; (4) expensive costs and wages for employing European laborers;[3] (5) consolidation of the Japanese labor force in Hawaii in terms of organized demands, competition, and strikes; and (6) the increasing mobility of plantation laborers to cities and the mainland because of deplorable work conditions in the plantations (Patterson, 1977; Choy, 1979:91–103). Thus, labor shortages in the sugar plantations became acute, especially inexpensive Asian labor.

To meet the demand, the possibility of bringing Korean laborers was discussed among Horace N. Allen, chief of the U.S. legation in Seoul, and representatives of the Hawaiian Sugar Planters Association at a number of meetings in San Francisco in March 1902. Koreans were apparently chosen to relieve the labor shortage as indicated in Allen's letter (dated December 10, 1902) to Stanford B. Dole, then the governor of Hawaii:

> I take the liberty of handing you duplicate copies of an edict recently issued by the Korean Government regulating the emigration of Korean subjects to foreign countries. My reason for sending you these copies is that I learn it is the intentions of a number of Koreans to try the experiment of emigrating to the Hawaiian Islands during the coming winter....
> The Koreans are a patient, hard-working, docile race; easy to control from their long habit of obedience. They are usually very keen on getting a foreign education, and this has taken quite a number to the United States where a few have become naturalized, while those who have returned are doing well and are a credit to their American education....
> Koreans are a more teachable race than the Chinese; they eat more meat than do the latter people, though their chief article of diet is rice.

If Koreans do get to the Islands in any numbers, it will be a God-send to them (Koreans) and I imagine they will be found to be unobjectionable and of good service as laborers. (Kim and Patterson, 1974:85-86)

The Korean king, Kojong, was eventually persuaded by Allen, and in November 1902 an American named David W. Deshler of the American Trading Company in Seoul was authorized to implement emigration of Korean laborers to Hawaii. Deshler promptly set up recruiting offices throughout major cities in Korea under the name of the East-West Development Company. The Korean government also established a new department called *Yu Min Won* (literally, People-Easing Bureau) to handle bureaucratic processes involved in the emigration of Korean laborers (Patterson, 1979:50). In order to attract the potential emigrants, the following advertisement was published by Deshler's company:

The climate is suitable for everyone and there is no severe heat or cold. There are schools on every island. English is taught and the tuition is free. Jobs for the farmers are available all the year around for those who are healthy and decent in behavior. Monthly payment is fifteen dollars in American money (sixty-seven won in Korean money). There are ten hours of work a day with Sunday free. The expenses for housing, fuel, water and hospital will be paid by the employer. (Choy, 1979:75)

Deshler's advertisement did not seem to attract enough Korean emigrants in the beginning, and American missionaries had to help: "It took Reverend George H. Jones' persuasive sermon to entice his congregation members to fill the first ship which left Inchon port on December 22, 1902, arriving in Honolulu on January 13, 1903. Nearly half of the 101 immigrants on the first ship were from Reverend Jones' Yongdong church in Inchon" (Sunoo and Sunoo, 1977:146). Most of the scholars on the Korean immigration history agree that American missionaries encouraged Koreans to emigrate to Hawaii (Warren Kim, 1971; Lyu, 1977; Sunoo and Sunoo, 1977; Choy, 1979; Patterson, 1979).

In short, the majority of Korean laborers came to the United States for better economic opportunity but not to settle down permanently. "Most of them came to Hawaii to stay temporarily. They wanted to return to their homeland as soon as they made enough money or the political climate of the Korean peninsula permitted them to go back" (Choy, 1979:77; cf. Patterson, 1979:9-10). Some of them indeed returned to Korea—964 men and 19 women by 1910—but the majority of them stayed (Warren Kin, 1971:11). They did not make a fortune nor did the political climate of Korea favor their return (in fact, there was no longer a "Korea" after the Japanese annexation in 1910). Thus, they became a typical Marginal Man.

Empirical research on the life conditions of the early Korean immigrants is lacking except for occasional interviews with the surviving immigrants that are available to researchers. Romanzo Adams' 1937 study on the interracial marriage in Hawaii contains many useful observations and statistical data but the study does not deal specifically with Korean immigrants' adaptation. Our discussion on the adaptation patterns of the immigrants is mainly based on historical documents and secondary data. Cultural, social, and economic adaptation of the immigrants are discussed in general terms without separating them categorically.

Several sources provide us with information that the early Korean immigrants were acculturated to the American culture slightly faster than their Japanese or Chinese counterparts, especially in the acquisition of the English language (Adams, 1937:187–188; Patterson, 1979:21–22). Aside from a myth that Koreans are superior in "native linguistic ability," Adams contends that such a rapid acculturation may be a result of the smallness of the immigrant group.

Whatever the reasons, the early Korean immigrant laborers left the plantation and moved to the cities and the mainland faster than their Japanese and Chinese counterparts (Patterson, 1979:23; Adams, 1937:186; Lind, 1938:254). The conditions on the plantations were deplorable for any worker—extremely hard work under the hot sun for low wages (65 cents for a man, 50 cents for a woman, for a ten-hour work day), no chance for promotion, and communal living quarters isolated from the outside world. By 1910 nearly one-third of the male laborers had left the plantation for the mainland United States (1,999 men and 12 women). During the period 1921 to 1926, the total number of Korean laborers on plantations was reduced by more than half (3,025) from the 1903–1905 period. Those who moved to Hawaiian cities and to the mainland were engaged as manual laborers at first but eventually managed to open small businesses, such as grocery stores, laundry shops, vegetable shops, and barber shop. Although very few of the Koreans could engage in semiprofessional jobs, some managed, however, to move into large-scale farming whereas others acquired big trucking firms or real estate businesses (Choy, 1979; 123–33).

Another noteworthy aspect of the immigrant's adaptation is their extensive involvement in Christian churches, which contrasts to the Japanese and Chinese immigrants whose involvement in the Christian faith has been rather insignificant. Prior to

A Historical Overview

their emigration from Korea, about four hundred of the early Korean immigrants were already baptized Christians. Within a decade, the number of Korean Christians grew rapidly and reached two thousands and eight hundred. Eventually almost every Korean in the Hawaiian Islands came to be identified with the Christian faith (Gardner, 1970; Warren Kim, 1971:29; Adams, 1937:188). The Korean ethnic church served the immigrant community as a social and cultural center as well as a religious center.

The early Korean immigrants were a minority of the minority in Hawaii, in particular, and in the United States in general. As of 1930, Koreans constituted only 1.8 percent (6,461) of the entire Hawaiian population of 347,799 whereas Japanese were the single largest ethnic group (40 percent), and whites (Caucasian or Haole) were the dominant group in terms of power though they too were a numerical minority (15.2 percent).

Such a small minority as the Koreans with their progressive acculturation and rapid mobility should have achieved a high degree of social assimilation, especially in the islands where a long tradition of racial amalgamation had been established. Their social assimilation, however, seems to have been extremely limited. Koreans are noted for their high exogamy (outmarriage) rate in recent years as indicated in the 1970 Census report (50 percent outmarriage rate in Hawaii according to U.S. Department of Health Education and Welfare, 1974:144), but a careful examination of data compiled by Adams (1937:195, 345) reveals that the early Korean immigrants' outmarriage rate was not higher than other ethnic groups except for the Japanese and Filipinos. In terms of exogamy, Koreans ranked seventh or eighth among ten ethnic groups in Hawaii (Hawaiian, part-Hawaiian, Spanish, Portuguese, other Caucasian, Puerto Rican, Chinese, Korean, and Japanese). Adams interprets his findings as follows:

> Peoples such as the Chinese, the Japanese and the Koreans with a tradition of familism including ancestor worship tend to marry within the group almost entirely for a generation if women are available. This is the result of the family authority or influence in the selection of brides and grooms. As the acculturation of such groups proceeds there is, more or less, a weakening of tradition and when the brides and grooms are of the native born generation a moderate increase in the outmarriage rate may be noted. (1937:198)

Adams' prediction turned out to be particularly true for Koreans some 30 years later, although it also applied to a lesser degree for other groups such as the Japanese, Filipinos, and Chinese (U.S.

Department of HEW, 1974:144).

At any rate, most of the early Korean immigrants were not socially assimilated either to the dominant group or to other minority groups. Even on the plantations, the barracks were racially and ethnically segregated. Aside from language difficulties, each ethnic group was there for a temporary sojourn, and there was no pressing need to assimilate in any direction. Even discrimination by whites was tolerated because "they believed they were helpless human beings living in the white peoples' society, and they dreamed of going back to their homeland as soon as Japanese domination ended" (Choy, 1979:78).

Consequently, their Korean's ethnic attachment remained strong; in fact, it became stronger as years went by. Korean language schools were established as early as 1905 and the children were taught Korean values, customs, history, and geography, as well as language. In addition to the Korean church, numerous ethnic organizations were founded, such as *dong-hoe* (self-governing village councils), patriotic societies, and even military training centers in support of the Korean independence movement to counteract Japanese imperialism (Lyu, 1977).

In sum, the patterns of the early Korean immigrants can be characterized as a considerable degree of acculturation, some occupational mobility, extensive religious involvement, virtually no social assimilation, and strong ethnic attachment. In many respects, the Korean immigrants' experience is similar to that of the first generation of all Asian immigrants (the sojourner's mode of adaptation), but the Koreans were unique in the sense that they were the only sojourners with no homeland to return to, even if they made a fortune (Siu, 1952). Their psychological plight has not been fully documented.

As mentioned before, the early Korean immigration to the United States officially ceased in 1924; however, a limited number of Korean students and political exiles continued to come to the United States and many of them eventually became permanent residents in the United States. Korean students started to arrive in the United States as early as 1899. According to Warren Kim (1971:23–26), the first group of 64 students of upper-middle-class background came to the United States between 1899 and 1909. They were mostly anti-Japanese activists and included Syngman Rhee who later became the first president of the Republic of Korea in 1948. Over half of these students remained in the United States as a result of possible persecution by the Japanese authorities at home. The second group of 541 political exiles came from Korea through China and Europe after the Japanese annexation of

Korea in 1910. They were admitted without passports because of the U.S. government's sympathy toward their nationalistic cause and plight. Some of the young Koreans attended American colleges but most were engaged in the Korean independence movement in the United States against Japanese colonial rule, and were thus often called "refugee students." Most of them became permanent residents and assumed leadership roles in the Korean communities in the United States. However, as "refugee students," they had to work for a living by hard labor on the farms, railroads, fisheries, and mines. "Those in the cities worked as cooks, kitchen helpers, waiters, house-boys, and janitors. Some had small businesses such as restaurants, vegetable stands, barber shops, second-hand furniture stores, rooming houses, groceries, but none had sufficient capital" (Warren Kim, 1971:26). No detailed follow-up studies on them are available except on a few "successful" professionals and businessmen (Choy, 1979:281-334).

The third group of 289 Korean students arrived with Japanese passports between 1921 and 1940. The majority of these students returned to Korea after the completion of their studies but some remained. Some of these are active leaders of the Korean community today. As of 1940, a total of approximately 600 Korean students were permanent residents in the United States.

The Interim Immigrants

The interim or post-Korean War immigrants who arrived in the United States between 1951 and 1964 are the most heterogeneous but least studied group among Koreans in America. This immigrant group can be divided into three categories, as mentioned earlier: Korean wives of American servicemen, war orphans, and professional workers.[4] The majority (77 percent) of this group consists of the first two categories (see Table 1.1). Based on the scanty data available, we discuss briefly the general demographic characteristics and adjustment patterns of the first two groups. The last category—professional and skilled workers—is discussed in the next chapter because of their similar socioeconomic background with the new immigrants. The very early wave of the new immigrants was largely composed of the third preference category (professional occupation).[5]

Intrusive sociological studies on the adaptation of Korean wives of American servicemen is urgently needed. During the period of 1950-1975, 28,205 Korean wives of American servicemen arrived in the United States, and yet they have been an "invisible" minority to sociologists. A few studies carried out mainly by social workers are available (Bok-Lim Kim, 1972, 1977; Sil Dong Kim, 1975; Trebilcock, 1973). Our discussion draws heavily on Bok-Lim Kim's review on the studies, which includes a comprehensive analysis of the adjustment problems encountered by the Asian wives of U.S. servicemen in general (1977).

Bok-Lim Kim summarizes the demographic profile of the typical intermarried Asian wife (Japanese and Korean) in America as follows:

> ...a relatively young to early-middle-aged woman who is more likely to be married, with a median education level of eighth grade. Her husband has an even chance of being either a few years older, or much older or younger than she. He is likely to be employed in military service or engaged in skilled or semi-skilled work. The couple has two or fewer children and have practically no organizational affiliations, with extremely limited participation in social activities. (1977:103)

In short, the Korean wife of an American serviceman is doubly marginal—from the American society and from the Korean immigrant community. Scholars on the subject seem to agree that social marginality and isolation are the most painful experiences for Asian wives in America (Bok-Lim Kim, 1977:103). "This group (the Asian wives) has been noted for its severe culture shock, lack of education, impoverishment, isolation, malcommunication in the family, lack of occupational skills, high divorce rate, and general alienation. It was also noted that the magnitude of problems were much greater among Korean wives than among Japanese wives" (Ryu, 1977:212). As Bok-Lim Kim emphasizes, there are successful and happy intermarriages between Korean women and American servicemen. Both happy and sad cases must be accounted for by extensive research, especially when the latter involves physical abuse, suicide or suicide attempts, and psychiatric disorders. At this point, we know very little.

We know even less about another category of the post-Korean War immigrants—the war orphans. No one knows how many orphans were produced by the Korean War. We do know, however, how many children were housed in various orphanages throughout Korea: in 1950 24,945 children were institutionalized in 215 orphanages in Korea (Chakerian, 1968:40). Of these children, 6,293 arrived in the United States through intercountry adoption (mostly through the Holt Adoption Agency) between 1955–66. About 46 percent of them were white Koreans, 41 percent were full Koreans, and the rest were black Koreans (Ministry of Health and Social Affairs, 1967; Hurh, 1972:16).

How have the Korean war orphans fared in American homes? To our knowledge, only one significant empirical study has been done on these children in the United States. Dong Soo Kim has recently conducted a nationwide research on the self-concept of adopted Korean adolescents (Dong Soo Kim, 1977). The carefully designed study on both the children and parents produced the following results: (1) Korean adopted children were generally placed in middle-class, white, Protestant families living in rural areas or small cities; (2) the reasons for adopting Korean children were mainly religious and humanitarian; (3) of the sample, about two-thirds of the children were full Koreans, most of the others were white Koreans and only a few were black Koreans; (4) numerous parents stated that they were very satisfied with their Korean children; (5) the children had relatively little Korean identity and identified themselves as Americans or more frequently Korean-Americans; (6) as a whole, the children's self-concept was remarkably similar to that of other Americans as represented by a norm group in the Tennessee Self-Concept Scale; (7) a supportive family environment did tend to affect a better self-concept formation among the adopted Korean children; and (8) as an adoption program, the placement of Korean children in American homes can be regarded as very "successful."

At the time of Dong Soo Kim's study, the average age of the children was fourteen years and one month. How will these young immigrants fare in the American society at large? Extensive studies are anticipated.

To summarize, the interim or post-Korean War immigrants were quite different from the early immigrants in terms of their demographic characteristics (mostly young women and children), push-pull factors (derived largely from the Korean War), and adaptation patterns (mostly familial and socialization problems). Particularly noteworthy is the striking difference in sex ratios: the early immigrants had a sex ratio of 10 males to 1 female, whereas the interim immigrants had a ratio of 1 male to 3.5 females. Another contrast is occupation. The majority of the interim immigrants (about 80 percent) reported no occupation other than that of housewife at the time of their admission to the United States (Hyung-chan Kim, 1974:30).

After World War II, a relatively large wave of Korean students reached the United States. It is estimated that about six thousands Korean students came to the United States between 1945 and 1965 (Warren Kim, 1971:26). How many of these students have changed their statuses from students to permanent residents is not certain. Moreover, a comprehensive longitudinal study on the Korean students' adjustment is completely lacking—either as residents in the United States or as American college graduates in Korea after their return. According to Choy (1979:219), there are approximately five thousands Korean students in the United States today, and yet the adaptation patterns of Korean students in the United States is another area that awaits a comprehensive sociological survey.

Having discussed the early and interim Korean immigration in historical and structural contexts, we now turn to the new immigration, a fresh chapter in the Korean immigrant history.

Notes

1. According to Choy (1979:72), some Korean laborers (fewer than twenty) had arrived in Hawaii in 1901 and 1902 through Japan. Whether they were bona fide immigrants (those who enter the United States with immigrant visas) is not certain.

2. Even prior to the passage of the Quota Act of 1921, immigration of Chinese and Japanese laborers had already been restricted by the Chinese Exclusion Act of 1882 and the Gentlemen's Agreement of 1907.

3. Transportation cost for each laborer: Norwegian, $130; Portuguese, $112; German, $100; South Sea Islander, $78.50; Chinese, $76.85; Japanese, $65.85 (Patterson, 1977:13). Including recruiting and other expenses, the total cost of bringing one laborer from Europe would be about $250 while the cost for one Asian laborer was only about $70, according to Choy (1979:92). Wages for European laborers were also substantially higher than that of Asian laborers (European wage—$18.20 a month Asian wage—$15) (Patterson, 1977:18).

4. We do not mean here that these three categories of immigrants ceased to arrive in the United States after 1964. On the contrary, several thousands of each category are admitted every year (U.S. commissioner of Immigration and Naturalization, 1965–1977). Proportionally, they were the largest immigrant categories among Koreans admitted during the period 1951–1964.

5. First preference: unmarried sons and daughters of U.S. citizens. Second preference: spouse and unmarried sons and daughters of an alien lawfully admitted for permanent residence. Third preference: members of professions, and scientists and artists of exceptional ability. There are altogether eight preference categories. For details, see Keely (1980:17–18). The spouse and parents of U.S. citizens over the age of twenty-one not subjected to numerical limitations.

2
New Korean Immigrants: Demographic Characteristics

The Immigration and Naturalization Act of 1965 abolished the national origins quota system, put a limit on immigration to the Western Hemisphere, and adopted a new preference system as well as revised labor certification procedures.[1] This new legislation has had diverse effects on immigration from various countries but its impact on the volume and composition of Asian immigration to the United States has been dramatic. The Asian share of total immigration to the United States increased from 7.6 percent (1961-65) to 27.4 percent (1969-73), equaling the European share (27.3 percent in 1969-73) for the first time in the American history of immigration.

The Korean share of the total United States immigration increased even more: from 0.7 percent to 3.8 percent between the same eight year period. The three Eastern Hemisphere countries from which the most immigrants came to the United States in 1965 were the United Kingdom, Germany, and Italy; in 1975, they were the Philippines, Korea, and China.

Detailed numbers of the recent immigrants from East Asia by country are given in Table 2.1. As is evident from the table, the increase of Korean immigrants in recent years has been phenomenal—an increase of about fifteen times during the decade 1965-1975. About one in every three immigrants from East Asia is now a Korean.

Of all Korean immigrants giving an occupation, the proportion that listed a professional occupation was very high in the 1961-65 period (71%), and increased in the 1966-68 period (75%), but declined noticeably in recent years (40% in 1974-77), similar to the trend with all Asian professionals admitted to the United States recently. Nevertheless, a substantial proportion (about 40%) of Asian immigrant workers are still drawn from professional, technical, and kindred occupational categories (U.S. commissioner of Immigration and Naturalization, 1961–67; cf. Keely, 1980: 19–20).

In terms of age and sex distribution, the majority of new immigrants from Asia are young and female. Koreans are more conspicuous in this regard—67.8 percent of all Korean immigrants during the period 1971–73 were under thirty as compared with 51.5 percent for the overall United States population in 1970 (U.S. Department of Commerce, 1977:23). Contrasting the period 1975–77 with that of 1971–73, the age structure of Korean immigrants is most conspicuous among the East Asian immigrants. During the 1975–77 period, about 44 percent of the Korean immigrants were under 20, whereas 17.5 percent of the Japanese, 26.9 percent of the Chinese, and 27 per cent of the Filipino immigrants were in the same age category. At the same time, the proportion of Korean young adults (age 20–39) was 44 percent, the lowest among all immigrants from East Asia (70.8% for Japanese, 47.6% for Chinese, and 47.4% for Filipinos). The overall sex ratio of Korean immigrants was 64.4 (64 males for 100 females) in 1977, as compared with 62.0 for the Japanese, 92.0 for the Chinese, 67.7 for the Filipino immigrants, and 95.1 for the U.S. national population in the same year.

In short, Koreans are one of the most rapidly growing new immigrant groups whose composition is strikingly different from the "old" immigrants from Asia (predominantly adult male laborers).[2] It is thus not surprising that the U.S. Census Bureau counted Koreans as a distinct ethnic group in the 1970 Census for the first time; earlier, Koreans were included in the "other Asians" category. According to the 1970 Census report, there were 70,598 Koreans in the United States. Eui-Young Yu (1977:122–23) contends that this figure was an underestimation because of miscalculation and misclassification, and the actual size of the Korean population in the United States could have been greater than 113,000. Nevertheless, the 1970 Census is the only comprehensive national statistic available on Koreans until the 1980 Census data are fully compiled and analyzed. Some crude data from the 1980 census are begining to be available, such as *Race of the Population by States: 1980* (PC 80-S1-3); however, potential errors in 1980 population counts are still being investigated by the U.S. Bureau of Census (U.S. Department of Commerce, 1981:4).

Based on 1970 Census data and other available secondary data, we first discuss the general demographic characteristics of Koreans in comparison to other Asians in the United States, and next, our primary data on Korean immigrants in the Los Angeles area in 1979 are analyzed as an updated sample survey. Our

1975–76 Chicago data are also referred to whenever they deserve particular attention.

Socioeconomic Characteristics of Koreans in the United States, 1970

In 1970, as compared with other Asian-Americans, the Koreans in the United States had the lowest sex ratio of 67.6 (68 males for 100 females) and the highest proportion of foreign born (54%) (see Table 2.2). Moreover, the majority (74%) of Koreans under the age of twenty were born in the United States, whereas a similar proportion (71%) of Korean adults were foreign born, mostly in Korea (Yu, 1977:125). In terms of age distribution, the proportion of the Korean population under 18 was 35 percent, about the same as it was for the entire United States population (34%); however, only three percent of the entire Korean-American population were elderly, the lowest proportion among all ethnic groups.

Koreans were also the most highly educated group among all groups—71 percent of them completed high school and 36 percent graduated from colleages, whereas only 11 percent of the total U.S. population were colleage graduates in 1970. The majority of Korean males (76%) and slightly less than half of the Korean females (42%) were employed, similar to the proportions for the entire U.S. population. Despite the highest degree of educational attainment among all the groups compared, the Koreans' income were not significantly higher than those of other groups in 1970. Since the data on the median family income are not available for the Korean group, an exact comparison cannot be made. Unfortunately, the 1970 Census did not provide us with the occupational distribution of Korean-Americans either.[3]

Similar to the ecological patterns of other Asian-Americans, Koreans were also concentrated in urban areas (67%); however, the proportion was the lowest among all groups compared, even lower than the U.S. national percentage (74%). As a result, Koreans were found to be more dispersed geographically than other Asian-Americans. Eui-Young Yu (1977:124–25) points out:

> While other Orientals are clustered in the western states and Hawaii, Koreans tend to disperse more widely in all states. Forty-one percent of all Koreans live in the western region, whereas 81 percent of the Japanese, 74 percent of the Filipinos, and 57 percent of the Chinese were found in the same region in 1970. Unlike other Asians, a large number of Koreans settle in the South. According to the census, 8 percent of the Chinese, 5 percent of the Japanese, and 9 percent of the Filipinos in the

United States were living in the South in 1970. On the other hand, 19 percent of the Koreans were residing in the South.

A demographic sketch of Koreans in the United States in 1970 can thus be made as follows: The majority of them were young, female, and born in Korea. Most of the adults had a high degree of educational and occupational backgrounds but were earning medium incomes. Unlike other Asian-Americans, who gravitate toward the Western states and Hawaii, the Koreans were relatively more dispersed in all states, and were also comparatively less concentrated in urban centers.

In order to provide a similar sketch of Koreans in the United States today, we must turn to our primary data obtained from a sample of Korean residents in the Los Angeles area in 1979, since it will take several years until the 1980 Census data are completely analyzed and available to the public. Approximately 13 percent of the total Koreans in the United States were living in Los Angeles County in 1970 (Yu, 1977:124). In 1980, it has been estimated that about 15 percent of the entire Korean population in the United States reside in the Los Angeles area.[4]

Demographic Characteristics of the Respondents in the Los Angeles Area, 1979

1. Age Distribution by Sex

The age distribution by sex for our sample is shown in Table 2.3 As a whole, our respondents' ages range from 20 to 84. For the male sample, the mean age is 42.2 with 63.3 percent in the age category of 31–50. On the other hand, for the female sample, the mean age is 38.8 with 65.5 percent in the age category of 21–40. The most conspicuous age category for both sexes is, therefore, 31–40, and the majority of our total sample (80%) are in the age category of 21–50.

The age distribution shown in Table 2.3 roughly corresponds to the findings of Lee's demographic study on the Korean population in the Los Angeles area in 1977 (Lee, 1979:43). According to Lee's survey, 80.5 percent of the Korean adult population (over 20) were in the age category 20–49. Another comparison can also be made to our previous study of Korean residents in the Chicago area in 1975. The median age of the Chicago sample was 36, the most conspicuous age category for both sexes was 31–40, and the overwhelming majority (94%) were in the age category of 20–50 (Hurh, Kim, and Kim, 1978: 17–18).

Since adaptation of immigrants to their host society is a social process, the *age at* immigration is a crucial variable in analyzing their adjustment patterns, such as acculturation and occupational entry. The majority (66%) of our respondents came to the United States when they were in the age category 21–40. Upon closer examination, we found that more than half of the male immigrants who fall in this category arrived in the United States when they were between 31 and 40; the majority of the female immigrants in this category came to the United States when they were between 21 and 30. In general, the average Korean immigrant starts his or her occupational career rather late in the new country. We discuss this occupational adjustment again later.

2. Marital Status and Family Size

Unlike the early immigrants from Korea, of whom about 80 percent were bachelors, the vast majority (483, 79%) of our respondents are married, 13 percent are single, and 6 percent are widowed. Very few are divorced or separated (1.3 percent for each category). The proportion of divorced persons in the 25–54 age category for the U.S national population was 8.5 percent in 1978 (U.S. Department of Commerce, 1979:82).

Although an overwhelming proportion of our sample is married, the size of the family (or household) is found to be moderate; the great majority of the sample (74.5%) do not have a household exceeding four persons. The mean number of persons living in a single household is 3.5. The average size of the American family in 1975 was 3.59.

According to Bok-Lim Kim, the household size of the Korean sample in her Chicago study was three to four on the average, similar so that of her Japanese sample. The largest size of the household among Asian-Americans was that of the Filipinos (four to five on the average, with 36.2 percent of the households containing five or more) (Bok-Lim Kim, 1978c:66, 111, 146).

3. Length of Residence in Los Angeles and the United States

Our respondents' length of residence ranges from several months to 53 years in the Los Angeles area and to 67 years in the United States. Nearly 81 per cent of our sample, however, have lived in the Los Angeles area for seven years or less, with a mean of 5.6 years. Almost two-thirds of our respondents have lived in the United States for seven years or less with a mean of 6.5 years (see Table 2.4).

Generally, our respondents within the Los Angeles area seem to have not settled. A small portion (9.5%) of our total respondents have lived more than five years at their current addresses whereas the majority (64%) have lived at their current addresses less than three years. Details on the residential distribution and mobility of Korean immigrants are given in Chapter 3.

In terms of housing, slightly more than half (56.9%) of our respondents rent apartment, whereas more than one-third (37.3%) own their own homes.[5] In the study of the Chicago area, it was found that about two-thirds of the Korean residents rented apartments, whereas only 18 percent owned their own homes in 1975. None of our residents live in nursing homes, although 25 senior citizens (71 and over) are included in our sample.

4. Educational Status

As revealed in the 1970 Census report (U.S. Department of HEW, 1974:134), the *Asian American Field Study* (U.S. Department of HEW, 1977), Bok-Lim Kim's study (1978c), and our Chicago study (Hurh, Kim, and Kim, 1978), the recent Korean immigrants are the most highly educated group among Asian-Americans. Data on the educational level achieved by our respondents in the Los Angeles area are supportive of the above findings.

Slightly more than half (male, 61%; female, 53%) of our respondents have already received college degrees in Korea before their emigration. One-third of our respondents (31%) have received some amount of education in the United States. Among those who studied in the United States, nearly half have received college degrees. Except for five females, none of our respondents went to elementary and high schools in the United States. The contrast between the proportion of college graduates among our respondents and that of the U.S. national population is striking. In terms of four years or more of college education, 64 percent of our respondents are represented, whereas only 20 percent of persons who were in the age category 25-34 and 12 percent of persons who were in the age category 45-54 in the United States in 1974 were so represented (U.S. Department of Commerce, 1977:302-313).

5. Occupational Status

Three-fourths of the respondents (74%) are found to be currently employed. As expected, more male respondents (85.8%) were employed than female respondents (64.1%). The proportion of the employed females in our research is, however, higher than that of American women (U.S Department of Labor, 1979).

The employed respondents are highly diversified in terms of the nature of their work and the organizational setting under which they work. For analytical purpose, we classify their occupations into the following five categories: (1) professionals and semiprofessionals, (2) proprietors and managers, (3) other white-collar workers, (4) skilled workers, and (5) semiskilled and unskilled workers.

One-third of the employed respondents (31.6%) are found to be proprietors or managers, one-fourth (23.4%) are professionals and semiprofessionals, and another one-fourth (24.8%) are semiskilled or unskilled workers. The remaining one-fifth are other white-collar workers (13.8%) or skilled workers (6.4%). The employed female respondents outnumber their male counterparts in two occupational categories, other white-collar workers and semiskilled or unskilled workers, whereas the reverse is true in the remaining three categories. As a whole, more than two-thirds of the employed respondents (68.8%) are in white-collar occupations. Occupational characteristics of our respondents are fully analyzed in Chapter 6.

In summary, a demographic profile of Korean immigrants in 1979 can be depicted as follows:

Generally, the immigrants are in early middle adulthood and are married and the average size of their family is 3.5. The majority came to the United States about six years ago. Approximately one-third of them reside in their own homes, whereas half rent apartments.

Most of the immigrants are highly educated. Currently, one-third of the employed are small business owners and/or managers, one-fourth are professionals and semiprofessionals, and another one-fourth are semiskilled and unskilled workers. The proportion of the employed female immigrants is higher than that of American women.

A closely related phenomenon to the demographic characteristics of the immigrants is their residential mobility. In the next chapter, we examine the residential distribution and mobility of Koreans in the Los Angeles area.

Notes

1. The Immigration Act of October 3, 1965 (P.L.89-236). This new law set an annual limit of 170,000 immigrants from the Eastern Hemisphere and 120,000 from the Western Hemisphere, with a maximum of 20,000 for any individual country, exclusive of any immediate relatives of American citizens. No one knows the rationale behind the figures of limitations. "They are simply pulled from the air, and bear no relationship to any theory or

principle at all" (Abrams, 1980:28). Concerning the labor certification procedures, "no worker shall enter the U.S. *unless* the Secretary of Labor certifies that there are *not* sufficient able and qualified workers in the U.S., and that the alien would *not* adversely affect wages and working conditions. It places the burden of proving no adverse effect upon the applyng alien" (Keely, 1980:16).

The Western Hemisphere includes South and North America and the Caribbean; the Eastern Hemisphere includes all other continents and islands.

2. In 1900 the Chinese immigrants had a sex ratio of 1,887 males per 100 females and the Japanese immigrants had a ratio of 349/100 in Hawaii and 2,370/100 in the mainland United States. (Lyman, 1974:88; Petersen, 1971:196). Between 1903 and 1905, the Korean immigrants had a sex ratio of 949.5 per 100 females as mentioned in our introduction.

3. The *Annual Reports* of the U.S. commissioner of Immigration and Naturalization contain information on the occupational distribution of immigrants at time of arrival; for instance, 72 percent of all Korean immigrants giving an occupation were professional, technical, and managerial workers during the period of 1965–73 (cf. U.S. Department of HEW, 1974:141). As noted earlier, this percentage has declined significantly in recent years. In 1977, the percentage was 39.1 percent.

4. In 1977, Lee identified 58,241 Koreans already living in the metropolitan area of Los Angeles and its continguous counties (1979:43). At that time, according to Yu's estimation, there were over 290,000 Koreans in the United States (1977:123). Yu's recent study indicates that about 60,000 Koreans of the estimated 400,000 Koreans in the U.S. were residing in 1979 in Los Angeles County alone (1980:78).

5. In 1979, 64.8 percent of the total U.S. housing units (75,280,000) were occupied by owners. Among the white-occupied housing units (66,111,000) 67.7 percent were occupied by owners, and of the non-white-occupied housing units (9,169,000) 43.7 percent were occupied by owners (U.S. Department of Commerce, 1979:785).

3
Settlement Patterns: Residential Distribution and Mobility

Although the Korean community in the United States has rapidly grown in recent years, its residential distribution and mobility have received scant attention from social scientists. The main difficulty for such a study is that Korean immigration to the United States is so recent that no relevant official statistics are available. This chapter attempts to identify the neighborhoods in the Los Angeles area where Korean immigrants have been concentrated and to analyze the residential mobility of Koreans as they settled in this new environment during the period 1972–1979.

Since no official data concerning Korean immigrants' residential distribution and mobility in the Los Angeles area are available, *The Korean Directories for Southern California* published in 1972, 1975, and 1979 were used for the study. The addresses published in the directories are by no means the total listing of Koreans in southern California as already discussed in the methodology section of this book. Without better alternatives, however, the directories may be the most comprehensive listings of Koreans available today.

Husbands, wives, and other family members are often listed separately because the directories list individual persons. In order to identify the residential distribution of Korean households more accurately, the present study has relied on the computer to eliminate duplicated telephone numbers in the directories so that the same telephone number is counted only once. The residential distributions of Korean households for 1972, 1975, and 1979 have been compared in order to recognize the changes in the residential mobility of Koreans and to analyze their geographical assimilation into an American city. The residential mobility of Koreans

This chapter is written by Dr. Siyoung Park, assistant professor of Geography, Western Illinois University.

in the Los Angeles area was examined by studying both the core area and the suburbanization of the Korean community.

Core Area of the Korean Community

A community is a group of people with some common identity of character of fellowship, within which there is communication and social interaction, but a community also consists of people who must be located in such a way that they can communicate (Everitt, 1976). The former is a community without propinquity and the latter is a community with propinquity. The term "Korean community" in this chapter represents the Korean ethnic community with or without propinquity.

The traditional model for residential mobility of an ethnic group involves three concepts: reception area, streaming area, and scattering (Stermole, 1980). The reception area is the place to which new immigrants gravitate. Streamings, either contiguous or noncontiguous to the reception area, represent a flow of people moving in a certain direction toward an area of increased concentration other than the reception area. Scatterings are often evidenced by low densities of the ethnic group in areas not contiguous to the center of concentration.

In 1972, about one-third of the Korean households listed in the directories were concentrated in the neighborhood along Olympic Boulevard, surrounded by Western Avenue, Hoover Street, Wilshire Boulevard, and Pico Boulevard. This reception area commonly known as "Koreatown" is generally divided into three districts—Pico Heights, Sanford, and Rimpau districts (zip codes 90006, 90005, and 90019). (See Figures 3 and 4 at the end of this chapter.)

As the latest immigrants to Los Angeles, without much knowledge of the city, Koreans had also scattered in low-rent districts of the ethnically mixed area surrounding the central business district of Los Angeles. This zone-in-transition in Burgess's terms (1925) included Dockweiler (90007, 90028), West Adams (90016), and Crenshaw (90008) in the south; Oakwood (90004), Los Feliz (90027, 90029), and Edendale (90026) in the north; and Boyle Heights (90033) in the east (see Table 3.1). According to the 1970 census, over 90 percent of the residents in the area south of downtown and the Olympic Area were black, and east of downtown was the largest Mexican neighborhood in Los Angeles. In 1972, Gardena (90247) was the only suburb with a relatively large Korean population.

The reception or core area remained unchanged through 1975.

The "Olympic Area" of the Pico Heights, Sanford, and Rimpau districts (90006, 90005, and 90019) continued to attract more Koreans. The Korean community, being an ecological entity, did experience some dynamic changes during these three years, however. The rank order of Korean-concentrated neighborhoods in Table 3.1 shows that the area adjacently north of the reception area—Los Feliz (90027, 90029), Wilcox (90038), and Edendale (90026)—doubled their Korean population, whereas the Korean population in the neighborhoods south of the reception area—West Adams, Crenshaw, and Dockweiler—declined. Additionally, some of the Korean population moved from the Mexican neighborhood of Boyle Heights. Hawthorne (90250) became an important Korean suburb, and Gardena (90247) continued to gain Korean residents (see Figure 5).

By 1979, a discrete Korean neighborhood had been established, and the northward streaming from the Korean reception area became more obvious. As shown in Table 3.1, Pico Heights, Sanford, Oakwood, and Rimpau (90006, 90005, 90004, 90019, 90020) had become a primary and yet transient Korean neighborhood or Koreatown, made up of 3,767 households, or 30 percent of the Korean immigrants. Neighborhoods north of the Olympic Area—Los Feliz (90029, 90027), Wilcox, Edendale (90026), and Hollywood (90028)—again doubled their Korean populations between 1975 and 1979 (see Figures 4, 5, and 6 at the end of this chapter for a comprehensive picture).

The transient nature of Koreatown in Los Angeles is well described by Eui-Young Yu (1980:79), a Korean demographer:

> Residential turnover for the Koreans is extremely high in Koreatown Los Angeles. An analysis of telephone directories in the area shows that only 11% of the Koreans who were residing in the area in 1972 still remained in 1977 (Yu, 1979a). Koreatown serves as launching station for many Korean newcomers. Very few of them stay very long. The zip code analysis of the Korean directories also shows that growth rates of the Korean population are much faster in the outlying and suburban areas than in Koreatown. The Koreatown Los Angeles will probably develop into a primarily Korean shopping and service area like Little Tokyo and China Town. Residentially, Koreans have not shown any single location of concentration. There is no sign yet that the Koreans will develop an ethnic neighborhood of their own as Italians and Poles did in the early stages of their immigration.

Suburbanization of the Korean Community

By 1979 more suburbs had emerged as important Korean neighborhoods. Both Hawthorne (90250) with 229 households and Monterey Park (91754) in the east had tripled their Korean populations during the four years since 1975. Additionally, Cerritos (90701) in the southeast, La Puente (91745) further east, and Gardena (90247) in the south near Hawthorne were suburbs that harbored over 100 Korean households in their respective municipalities in Los Angeles County.

Table 3.2 shows the distribution of Korean households in Los Angeles, Orange, Riverside, and San Diego counties in Southern California. Between 1972 and 1979, the number of Korean households in Southern California grew from 3,430 to 12,722. Both in 1972 and 1975, almost all (96 percent) Korean households were located in Los Angeles County, and only a negligible number of Koreans lived in Orange, Riverside, and San Diego counties. Also about 70 percent of the Korean immigrants were settled within the city limits of Los Angeles.

By 1979, however, rapid suburbanization was occurring. Only half of the Korean immigrants remained within the city boundaries of Los Angeles, whereas 38 percent of the Korean households were located in the suburbs of Los Angeles County. The other 12 percent, about one hundred and forty households, were scattered primarily in Santa Ana and Anaheim of Orange County, and San Diego. The suburbanization process will undoubtedly continue as the Korean community in Los Angeles expands.

Residential Distribution and Other Korean Institutions

The changes experienced in the neighborhoods of Koreatown and in the suburbs are now compared with the distribution of other activities of ethnic communality. Religious institutions and business operations have been the center of important cultural, social, and economic activities for any ethnic community; therefore, the geographical distribution of Korean churches and retail stores or services should also reflect the residential mobility of the Korean community in Los Angeles.

1. Distribution of Korean Churches

According to *The Korean Directory of Southern California,* forty-two Korean churches were located in the Los Angeles area in

1972. By 1975, 75 Korean ethnic churches were scattered both in Los Angeles and in the surrounding counties. Yet they were mainly concentrated within the Los Angeles city limits, especially in the Olympic Area of Dockweiler, Oakwood, and Rimpau, where 34 Korean churches were located. In 1979, according to the Korean directory, 180 Korean churches were in existence all over southern California. Among them, 104 churches were located within the Los Angeles city limits, and the majority were concentrated in the Olympic Area and in the neighborhoods to the north, which coincides with the residential distribution of Koreans in Los Angeles. The location of churches built in the suburbs followed a pattern similar to that of residential mobility. Gardena and Torrence in the south, Cerritos and Downey in the southeast, Pasadena in the northeast, Van Nuys in the northwest, and Monterey Park and La Puente in the east each added new churches in their respective municipalities during the four years while more Korean churches were founded in Santa Ana, Anaheim, and San Diego.

In 1979, there were only seven Korean Buddhist temples in Los Angeles, even though the number of Buddhists in Korea is disproportionately large. One of the probable explanations for this phenomenon is that to establish a Buddhist temple demands the ownership of the entire building because the temple requires a completely different and unique interior design and architectural style. On the other hand, a Christian church can simply be rented for Sunday afternoon services from other ethnic churches of the same denomination, a common practice in ethnically mixed metropolises (Park, 1980.)[1]

2. Distribution of the Korean Business Establishment

In an urban landscape, business establishments with their advertising in different languages frequently offer clues to the presence of different ethnic groups. The concentration of business establishments along Olympic Boulevard has imprinted a strong visual mark on the Los Angeles landscape (*Newsweek*, May 26, 1975; Sherman, 1979). Several detailed studies of Korean businesses in Los Angeles are available (see Chapter 6), and the present discussion is limited to only the geographical distribution of Korean business establishments with reference to Korean neighborhoods.

In 1972, 401 Korean business firms were listed in the yellow pages of *The Korean Directory of Southern California*. Small retail stores, auto-related services, food services, and trading companies were primarily concentrated near the central business district, and the Olympic Area already had several scores of Korean business firms. By 1975 the number of Korean-operated businesses had risen throughout Los Angeles to over 1,300. The largest concentration of businesses was in a three-mile stretch along Olympic Boulevard between Hoover Street and Crenshaw Boulevard. In 1972 the northern and southern boundaries of the Koreatown business district were Wilshire Boulevard and Washington Boulevard, and by 1975 the northern boundary had extended further north to Beverly Boulevard. The most common types of business were food-related enterprises (e.g., grocery and liquor stores), followed by professional and semiprofessional services (e.g., employment and accounting services), and other retail establishments (e.g., gift shops and furniture stores). Southward expansion of the Korean business district was limited, however, and followed the same pattern as was observed in the residential distribution of the Korean community in 1975 (Kim and Wong, 1977). Kim and Wong have indicated that the south side harbored only a small concentration of Koreans because of the less attractive land characteristics, the lower socioeconomic environment, the higher crime rate, and, hence, the higher insurance rates.

In 1979 the total number of business firms listed in the Yellow Pages of *The Korean Directory of Southern California* was 2,337, and they were spread out over the sixty-mile radius of greater Los Angeles. Korean business cater to two types of clientele: (1) other Koreans and (2) local customers in the business district. The majority of businesses in the Olympic Area serve Korean ethnic needs, whereas businesses in the black neighborhoods of south Los Angeles (along the Harbor Freeway) or the Mexican neighborhoods of east Los Angeles (Boyle Heights) serve the needs of local residents. An entrepreneur may change thus the ethnicity of his or her customers during the course of his or her career (e.g., from an Oriental grocery shop to a liquor store). Korean businesses that do not cater to other Koreans tend to have a disproportionately large share of disadvantaged people as clientele, and these businesses are concentrated heavily in a small-scale retail and services (Bonacich, Light, and Wong, 1980). It is less likely, however, that those small businesses dealing with non-Koreans advertise extensively in the Korean directory; as a consequence, the number of such businesses in the directory might have been underrepresented. In any case, the distribution of Korean business firms does not always coincide with Korean residential neighborhoods, especially in the inner city.

The Korean business district in the Olympic Area expanded its territory in every direction recently, including into previously black neighborhoods to the south. In the suburbs, however, Korean business establishments are primarily concentrated in the municipalities of Korean concentration. The number of businesses located in Hawthorne, Gardena, Torrence, Monterey Park, Downey, and Van Nuys indicate the presence of a growing Korean community in those areas.

In 1979, the most rapidly growing types of businesses were professional and semiprofessional services and import-export trading companies.[2] Within the Korean retail or service job categories, levels of goods and services became more diversified. Harris (1971) points out that it is an indication of the dynamic growth of an ethnic community when the quality and level of goods and services becomes diversified and improved. Similarly in Chicago, as the Korean community grew larger, more specialty stores, such as herbalists, acupuncturists, jewelers, opticians, piano tuners, and surveyors of electric and photographic products, which were nonexistent in 1974, opened for business in 1978.

Summary and Implications

Los Angeles is one of the most dispersed cities in the United States, and the Korean immigrants who settled in Los Angeles rapidly spread outward to the suburban areas. Between 1972 and 1979, the Korean community in Los Angeles grew in two aspects: the establishment of a discrete "Koreatown" in the Olympic Area and the rapid suburbanization within a sixty-mile radius of Greater Los Angeles. The Olympic Area located west of downtown Los Angeles has been a reception area for Korean immigrants, and churches, business establishments, and homes of newly immigrated Koreans are located there. As the Korean community has grown, the suburbanization process has proceeded sectorally following the major freeways: Hawthorne and Gardena in the south along the San Diego Freeway, Downey and Cerritos in the southeast along the Santa Ana Freeway, Monterey Park and La Puente in the east near Pomona and San Bernadino freeways, and Van Nuys in the northwest along the Golden State Freeway.

If the present trend continues, Korean residential neighborhoods may experience the following changes:

1. The present continuous streaming to the north of the Olympic Area will continue, and more Koreans will settle in the Los Feliz, Wilcox, and Hollywood areas of the Los Angeles downtown vicinity. The streaming process will, then, become stabilized because of the physiographic barriers—mountains and Griffith Park—in the north.

2. Because of the physiographic barriers and the less attractive neighborhoods surrounding downtown Los Angeles, the emergence of contiguous streaming in other directions might be difficult. One noncontiguous streaming pattern now occurring is to the south; the Hawthorne and Gardena areas may continue to grow, and the suburbs of Torrence and Palos Verdes may become important Korean neighborhoods.

3. The Korean neighborhoods in Monterey Park and La Puente in the east and Artesia and Cerritos in the southeast seem to be in the scattering process. The future intraurban migration of Koreans toward the southeast or east should be closely examined to identify possible streaming processes. Especially important is a corridor developing toward the southeastern areas, such as Downey, Artesia, and Cerritos, which are located at the gateway to Orange County. Both Santa Ana and Anaheim in Orange County housed most of the Koreans residing outsie of Los Angeles County in 1979—over 8 percent of Koreans in southern California.

Scattering process have generally been interpreted as evidence of diminished ethnic affiliation or of assimilation by the dominant ethnic group. However, Koreans scattered into various suburbs of predominantly white neighborhoods often move to the suburbs that other Koreans previously entered. Would this mean then that the Korean immigrants' ethnic attachment is unaffected by their residential scattering to various suburban areas where whites predominantly reside? If so, this phenomenon of geographic assimilation without weakening ethnic social ties may be called "adhesive adaptation in residential mobility." This issue is explored in Chapter 5.

Notes

1. For details on the religious participation of Korean immigrants, see Chapter 8.
2. For example, advertising companies, attorney's offices, banks, CPA services, construction companies, travel services, etc.

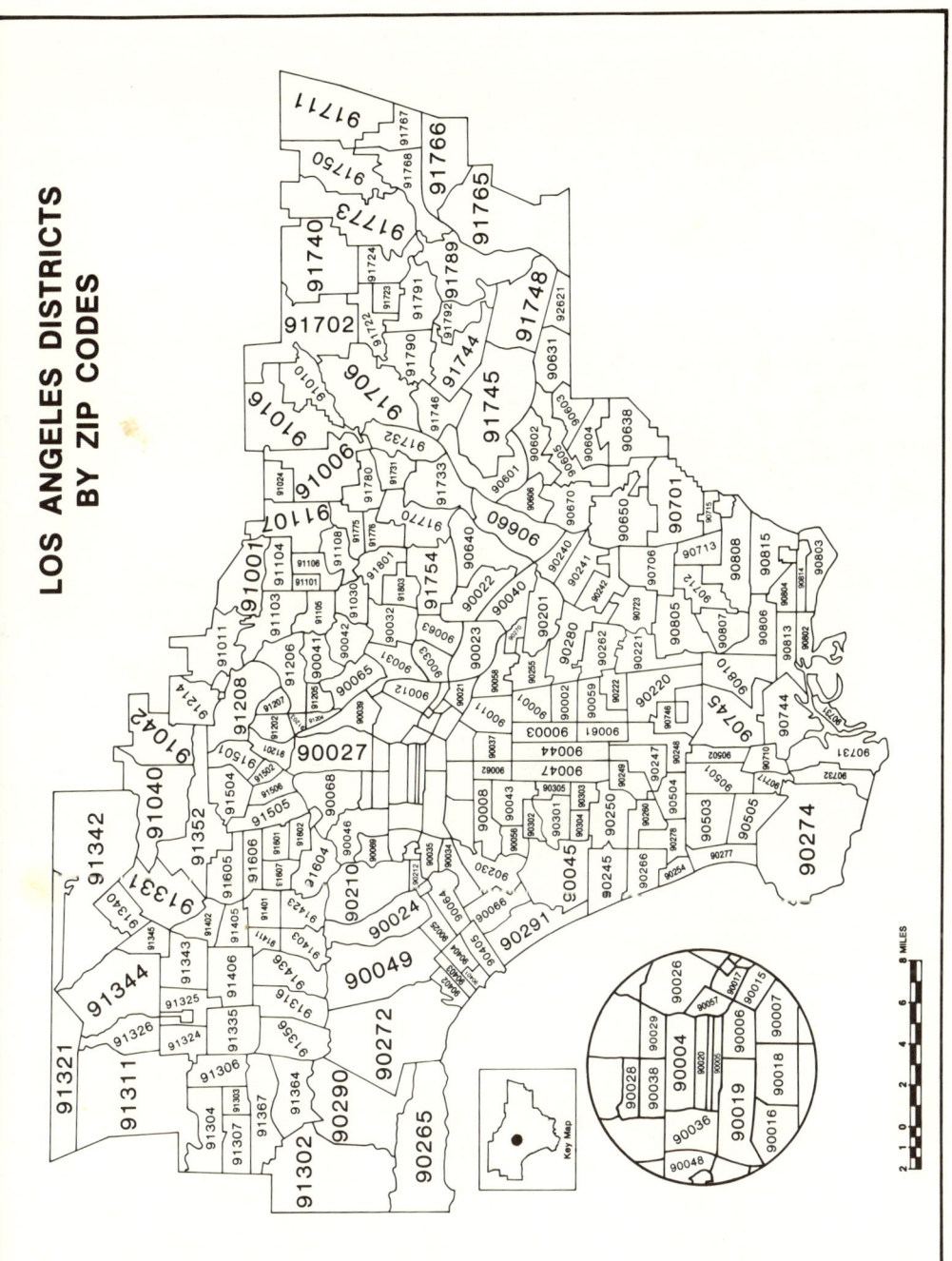

Figure 3. Los Angeles Districts by Zip Codes

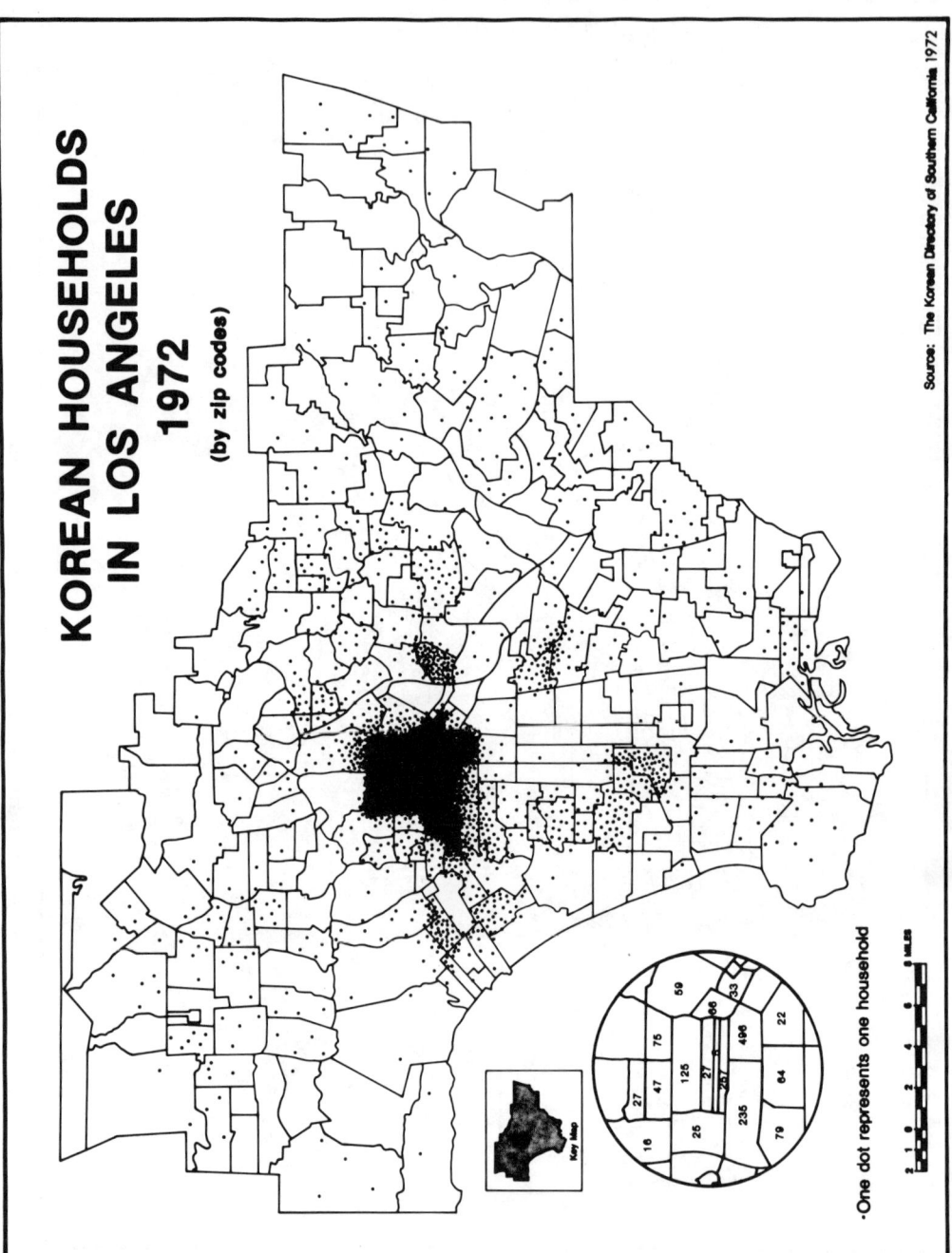

Figure 4. Korean Households in Los Angeles 1972 (Total 3,430)

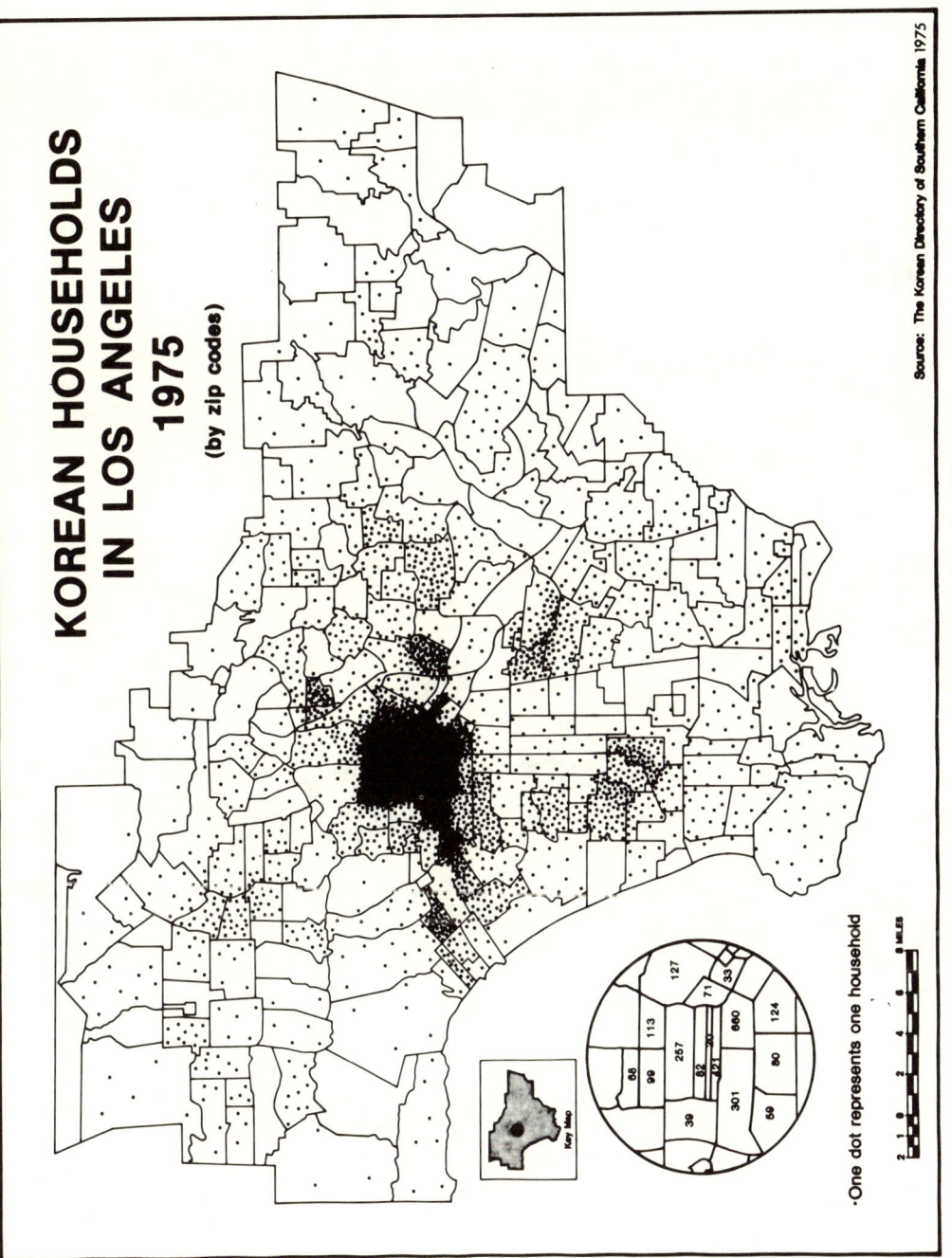

Figure 5. Korean Households in Los Angeles 1975 (Total 5,036)

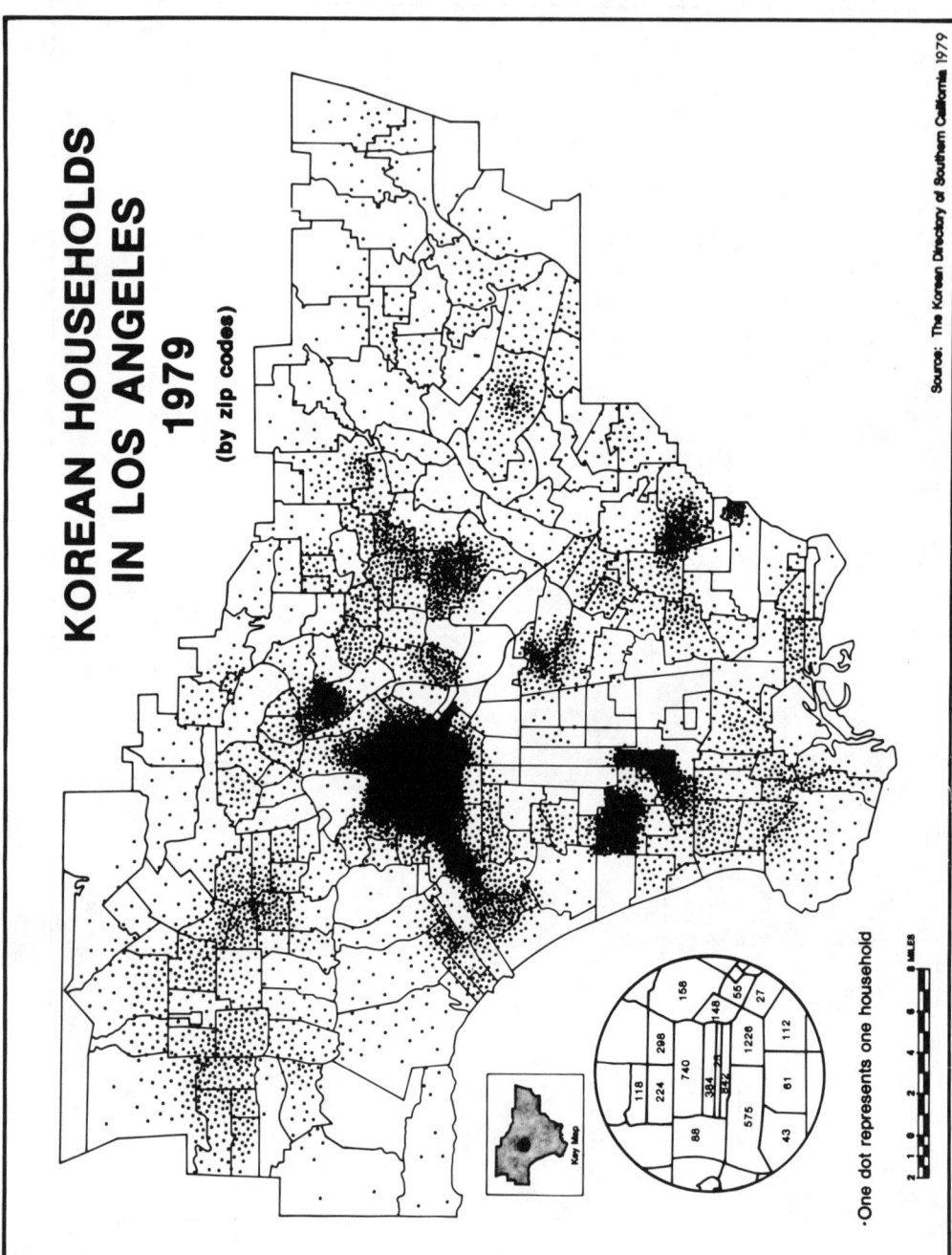

Figure 6. Korean Households in Los Angeles 1979 (Total 12,722)

4
Acculturation: Adhesive Adaptation to American Culture

Having described the historical and demographic backgrounds of Korean immigrants in the United States, we now turn to various dimensions of their adaptation in their new country. As we observed in the introduction, the adaptation of immigrants is the *process* in which immigrants modify their attitudinal and behavioral patterns in order to maintain and improve their life conditions in a manner that is compatible with the new environment. Included in the adaptation process are various subprocesses or dimensions such as cultural, social, economic, and psychological. Among these adaptive subprocesses, acculturation (or cultural assimilation) is usually the first to occur after immigrants arrive in the new country and may not necessarily lead successfully to other adaptive processes, especially social assimilation. Gordon points out aptly:

> Cultural assimilation, or acculturation, is likely to be the first of the types of assimilation to occur when a minority group arrives on the scene; and cultural assimilation, or acculturation, of the minority group may take place even when none of the other types of assimilation occurs simultaneously or later, and this condition of "acculturation only" may continue indefinitely. (1964:77)

In this chapter, we (1) describe the various patterns of the immigrants' acculturation, (2) analyze the typical mode of their acculturation in terms of its structural and situational sources, and (3) advance some theoretical propositions that are generally relevant to the nonwhite immigrants' cultural adaptation in the United States. Accomplishment of the these tasks first requires a clarification of the conceptual problems involved in the study of cultural adaptation in general, and acculturation, in particular.

Conceptual Problems in Acculturation Studies

For the purpose of our study, cultural adaptation is conceived as a broad concept to include its various modes, such as acculturation, cultural assimilation, deculturation, and cultural pluralism. Among these, however, acculturation is the central concept.

Acculturation, a term more widely used by anthropologists than sociologists, is the process by which "the culture of a society is modified as the result of contact with the culture of one or more other societies" (Gillin and Raimy, 1940:371; cf. Teske and Nelson, 1974:351; Thurnwald, 1932:557). As a social process, acculturation takes place in a variety of ways. It may occur unilaterally or bilaterally; voluntarily or involuntarily; and partially or wholly. Depending on the pattern or a combination of patterns, many different types of acculturation emerge. For instance, a combination of unilateral and voluntary acculturation is what sociologists call *cultural assimilation*; a combination of unilateral and involuntary acculturation would be *deculturation* (deprivation of native culture and forced integration into dominant cultural patterns); and a combination of bilateral and voluntary acculturation may be *cultural pluralism* or "democratic acculturation" (Teske and Nelson, 1974; Kramer, 1970:188–212). Teske and Nelson (1974) have recently advanced a comprehensive typology of acculturation that introduces many types of acculturation other than the ones mentioned, e.g., "controlled acculturation."

However, we first examine the immigrants' cultural adaptation in the *generic* conceptual framework of acculturation, rather than confine ourselves to a specific type of acculturation. As we analyze various patterns of the Korean immigrants' acculturation, a typical mode of their cultural adaptation eventually emerges that is then analyzed in the structural context of the "new immigration."

Patterns of Korean Immigrants' Acculturation

According to past studies, the following factors generally affect the acculturation rate of immigrants: (1) racial and cultural similarity between the dominant and immigrant groups, (2) demographic and socioeconomic characteristics, (3) nature and area of immigrants' settlement, (4) proximity to homeland, (5) mutual attitudes of the dominant and immigrant groups, and (6) the length of immigrants' residence in the United States (Warner and Srole, 1945; Eisenstadt, 1951; Weinstock, 1964; Gordon, 1964;

Vander Zanden, 1966:308–313; Berry and Tishler, 1978:280–287; Hurh, 1977a; Schaefer, 1979:42–45).

Particularly because of the first factor (racial and cultural dissimilarity), the degree of cultural ambivalence and conflict seems relatively higher for Asian immigrants than for European immigrants. For instance, our Chicago study revealed the Korean immigrants' strong ambivalence between their desire to discard some specific aspects of their traditional culture and, at the same time, their desire to preserve their own ethnic heritage through generations (Hurh, Kim, and Kim, 1978:92).

We now examine various patterns of the Korean immigrants' acculturation in light of our Los Angeles data. In order to measure the degree of the immigrants' acculturation, the following variables were used: English proficiency, exposure to American-printed mass media, and Anglicization of Korean names (first names).

1. Proficiency in English Language

One of the most important variables affecting cultural adaptation is language. There are three possible ways to assess one's language ability: objective tests, subjective self-evaluations, and observations of linguistic behavior. A combination of all of these would be ideal, but in this study, the first method was not feasible because of the "ego-threatening" latent function of such tests that would most likely jeopardize the interview situation (Gorden, 1975; and also see Appendix B). Because of the limited contact between interviewers and respondents, the third method was also not appropriate. Thus, our data draw on the respondents' self-evaluation of their English proficiency measured by the responses to the following questions: (1) Reflecting on your experience in America, how well do you think that you can express yourself in English? (2) How well can you read American newspapers and magazines? (3) How well can you write letters in English?

As Table 4.1 reveals, about two-thirds of our respondents rate their English ability as "about half" or less in all three dimensions (speaking, reading, and writing). This is true for both male and female respondents. The rating of the Los Angeles respondents is even lower than that of our Chicago sample. Three factors may explain this difference. First, more elderly immigrants are included in the Los Angeles sample than in the Chicago sample. Second, the educational achievement level of the Los Angeles sample is considerably lower than that of the Chicago sample. And third, the Korean ethnic enclave is more firmly and extensively established in Los Angeles than it was Chicago in 1975. In fact, one does not have to speak a word of English to satisfy one's daily needs in Los Angeles' Koreatown (Olympic Boulevard and 8th Street).

One may wonder why such a large proportion of the immigrants experience language problems when the majority of them had some college education prior to their emigration from Korea. English is taught in high schools and colleges in Korea, but its practical use in Korea is extremely limited because of the emphasis on written English. As a result, even a college graduate in Korea is frequently not competent in engaging in simple conversations in English. In addition, unlike the Filipino and other Asian immigrants (e.g., Indians and Chinese from Hong Kong) who have had Anglo-American colonial experiences, the Korean immigrants have never been accustomed to the use of English, especially conversational English.

With such a limited ability in English, the majority (60%) of the employed immigrants indicate that they work in places where English is always required (310, 61.3%) or often required (59, 11.7%), whereas one-fourth (137, 27%) of the employed work where virtually no English knowledge is needed.

In contrast, at home, the overwhelming majority of the Los Angeles sample (about 80%) did not generally use English. They used English more with their children than other members of the family, but only 7.5 percent used it always (Hurh and Kim, 1979b:24). In short, the majority of Korean immigrants must be bilingual—English at work and Korean at home.

2. Exposure to American-Printed Media

The degree of immigrants' exposure to American-printed mass media was measured by the responses to the following questions: (1) Do you read any American newspaper(s)? (2) If you read American newspaper(s), what section do you mainly read? (3) Do you read any American magazine(s)?

Our data reveal that only 22 percent of the respondents (134) subscribed to American newspapers regularly, whereas 78 percent (475) regularly subscribed to Korean newspapers. About one-third (207, 33.7%) of our respondents bought American newspapers at newsstands occasionally. In fact, nearly half (273, 44.5%) of our respondents did not read American newspapers at all. No significant sex difference is observed in the general readership of newspapers.

For those who read American newspapers, their favorite newspaper sections appear to be predominantly the advertisement (217, 63.6%), social (206, 60.4%), and political sections (188, 55.1%). A sex difference emerges when the readership of American newspapers concerns particular favorite sections: male readers tend to favor the economic (85, 31.8%) and sport (77, 47%) sections, whereas female readers favor the cultural life (86, 48.6%) and family affairs (71, 40.1%) sections. As mentioned, advertisement is the most favored sections in American newspapers for the Korean immigrants as two-thirds of the female readers (121, 68.4%) and slightly more than half of the male readers (96, 58.5%) read this section.

Approximately one-fourth (157, 25.8%) of our total respondents regularly subscribed to American magazines and slightly less than one-fourth (142, 23.3%) bought them at newsstands occasionally. The magazines with the largest circulation among our sample are *Time, Newsweek*, and *Reader's Digest*, in that order. Similar to the newspaper readership, about half of our sample did not read American magazines at all. Comparative data on the readership of Korean magazines are lacking because domestic subscription service for Korean magazines is not available in the United States, and one has to either buy Korean magazines at Korean bookstores or place an order to Korea directly through overseas mail.

In sum, Korean immigrants have a limited exposure to American-printed mass media. This is probably the result of a combination of the following factors: the immigrants' language problem, limited participation in the American society (ethnic confinement), and their persisting interest in Korea and primary concerns on the local Korean ethnic community (ethnic attachment). Ethnic confinement and attachment of Korean immigrants are analyzed later.

3. Attitude Toward Anglicizing Korean Names

Anglicization of Korean first names is one of the most conspicuous ways toward Americanization or acculturation since it involves modification of one's symbolic identity (Kang, 1971). Name changes would not have occurred or would not have become an issue if our respondents had not emigrated to America. To measure the respondents' attitudes toward the name change, the following question was asked: How do you feel about Koreans' changing their names to American names? About half (315, 52%) of our respondents approved, whereas 40 percent (242) disapproved of adopting American first names. Since the margin of different is not too great, we may consider our respondents' attitude toward such a practice as ambivalent at best.

The reasons for approving the Anglicization of first names are found to be (in rank order): "it is easier and convenient to pronounce and remember for Americans," "for the sake of children," "for faster assimilation," "familiar to Americans," "it's natural to adopt American names when you get citizenship," "since I have many occasions to contact Americans." Those who disapproved Anglicizing names gave the following reasons (again in rank order): "there is no need to change my name," "to preserve Korean identity," "skin color would not change by Anglicization of names," "since my name was given by my parents," "simple don't like to discard my own name." None of our respondents expressed, in evaluative terms, whether he or she "liked" American names or Korean names better. Practical expediency and preservation of what is given dominate the issue of Anglicization.

In general, our data on the three acculturation dimensions (language, mass media, and name change) of the Los Angeles sample reveal that the respondents are not highly acculturated mainly because of their very recent arrival in the United States (a mean of 6.5 years). As a counterpart to such an early stage of adaptation, one may expect a high degree of ethnic attachment among the immigrants. We next examine some ethnic attachment variables that could have a bearing on the immigrant's acculturation.

4. Ethnic Attachment Variables Related to Acculturation

As we have already defined in our introduction, in our study ethnic attachment refers to the immigrants' subjective identification with their Korean heritage, preservation of Korean culture, and active maintenance of their intimate social ties with Koreans. Ethnic attachment can be measured in many ways as Greenstone suggests (1975:3-4):

> First, the strength of the individual's loyalty or subjective identification with an ethnic group. Second, the degree to which an individual's parentage locates him in a single ethnic group rather than in two or more groups as a result of mixed marriages. Third, the degree to which an individual conforms to a group's traditional customs (or if we somewhat redefine ethnicity, the individual's commitment to the group's traditional religious affiliation, (for example, Judaism for Jews, Roman Catholicism for Poles and Italians). Fourth, the extent to which an individual's friendship pattern is concentrated among members of his own ethnic group. Fifth, the extent of affiliation with and activity in ethnic organizations such as B'nai B'rith or the Polish National Alliance.

In this chapter, we examine, however, only attitudinal aspects of the immigrant's ethnic attachment; behavioral aspects are analyzed in the next chapter. Our respondents were asked to express the degree to which they agreed or disagreed with the following five statements dealing with familism, ethnic inferiority (or ethnic pride), native language, ethnic association, and the ethnic church:

1. When my personal interest is in conflict with my family need, family duty should be given priority (familism).
2. I am ashamed of being born a Korean (ethnic inferiority or ethnic pride).
3. It is necessary for children of Korean immigrants to speak Korean language well (native language).
4. Although Korean immigrants need to adjust themselves to the American society occupationally, they must associate mainly with Koreans in other areas of life (ethnic association).
5. After Korean immigrants are accustomed to American life, it is better for them in many respects to attend American churches than Korean churches (ethnic church).

The highest consensus among the respondents were found on the first three statements. Regardless of sex, most of the respondents indicated that family duty should be given priority (252, 89.7% of the male and 306, 91.6% of the female); children should be taught Korean language (254, 90.4% of the male and 296, 89.2% of the female); and they did *not* feel ashamed of being born a Korean (266, 94.7% of the male and 315, 94.4% of the female). Concerning the statement on associations with Koreans, the respondents were evenly divided, whereas the great majority (414, 68.7%) preferred the Korean ethnic church over the American church.

Through the foregoing observations, it becomes apparent that the Korean immigrants' attachment to their native culture and society is generally strong. Their ethnic attachment is further augmented by their responses to the following additional questions: (1) Do you approve of Korean-American (white) marriage? (2) How do you feel about returning to Korea eventually and spending the rest of your life there? Negative attitudes on intermarriage and positive attitudes on return migration would indicate their strong ethnic attachment. More than 60 percent (368) of our respondents disapproved of intermarriage, whereas only one-third approved (199, 32.6%). These findings are strikingly similar to the data obtained from our Chicago study. There are very few differences between sexes on this attitude. Furthermore, the respondents' negative attitudes on the interracial marriage are largely unaffected by their lengths of residence in the United States and levels of education.

When our respondents were asked to give reasons for their attitudes, the following were prevalent among 491 respondents:

Reason for Disapproval	Frequency N	%
Differences in feelings, thinking, and customs between races	212	43.4
Koreans must marry Koreans	48	9.8
Dislike mixing blood	31	6.3
To preserve pride, purity, and heritage of Korean race	15	3.1
Misfortune of mixed-blood children	12	2.5
Causes conflicts between families	4	0.8
For better human relations among Koreans	4	0.8
Would lead to unhappy marriage	4	0.8
Would dilute racial origin	4	0.8
Even through interracial marriage one can't be assimilated anyway	4	0.8

Reasons for Approval	Frequency N	%
As long as they love and understand each other	106	21.8
As long as they live in America, there is no reason to discriminate	16	3.3
All human beings are the same	13	2.6
For better assimilation	9	1.8
The second-generation Koreans will become Americans anyway	9	1.8
Total	419	100.0

As to the question of return migration, about half (50.1%) of the respondents expressed their desire to return to Korea for various reasons, whereas about one-third (33.8%) would remain in the United States. About 15 percent of the respondents were undecided. The reasons for each group are shown on page 81.

Would Return	Frequency N	%
I would like to return.	198	35.5
I plan to return.	41	7.4
After my children finish school, I will return.	13	2.3
Of course, I must return (this place is not good for old people).	11	2.0
I will return, when the Korean society is stabilized.	4	0.7
Other reasons	12	2.2
Would Remain		
I have no intention to return. I will spend the rest of my life here.	121	21.7
Since my family is here, I don't plan to return.	27	4.8
Realistically, it's impossible to return. I wish I could, though.	12	2.2
I would like to visit Korea, not to live.	21	3.8
Other reasons	7	1.3
Undecided		
I have not thought about it.	59	10.6
I thought about it, but I can't decide now.	28	5.0
It does not matter to me either way.	3	0.3
Total	557	100.0

Finally, the immigrants' strong ethnic attachment does not mean their total blind commitment to their native culture. As with the case of acculturation, ethnic attachment is selective. In order to identify certain aspects of Korean culture and behavioral traits that Korean immigrants themselves desire to change in the course of their immigrant life, we asked the respondents an open-ended question: "In your life in America, do you feel some aspects of Korean culture (habit, customs) need to be modified? If so, what are they?" Awareness of such needs themselves can also be considered a part of the acculturation process. The following is a summary of responses in order of frequency:

Korean Cultural and Behavioral Traits Need to be Modified	Frequency
Male dominance	53
Prying into other's private life	51
Downgrading others	40
Cumbersome Korean cookery	36
Lack of public etiquette	36
Lack of punctuality	34
Men not helping in the kitchen	30
Rudeness (expressionless face)	25
Power struggle for offices	24
Lack of cooperative spirit	23
Sudden visit without prior notice	21
Pretentiousness	18
Parents-centered education of children	17
Indecisiveness (yes and no is not clear)	13
Too loud talk in public	13
Ostentatious ceremonies (wedding, funeral, ancestor worship)	12
Gossiping	11
Ancestorship	10
Self-centered way of thinking	8
Jealousy	7
Asking burdensome favors	7
Making noise while eating (e.g., smacking)	7
Lack of social activity together between wife and husband	7
Craving for power	7
Disorderly conduct	6
Irresponsible behavior	6
Lack in expressive skills	5
Ignoring fellow-Koreans	5
Bribing superiors	5
Extended family system	5
Mistreatment of elderly persons and parents	5
Bragging	5
Calling people late at night	5
Authoritarianism	4
Speaking Korean in front of Americans	4
Not keeping promises	4

The above analysis is based on the response of 421 respondents.

Some of the cultural and behavioral traits listed are not necessarily unique to Koreans. It is, however, a matter of degree and reflects to what extent Koreans feel a need for modification because they are living in America. Whether progressive acculturation would modify these traits is a moot question.

So far, we have described various patterns of Korean immigrants' acculturation in the United States. As we have seen, some of the patterns are discrete but, in general, a common or typical mode of adaptation seems to emerge for all major acculturation dimensions. The mode is "adhesive adaptation" as briefly mentioned in our introduction. Certain aspects of American culture are added onto the Korean culture, without replacing or modifying any significant part of it. Varification of this adhesive mode calls for an intrusive cross-analysis of relevant variables.

Cross-Analysis of Acculturation Variables

The previously mentioned "adhesive adaptation" suggests an idea that acculturation and ethnic attachment are not necessarily mutually exclusive. In order to examine the relationship between the two, our respondents were divided into various categories by two main blocks of structural variables—the length of the respondents' residence in the United States and the level of their educational attainment.

In terms of the length of residence, our respondents were divided into six categories as shown in Table 2.4: (1) 2 years or less, (2) 3-4 years, (3) 5-6 years, (4) 7-8 year, (5) 9-10 years, and (6) 11 years or more. By this division, our respondents were found to be fairly well spread in all six categories.

According to their levels of education, the respondents were divided into four categories: (1) noncollege graduates, (2) Korean-college graduates, (3) American-college graduates, and (4) college students. Noncollege graduates refer to those who never obtained any college degrees. Korean-college graduates refer to those who obtained college degrees only in Korea. American-college graduates are those who obtained undergraduate or graduate degrees in the United States, regardless of their educational achievement in Korea. College students are those who are currently attending American colleges and universities.

Korean-college graduates are the model category for both male and female respondents. Hence, numerically small categories are American-college graduates and college students. Table 4.2 shows a comprehensive picture of each category in terms of current age, age at immigration, current occupation, and length of residence.

Because of their transitory status, those respondents who are still attending colleges are excluded in the further analysis. Among the remaining three categories, American-college graduates are considered as the best educated and noncollege graduates as the least educated, under an assumption that American colleges would provide the immigrants more *appropriate* knowledge and skills for *adaptation in the American society*.[1] At the same time, American-college graduates are the youngest group whereas noncollege graduates are the oldest in terms of both current age and age at immigration. Moreover, occupational categories also correspond to the levels of education. The majority of American-college graduates are found to be professionals and semi-professionals; the majority of Korean-college graduates are proprietors and managers of small businesses; and noncollege graduates are mostly blue-collar workers. Regardless of sex, American-college graduates have also been in the United States considerably longer than any other categories. These observations confirm that the three categories of our respondents based on educational levels are equivalent to three distinct socioeconomic status groups within the immigrant community.

We now examine the relationship between structural variables and acculturation variables. As Tables 4.3 and 4.4 indicate, all three dimensions of acculturation (English proficiency, exposure to American mass media, and Anglicization of Korean names) are positively related to the length of residence. Similarly, the immigrants' levels of education (socioeconomic status) are also positively related to the degree of acculturation (see Table 4.7).

Since both the length of residence and level of education are positively related to the three acculturation dimensions, the relationship between the length of residence and the degree of acculturation is further analyzed for each of the three groups of respondents classified by educational levels (noncollege graduates, Korean-college graduates, and American-college graduates). For all groups, the length of residence is found to be positively related to the three dimensions of acculturation. There is, however, an exception: among noncollege graduates, the length of residence is not related to the degree of exposure to American mass media. Regardless of the length of residence, about two-thirds of the noncollege graduates do not subscribe to American newspapers, and three-fourths of them do not subscribe to American magazines. In general, the immigrants become more acculturated as their length of stay in the United States extends and their socioeconomic conditions improve.

In sharp contrast to the findings on acculturation, most of the dimensions of ethnic attachment are *not* related to the length of residence in the United States. As is evident from Tables 4.5 and 4.6, regardless of the length of residence, a high proportion of our respondents subscribe to Korean newspapers, prefer to associate with Koreans, and prefer to attend the Korean ethnic church. Almost all of them also indicate their strong sense of family priority, ethnic pride, and preference for teaching Korean language to their children (Table 4.6). The educational statuses also have no bearing on the degree of ethnic attachment (see Table 4.7). Generally, most of the respondents show strong feelings of ethnic attachment regardless of the levels of their education (Table 4.7).

With the exception of the female respondents, reading a Korean newspaper is significantly related to their level of education. The relationship, however, does not show any meaningful pattern. It merely reflects that one group (Korean-college graduates) of the respondents read Korean newspapers proportionally more than the other groups. Another exception to the cross-analysis of levels of education and ethnic attachment is on the item of association with Koreans. Those respondents who were more educated were significantly less inclined to agree with the statement that Koreans should exclusively associate with other Koreans on the primary group level.

When the immigrants show strong ethnic attachment regardless of the length of their residence in the United States and their level of education (socioeconomic status), it is probable that their progress in acculturation will not weaken their ethnic attachment either. The degree of the immigrants' acculturation is indeed *not* related to the degree of their ethnic attachment. For example, the respondents' exposure to American mass media is not related to their attitudes toward Korean traditional values and their preference of attending Korean ethnic churches (see Tables 4.8 and 4.9).[2] Similarly, the respondents' proficiency in English and their attitudes toward the Anglicization of Korean names have no relationship with their preference of associating with fellow Koreans and/or attending Korean churches (see Tables 4.9 and 4.10).

In short, the immigrants' strong attachment to their native culture and society is largely *unaffected* by their length of residence, socioeconomic status, and acculturation. Or, to put it differently, progress in time, status, and acculturation does not accompany regress in ethnic attachment.

Until the early 1960s when theories on ethnic pluralism began to emerge (e.g., Glazer and Moynihan, and Gordon),[3] most of the studies on American ethnic minorities assumed the notion that the minorities' progressive acculturation and assimilation would mean at the same time their regressive ethnic attachment. For example, Korean immigrants' learning of the American way of life would require unlearning of their native culture, and increased social acceptance of Koreans by Americans would also entail a decrease in Koreans' association with their own ethnic group, or vice versa (cf. Dohrenwend and Smith, 1962:35; Eisenstadt, 1954b:12–14; Kramer, 1970:211–212).

As we have cross-analyzed acculturation variables, our findings clearly reject such a zero-sum model of assimilation, but rather strongly confirm our original theoretical framework of an adhesive or additive model. Although we have so far examined only the cultural dimensions of the immigrants' adaptation, a similar adhesive or even more accentuated form is anticipated in the social dimensions of adaptation as we see in the next chapter. Why does this adhesive model emerge for the Korean immigrants?

To conclude this chapter, we briefly discuss the structural and situational sources of adhesive adaptation. Theoretical and practical implications of adhesive adaptation in the context of the

American social structure are extensively discussed in the concluding chapter of this book. Adhesive adaptation seems to emerge basically from the confluence between structural and situational factors and one's perception of it. For the Korean immigrants' adaptation, the most relevant structural factors are ethnic segregation inherent in the American social structure and the Korean immigrants' limited adaptive capacities (e.g., radically different cultural heritage including language). Situationally significant factors are a large influx of new immigrants from Asia, ecological concentration of Koreans in their own ethnic enclaves, political relations between Korea and the United States, overall economic recession, and an unfavorable labor market.

These structural limitations and situational problems interact with one another to further ethnic segregation and confinement, whether they occur voluntarily or involuntarily, or both. As we mentioned in our introduction (theoretical framework), the immigrants' perception of such structural limitations and definition of their own limited adaptive capacities and resources would invoke in the immigrants a defense—their desire to maintain and even enhance their ethnic attachment and identity.

It becomes, therefore, apparent that by adhesive adaptation, the immigrants do not resist acculturation or assimilation but rather seek to adopt the new culture and society whenever possible without discarding the old. They cannot afford to discard the old, not because it is necessarily better than the new but rather because it provides them mutual aid and support in times of personal crises and external group threat (cf. Glazer and Moynihan, 1963:xxxiii). In spite of progressive acculturation together with improved socioeconomic conditions, ethnic attachment thus provides the immigrants with a sense of security, primary-group satisfaction, and group identity as long as they are excluded in principle from the mainstream of the American social structure. Ethnic confinement is more pronounced in intimate social relations of Korean immigrants as we examine in the next chapter.

Notes

1. We do not mean here that the American college would generally provide superior knowledge and skills than the Korean college would. It is merely assumed that American-college graduates may be more readily accepted than Korean-college graduates in the American labor market.

2. Subscription to American newspapers is negatively related to preference of associating with Koreans (Table 4.9). However, it is also found that those who subscribe to American newspapers subscribe proportionally more to Korean newspapers.

3. This is not to say that the idea of ethnic pluralism did not emerge prior to these authors. The idea of "cultural pluralism" was espoused already by many scholars in the early 1900s; for instance, Kallen (1915, 1924) and Bogardus (1949). Cf. Newman, 1973:67-96.

5
Social Relations: Ethnic Segregation and Confinement

Intimate Social Relations

The importance of intimate social ties (or the primary group relations) for human adaptation has repeatedly been emphasized by many social scientists since Toennies (1957) and Durkheim (1951). Through intimate social relations, we satisfy our sociopsychological needs such as companionship, emotional support, assistance, and validation of our beliefs and opinions (Sutcliffe and Crabbe, 1963; Homans, 1950 and 1961). Intimate social relations also serve as a buffer, protecting individuals in the mass society (Cutler, 1973). According to Lauman, "the intimate face-to-face group is often held to form the critical primary environment by which an individual is related to the larger society" (1973:111). Intimate social relations thus provide a basic social condition for human adaptation.

In this chapter, we first discuss the Korean immigrants' intimate social relations outside their workplace and next their participation in voluntary associations as an extension of their intimate social relations. A crucial factor in this analysis is the immigrants' mobility. In addition to their initial cross-national (geographical) mobility, the Korean immigrants have experienced a considerable occupational mobility in the United States as discussed in the next chapter.

It has been argued that, in theory, mobility disrupts and weakens intimate social relations with the kin and nonkin (Durkheim, 1951; Toennies, 1957; Wirth, 1938; Parsons, 1949). Emprical studies confirm this disrupting effect of mobility. Several studies, however, show that nonkin who can easily realign their interpersonal relations usually form new social ties in their new environment even though the old ties have been broken

(Bruce, 1970; Hendrix, 1976). Kinship contact is also found to persist in spite of mobility (Adams, 1970; Sussman, 1968).

In light of the growing evidence of kinship contact, Litwak (1959–60) presents a new theory of family system, the modified extended family, which he thinks exists in the United States and other industrialized countries. According to him, the modified extended family consists of "a series of nuclear families joined together on an equalitarian basis for mutual aid" (1959–60:178). A great advantage of this family system is that it is not bound together by demands for geographic propinquity or occupational similarity among kin. Thus, the new family system can adjust to the demands of industrial society, but allows kin to keep close ties.

This review of the literature leads us to expect that in spite of their mobility, Korean immigrants may reestablish close social relations with nonkin and also maintain contact with kin. This position is further strengthened by two additional observations. First, when minority groups are subjected to discrimination, they are found to develop strong kinship ties within their respective groups (Barnett, 1960; Hays and Mindel, 1973; Winch, 1968). These kinship ties are interpreted as a supportive structure in a somewhat hostile environment (Hays and Mindel, 1973:47). Korean immigrants as a racially distinct group would face a similar situation in the United States.

Second, the current U.S. immigration law gives a preferential treatment to the relatives of U.S. citizens and permanent residents as discussed in Chapter 1. Taking advantage of this law, Korean immigrants have invited their kin from Korea to the United States. This practice sets a pattern of kinship aid. Once the invited kin arrive in the United States, the old immigrants would have to help the newly arrived kin in their initial settlement. Then, the newly arrived kin would feel a sense of indebtedness that would strengthen kinship solidarity.

We would therefore expect Korean immigrants to establish or reestablish and maintain intimate social relations with kin and nonkin. This would be particularly true in an area like Los Angeles where Koreans are heavily concentrated. Our descriptive study of their intimate social relations empirically tests this conjecture. In addition to the descriptive study, we explore the following two questions: (1) How well do the immigrants manage to include whites among their personal friends? (2) If the immigrants maintain intimate social relations with both kin and nonkin, are these intimate groups compensatory to, or independent of, each other? Theoretical bases for the two questions are elaborated.

As discussed in our introduction, social assimilation refers to the acceptance of racial or ethnic minority members by the dominant group on the primary group level. For Gordon, social (structural) assimilation is "the keystone of the arch of assimilation" (1964:81). He contends that social assimilation will eventually lead to many other types of assimilation: "Once structural assimilation has occurred, either simultaneously with or subsequent to acculturation, all of the other types of assimilation will naturally follow" (1964:81). Social assimilation is also a crucial factor for the analysis of such secondary group relations as employment and occupational careers in the labor market (Kim and Hurh, 1980c).

In the United States, white Americans are members of the dominant group. Therefore, the study of social assimilation should focus on the extent to which the immigrants include whites in their intimate social relations. Since virtually all kin of the Korean immigrants are also Koreans, our analysis of social assimilation examines the extent to which the immigrants participate in American voluntary associations and include whites in their personal friends and close neighbors.

In his study of the aged, Rosow (1967) raises the issue of whether family members, friends, and neighbors of the aged are a compensatory (reference) group. He maintains that if the groups are compensatory to each other, they will be a functional substitute for each other and "affiliation with one group tends to come at the expense of association with the other and each group can significantly compensate for the absence of the other group" (Rosow, 1967:195). According to Rosow, an alternative idea is that "kin and friends are basically independent, unrelated membership groups" (1967:199). If the groups are independent, it is expected that involvement with one would not affect activity with the other.

Participation in Voluntary Associations

As an extension of our analysis of intimate social relations, we probe the immigrants' participation in voluntary associations based on our Los Angeles study. Voluntary association refers to a group of people organized for some common interest other than profit-oriented ones. A major feature of voluntary association is that its existence and activities reflect the will of its members (Seligman and Johnson, 1954:283). Voluntary associations may involve secondary social relations in the United States; however, voluntary associations of ethnic minorities are usually dominated by the small and primary group atmosphere (Sklare, 1955; Greeley, 1972). In this sense, Korean immigrants' voluntary associations can be treated as an extension of their intimate social relations.

The immigrants' experience of voluntary association is analyzed in terms of (1) the rate of affiliation with voluntary associations, (2) the intensity of participation, and (3) the activities within the voluntary associations.

The Immigrants' Intimate Social Relations with Koreans

Three-fourths of our Los Angeles sample (210, 74.7% of the males and 252, 75.4% of the females) reported having kin in the Los Angeles area—the geographically accessible kin. The majority (53, 58.8%) of those who specified their relationship with the kin showed that their kin in the Los Angeles area were sisters and/or brothers. Other kin in the area were parents (68, 15.8%), married children (19, 4.4%), uncles and/or aunts (56, 13%), in-laws (61, 14.2%), and other relatives (146, 33.9%).

Half of the respondents (50.8%) who had kin in the Los Angeles area indicated contacting their kin once a week or more often. Most of them (80.1%) contacted their kin at least once a month. This observation shows that kin constitute an important part of the respondent's intimate social relations in the Los Angeles area.

Three-fourths of the respondents were also found to have close neighbors. Most of them indicated that their close neighbors were exclusively Koreans (341, 74.8%). A few of them had both whites and Koreans as their close neighbors (58, 12.7%). Altogether, nearly nine-tenths of the respondents had Koreans as their close neighbors. Consequently, very few respondents had exclusively whites (42, 9.2%) or non-Korean minority members (15, 3.3%) as their neighbors.

Taking advantage of geographical propinquity, the respondents with close neighbors contacted their neighbors frequently. Among these respondents, one-fourth of the males (42, 25.1%) and one-third of the females (80, 34%) saw their neighbors every day. As a whole, about four-fifths of the respondents (150, 80.2% of the males and 203, 86.4% of the females) contacted their close neighbors once a week or more.

In this study, *friends* refer to those with whom the respondents feel they share something together and like each other. Sharing and affectivity, therefore, characterize friendship. To test the respondents' experience of friendship, the following questions were asked:

Do you have any person(s) in the Los Angeles area with whom you maintain an intimate relation and with whom you feel you share something together? Some have one or two such persons. Others may have several such persons or none at all. How many such persons do you have? If you have such persons, select some of them (5 or less) and answer the following questions about them: their name (first or middle), place of first meeting, age, length of association, final education and current occupation.

We asked these questions separately for Korean and non-Korean friends. By this measure, nine-tenths of the respondents (263, 93.6% of the males and 300, 89.8% of the females) were found to have Korean friends. The respondents provided detailed information on 1,763 of their Korean friends. Analysis of these Korean friends shows that one-fifth or more of them were kin of the respondents (see Table 5.1). However, virtually all of the respondents who have kin-friends also reported to have one or more non-kin friends.

The male respondents mentioned that one-third of their friends were old friends (118, 14.6%) or alumni (133, 16.4%), whereas the female respondents indicated that one-fourth of their friends were old friends (101, 10.6%) or alumni (130, 13.6%). *Old friends* usually refer to those who were already friends of the respondents prior to their emigration from Korea. *Alumni* are those with whom the respondents went to the same high school or college in Korea. These observations, then, identify three types of preimmigration friends, although they may not be mutually exclusive: kin-friends, old friends, and alumni. Because of their preimmigration social ties, the respondents knew three-fourths of their preimmigration friends for nine years or more (305, 76.4% of the preimmigration friends of the male respondents and 346, 76.4% of the preimmigration friends of the female respondents). As a whole, the preimmigration friends were found to be half of the respondents' current friends.

The respondents met the majority of their postimmigration friends at church or workplace (see Table 5.1). Church was the most common place to meet their postimmigration friends. The respondents met other postimmigration friends at school, neighborhood, or other places. Because of their postimmigration social ties, the respondents knew the majority of their postimmigration friends for four years or less (230, 59.4% of the postimmigration friends of the male respondents and 290, 60.3% of the postimmigration friends of the female respondents).

The Immigrants' Intimate Social Relations with Non-Koreans

Although most of the respondents had Korean friends, only one-third of the respondents (95, 33.8% of the male and 106, 31.7% of the female) were found to have white friends. Altogether, slightly less than half of the respondents (128, 45.6% of the male and 150, 44.9% of the female) had non-Korean friends, including Asian, Mexican, black, or others. The respondents provided detailed information on 526 non-Korean friends, most of whom were white (376, 69.8%).

Unlike the case of the postimmigration Korean friends, the respondents initially met most of their non-Korean at their work place or at school. The work place is found to be the most common place to meet their non-Korean friends, regardless of the ethnicity of the non-Korean friends (see Table 5.2). The female respondents met their non-Korean friends in their neighborhood proportionally more than the male respondents. Since the respondents met their non-Korean friends after their immigration to the United States, the respondents knew the majority of their non-Korean friends for four years or less (147, 65% of the non-Korean friends of the male respondents and 215, 72.9% of the non-Korean friends of the female respondents).

In general, the level of education is positively related to the degree to which our respondents are socially assimilated. This is demonstrated by the fact that regardless of sex, American-college graduates have proportionally more white friends and participate more in American voluntary associations, whereas the reverse is true among noncollege graduates (see Table 5.3). The length of residence in the United States is also positively related to the respondents' social assimilation regardless of sex (Table 5.4). However, our data also reveal a restrictive nature of the immigrants' social assimilation; even among American-college graduates, half have no white friends. A similar pattern can be observed from those who have been in the United States for eleven years or longer.

Since the two interrelated variables (the length of residence and the level of education) are positively related to the degree of social assimilation, we analyzed further the relationship between the length of residence and the degree of social assimilation for each of the three groups of respondents classified by educational levels (noncollege graduates, Korean-college graduates, and American-college graduates).

Their length of residence of the noncollege graduates in the United states is not related to their degree of social assimilation (see Table 5.5). Regardless of the length of residence, the degree of noncollege graduates' social assimilation was found to be highly limited.

In contrast, Korean-college graduates show that their length of residence is positively related to the degree of social assimilation: those who have been in the United States for a longer period of time have proportionally more white friends and participate more in American voluntary associations. Since there are few noncollege graduates and Korean-college graduates whose length of residence exceeds 11 years, two time intervals—9–10 years and 11 years or more—are combined for our analysis.

On the other hand, very few of the American-college graduates have been in the United States for less than four years (N=8). Thus, three time intervals—two years or less, three to four years, and five to six years—were combined. This combination of time periods severely limits the range of the American-college graduates' length of residence to be tested. Our limited test indicates that the length of residence is not related to the degree of social assimilation among American-college graduates. Regardless of the length of residence, the degree of their social assimilation is *relatively* high; about half of them had white friends and one-fourth of them joined American voluntary associations. These findings suggest that the American-college graduates' friendship with whites develops to a certain level within several years after their arrival in the United States, mainly through their schools and workplaces (Table 5.2), and this level seems to maintain steadily thereafter. In this process of developing friendship with members of the dominant group, the immigrants' first few years in the United States appear to be crucial. Unfortunately, however, our analysis cannot cover this period adequately because of the reasons mentioned.

We now examine the respondents' social relations with members of their own ethnic group. Neither the length of residence in the United States nor the level of education is related to the proportion of the respondents who associated with Korean intimate groups in the Los Angeles area (friends and kin) and who joined Korean voluntary associations (see Tables 5.6, 5.7, and 5.8).[1] Irrespective of their length of residence or level of education, the respondents maintain a strong attachment to their own ethnic social ties. Even among the old settlers (11 years or more), more than four-fifths (85.1%) of them had Korean friends, and there is no sign that the respondents reduced the frequency of their contact with kin as their length of stay in the United States extends. An exceptional case is found, however, among the female respondents, for whom the level of education is inversely related to the proportion of those who joined Korean voluntary associations.

Differentiation of the Intimate Groups

As shown in Table 5.9, association with kin in the Los Angeles area is not related to the chance that the respondents associate with Korean friends or join Korean voluntary associations. This confirms the "independent" theory mentioned earlier (Rosow, 1967:199). Those who have Korean friends indicate, however, a significantly higher chance of joining Korean voluntary associations, which include churches. About two-thirds (188, 62.7%) of the male and female (167, 63.5%) respondents who had Korean friends also participated in Korean voluntary associations. This relationship seems to reflect the fact that the respondents have met a high proportion of their postimmigration friends at the church. Korean friends and voluntary association do not appear to be compensatory to one another in terms of their functions.

Association with white friends is also not related to the chance of the respondents having Korean friends and contacting kin in the Los Angeles area or joining Korean voluntary associations with one exception among female respondents (Table 5.10). This pattern clearly demonstrates that *the social assimilation of the respondents is not accompanied by their dissociation from Korean intimate groups*.[2] As the immigrants are more socially assimilated to the American society, they *expand* the overall dimension of their intimate social relations, rather than replacing one dimension with another. This pattern of social adaptation has been observed from both Korean-college and American-college graduates, although the two groups reveal somewhat different mode of social assimilation with respect to their length of residence.

Are these intimate social groups of the immigrants functionally differentiated as the independence theory seems to suggest? Unless the social groups are functionally differentiated, our respondents would have little incentive to associate intimately with various groups of people (Litwak and Szelenyi, 1969). We examined this issue by analyzing the responses to the following question: "When you have difficult personal problems, with whom do you mainly discuss them?" Then, the following response categories were presented: spouse, parents, children, other kin (specify), Korean friends, American friends, colleagues at work, minister or priest, and others (specify).

The spouse is found to be the person who was most frequently consulted by the respondents in times of personal crisis. Three-fourths of the male respondents and two-thirds of the female respondents indicated discussing personal problems with their spouses (see Table 5.11). Many also discussed their problems with their parents, children, and other kin. Most of the other kin are found to be sisters or brothers of the respondents. This indicates that the respondents heavily rely on their immediate family members for communicating their personal problems.

A high proportion of the respondents were also found to discuss their problems with their Korean friends. Thus, Korean friends emerged as the most trusted nonkinship members in time of personal crisis. Korean ministers or priests were also consulted by many respondents. However, only a small proportion of the respondents discussed their problems with American friends or colleagues at work. In spite of frequent contact, close neighbors are virtually not mentioned, even in the category "others."

Analysis of job information transmission provides another opportunity to examine the nature of contact that the respondents have with their intimate groups (see Chapter 6 for a detailed discussion). To the question, "How did you obtain job information which led you to your current employment?" about half of the respondents (191, 51.8%) indicated obtaining their job information from other persons. Among these respondents who obtained job information from others, nearly half did so from their Korean friends (90, 47.6%), and a small proportion from their kin (31, 16.4%). Again, neighbors were rarely mentioned as a source of job information.

The preceding analysis reveals different roles played by each type of intimate group. Although kin are most frequently consulted for personal problems, friends are mostly used for obtaining help in the labor market. Neighbors are conspicuous by their absence in these two activities (confiding personal problems and job information transmission).

Participation in Voluntary Associations

The definition of voluntary association is an unsettled issue. Therefore, it is debatable whether the church and the labor union should be included as voluntary associations (Babchuk and Thompson, 1962). In this study, the labor union is no problem because no respondent mentioned it. A high proportion of the respondents, however, were found to be affiliated with the Korean church, so that in this study, the church is included as a voluntary association, and meets the definition of a voluntary association adopted in this chapter. Furthermore, the Korean church is found to perform several vital functions of the voluntary association (e.g., social, symbolic, ideological).

A great majority of the respondents (468, 76.1%) were found to participate in Korean voluntary associations that consist mainly of Koreans and use the Korean language. Of these respondents, the vast majority (87.7%) joined one association and the remaining respondents (12.3%) joined two or more associations. The Korean church was found to be the most popular association (see Table 5.12). Social club, alumni group, religious group and senior citizen's group are also mentioned by many respondents. The social club includes tennis club, hiking club, *go* club, golf club, woman's club, volleyball club, YMCA, Lion's Club, Kiwani's Club, and others.

There is a sharp difference in the extent to which the respondents attended the church and other voluntary associations. Most of the church affiliates (359, 84%) were found to attend their church at least once a week, whereas two-thirds of those who participated in other voluntary associations (71, 64.5%) attended their association less than once a week. A small difference is, however, found in the proportion of those who held a staff position or carry some official duties. One-third of the male church affiliates (56, 30%) and one-fourth of the female church affiliates (55, 22.8%) held staff positions in their church. Many church affiliates (65 males and 81 females) also performed various duties in their church, such as Sunday school teachers, choir members, leaders of youth groups, members of evangelical service, clerks, or financial officials (see Chapter 8 for details on church participation). Among those who participated in other voluntary associations, one-third (33, 30%) held staff positions or carried some official duties.

A very small proportion of the respondents participated in American voluntary associations that mainly consist of non-Koreans and use the English language (see Table 5.12). Most participated only in one association (93.1%). The types of American association that the respondents joined the most are social clubs, churches, and other religious groups. One-third attended their American voluntary associations once a week (39.3%) and another one-third attended less than once a month (32.1%). Very few were found to hold a staff position or carry an official duty (12.3%).

The preceding analysis reveals that a high proportion of the respondents join the Korean voluntary associations, and the intensity of their participation is generally high among the church affiliates. But participation in American voluntary associations is severely limited in its scope and intensity. This observation is comparable to the finding of our Chicago study: "Social relationships among the respondents are built around ethnic organizations, especially church, within the well-defined boundaries of a Korean enclave" (Hurh, Kim, and Kim, 1978:30).

Perception of Social Assimilation

As a supplementary analysis, the respondents' subjective perception of social assimilation was examined. For this analysis, the following three questions were asked: (1) Do you think it is generally difficult to make friends with white Americans? (2) Would you feel more comfortable living in a predominantly white neighborhood rather than Korean? (3) How strongly do you agree or disagree with the following statements: (a) When I am with Americans, I often feel "left out" or isolated; (b) Most Americans whom I personally know do not seem to understand how I feel about things. For these questions, the following five response categories were represented: strongly agree (definitely yes), agree (yes), don't know, disagree (no), and strongly disagree (definitely no).

Our respondents were widely distributed in their responses to these questions. Interestingly, however, their responses were generally related to their actual experience of social assimilation as measured by the question of whether they have white friends. Those who had white friends showed a significantly more positive response to social assimilation than those who did not. Thus, compared with the latter, the former had less difficulty in making friends with whites and felt less left out or not understood.

Only one exception comes from their response to the question on whether they would feel more comfortable living in a white neighborhood. To this question, their actual experience of social assimilation is not related at all. But the numerous remarks they made with respect to this question reveals a complicated motivational structure behind their desire to live in a white or Korean neighborhood. Those respondents who favored a white residential area were motivated by their desire to avoid Koreans ("Koreans make too many slanderous comments on others," "Koreans interfere with other's privacy") and/or their desire to associate with whites ("Whites are courteous, kind, and cheerful," "Whites live in a clean, quiet, and safe area"). Those who do not desire to live in white residential areas were also motivated by their desire to avoid whites ("Koreans are discriminated against in white residential areas," "We have language or cultural problems with whites") and/or their desire to associate with fellow Koreans ("I feel comfortable with Koreans," "We can eat *Kimchi* and other Korean foods without any fear of complaints"). These two sets of desires suggest that some complicated motivations affect their attitude toward association with Koreans and whites.

Summary and Conclusions

We have observed that the Korean immigrants in the Los Angeles area manage to establish a complex web of intimate social relations with others in spite of their extensive mobility. Most of those in the immigrants' intimate networks are, however, Koreans. Furthermore, such ethnic attachment remains largely unaffected by their length of residence in the United States or the level of education. In contrast, their intimate association with whites varies with these two factors, and is in general, limited. This limited social assimilation and the ethnic attachment among the Korean immigrants indicate that their intimate social contact is generally confined to the members of the same ethnic group.

In this chapter, we have examined three types of intimate social relations: kin, personal friends, and close neighbors. For the vast majority of the respondents, kin constitute an important intimate group. This is demonstrated by the proportion of those who have kin in the Los Angeles area, the frequency of their kinship contact, and the proportion of those who discussed personal problems with kin.

Analysis of the kinship contact in the United States reveals two interesting points. First, most of their kin in the Los Angeles area are the primary relatives of the respondents—parents, brothers, sisters, sons, and daughters (and spouses). Those kin who are consulted for personal problems mostly are also the primary relatives of the respondents. This indicates that for the immigrants, the range of kinship contact is usually limited to the primary relatives.

Second, the number of some primary relatives (e.g., parents) who are consulted by the respondents for their personal problems exceeds the number of the same type of primary relatives reported living in the Los Angeles area. This reveals that many primary relatives who do not live in the Los Angeles area are also consulted by the respondents. Thus, our Los Angeles sample supports the contention of Litwak that today, kinship contact does not necessarily require geographical propinquity.

Korean friends are another important intimate group for the

respondents. For their friendship, both pre- and postimmigration social ties play a crucial role. Our respondents also showed that their close neighbors were mostly fellow Koreans.

The two types of intimate groups (kin and friends) reviewed in this chapter indicate some degree of functional differentiation. The respondents relied mostly on kin when they had personal problems, but their friends are most active in the job information transmission. Since the solution of personal problems requires an intimate personal knowledge of the respondents, kin seem to be in a better position than any other types of persons. But transmission of job information requires similarity between the informer and receiver of the information in their career and occupational orientation. In this respect, friends may be in a more suitable position than kin who are differentiated in terms of sex, age, and generation. This interpretation suggests that functional differentiation among intimate groups results, in part, from their differential resources to assist the respondents.

We have observed that the respondents' chance to associate with one intimate group is independent of their chance to associate with other intimate groups. This shows that their association with one intimate group neither deters nor facilitates their chance of associating with other intimate groups. Under this condition, the respondents can associate with some or all of the intimate groups on the basis of the availability of such groups and their willingness or necessity to associate with the groups. In reality, it has been observed that virtually all of the respondents have personal friends, and most of them have, additionally, kin and/or close neighbors.

The independent association is also extended to the chance of associating with whites. Under this condition, association with any Korean intimate group neither deters nor facilitates the respondents' chance of associating intimately with whites and vice versa. Therefore, we see no evidence that association with whites is accompanied by disassociation from intimate contact with Koreans. This observation again confirms the adhesive pattern of adaptation. As already mentioned, almost all of the immigrants maintained close social ties with other Koreans. Additionally, some of them maintained intimate association with whites without jeopardizing their chance of associating with Koreans.

The Korean church dominates the immigrants' experience of voluntary association in the United States. In this chapter, we have observed that in addition to its religious function, the church has some social function to satisfy the personal needs of its members. The church serves as a ground to meet friends, and it offers an opportunity for church affiliates to hold staff positions, to satisfy their needs for social recognition and self-expression, or to use their ability or power. The roles of the Korean ethnic church are discussed fully in Chapter 8. Other Korean associations such as social clubs, alumni groups, religious groups, and senior citizen's associations are also designed to satisfy the various personal needs of their members—recreational, social, and symbolic. The American voluntary associations in which the immigrants participate are similar in their functions to the Korean associations. These associations are mainly expressive ones that exist to satisfy immediate personal needs of the members, but not instrumental ones, which are designed to influence the existing social system or policies of the government or other public agencies (Babchuk and Edwards, 1965).

The respondents' perception of their relationship with whites was found to be generally related to their actual experience of social assimilation. Thus, those who had white friends expressed more favorable experiences with whites than those who did not. This holds true except in one case: the respondents' desire to live in white neighborhoods. In this case, the respondents exhibited complex attitudes toward their desire to associate with Koreans or whites. Those who desired to live in the Korean neighborhoods were motivated by their attraction to fellow Koreans and/or their desire to avoid whites. Those who desired to live in the white neighborhoods were motivated by their attraction to whites and/or their desire to avoid Koreans.

Notes

1. Data on association with close neighbors are excluded from the subsequent analyses. As discussed, almost all of the respondents with close neighbors reported to have Koreans as their close neighbors. This means if they did not have Koreans in their neighborhood, they were likely to have no close neighbors at all. Under these circumstances, when the respondents reported to have no close Korean neighbors, this would not necessarily mean a lack of social attachment to their own ethnic group. This point is particularly pertinent to those respondents who have been in the United States for a longer period of time. As the "old timers" increasingly move to suburban areas, they may not find any Koreans in their neighborhood. Thus, association with close Korean neighbors is not a good indicator of the respondents' attachment to their ethnic social ties.

2. A similar pattern is observed from the respondents' participation in American voluntary associations in relation to their association with Korean friends and kin, and participation in Korean voluntary associations. However, the numbers of the respondents in some categories are too small for a meaningful cross-analysis, since the total number of the Koreans who participate in American voluntary associations is small to begin with.

6
Occupational Career: Containment in the Segregated Labor Market

As already indicated, most of the Korean immigrants as a racial minority came to the United States with a high socioeconomic status, and some of them have also been highly educated in the United States (see Chapter 2). Such racial and socioeconomic backgrounds seem to complicate the immigrants' adjustment in the American labor market. On the one hand, one would expect that the Korean immigrant would be well accepted in the American labor market because of their relatively high socioeconomic background and skills. On the other hand, one suspects that they are subjected to the various forms of discrimination in the racially biased labor market in the United States.

The Korean immigrants' problem can be further aggravated by the fact that they are the first-generation immigrants. As immigrants, they face a variety of problems associated with their immigrant status such as a language problem, unfamiliarity with the American way of life, and the lack of a solid socioeconomic base in the United States. Under these circumstances, one would question how the Korean immigrants adjust themselves in the American labor market.

Two theoretical approaches appear promising for the analysis of this issue: individual and structural. The human capital theory represents the former and the schools of labor market segmentation and job information transmission represent the latter.

As an individual approach, the human capital theory is concerned with the income of workers. The theory contends that wages or salaries of workers are mainly determined by their productivity at work, which is in turn explained by their stock of human capital accumulated through their formal education and on-the-job experiences (Blau and Jusenius, 1976; Bowman, 1966; Mincer, 1970; Schultz, 1961; Thurow, 1969, 1975). According to this position, the more stock of human capital the workers accumulate, the more wage or salary they can earn.

An extension of the human capital theory is that income and other occupational rewards that workers receive at work depend on the workers' individual productive resources. If they possess a great deal of such resources, they will be rewarded accordingly from the initial placement to the subsequent mobility, monetary compensation, and so on. From this perspective, employment and other occupational problems of workers come from their lack of marketable resources, unless the demand for labor is drastically reduced. Thus, if the Korean immigrants cannot find jobs, this approach would assert that their employment problem may, for example, come from their language problem. As a medium of communication, language ability (English proficiency) is a crucial component of the required ability at work. Therefore, their language problem makes them relatively unattractive to prospective employers. In sum, the human capital school asserts that the individual productive resources of the workers ultimately explain their experience of occupational reward and achievement in the labor market.

In the area of occupational sociology, there are two major analytical focuses that analyze the structurally generated problems of minority-group employment: the labor market segmentation and the job-seeker's method of job information acquisition. The former focuses on the division of the American labor market in terms of "the Balkanization of labor markets," "dual labor markets," "the split labor market," or "segments and shelters of labor markets" (Bonacich, 1972; Doeringer and Piore, 1971; Freedman, 1976; Kerr, 1954; Piore, 1969). According to this analytical focus, the system of labor distribution in the United States has been segmented into multiple markets, which are observed across occupations and/or industries. The segmentation distinguishes one labor market (e.g., an employing organization or a set of employing organizations) from other labor markets through job-related rewards, such as job security, pay, promotions, opportunities for training or skill upgrading, prestige, and respect of due process in labor grievances. In some cases, the segmentation proceeds even further to divide the same labor market into multiple submarkets that operate distinctly for different types of workers or employers.

Such labor market segmentation is systematically related to the race, sex, or age of workers (Doeringer and Piore, 1971; Bonacich, 1972; Freedman, 1976). Needless to say, racial and/or ethnic minorities tend to be concentrated in relatively unfavorable labor markets. In other words, the labor market segmentation highlights the institutional mechanism that discriminated against racial and/or ethnic minorities in employment.

Freedman contends that labor market segmentation develops by a variety of sheltering mechanisms in labor markets. Such mechanisms spare those who are already employed from the competition with the potential job seekers, and also protect the employed "against adversity and mitigation of the effects of unemployment, disability, illness and old age" (1976:113). For developing the sheltering mechanisms, employees take advantage of favorable structural elements (large establishment size, internal promotion ladder), occupational licensing and accreditation, and unionization. According to Doeringer and Piore, segmentation results from the internal labor market in an administrative unit (e.g., a local plant) which accords special rights and privileges to employees. Through the operation of the internal labor market, employers want to reduce the cost of training and labor turnover and increase work efficiency, whereas employees try to keep their jobs and protect their opportunities for promotion, training, and other benefits.

Once the internal labor market and/or sheltering mechanism operates, such conditions reward employees but penalize job seekers. For job seekers, it is difficult to penetrate into the labor market where such an internal labor market or sheltering mechanism has already been well institutionalized. This condition forces members of minority groups to gravitate to the easily accessible but relatively unfavorable labor markets or to remain unemployed.

The study of job information transmission is concerned with the problem involved in the job search. According to this school, there are basically two methods of job information acquisition: formal and informal. The formal method refers to the acquisition of job information from mass media, public or private placement centers, or university-professional placement services. This method is characterized by the use of established channels of job information transmission. The informal method refers to the process of obtaining job information from sources other than the established channels of job information transmission. The informal method is further subdivided into two types: personal contact and direct search. Personal contact refers to the process of obtaining job information from relatives, friends, past or current work associates, a prospective employer, immediate superior, or other persons. Direct search means that a job seeker writes directly to prospective employers concerning job opportunities or applies for a job in person.

Of the three methods described, personal contact is used most frequently by both blue-collar and white-collar workers and generally introduces better jobs than other methods (Brown, 1965; Crain, 1970; Granovetter, 1974; Rees, 1966; Reid, 1972; Sheppard and Belintsky, 1966; Ullman, 1968). The advantages of personal contact as a method of job information acquisition may be attributed to several factors. First, as Rees (1966) indicates, personal contact can convey more information about a job than formal method or direct contact. Second, if job information comes from someone the job seeker knows well or trusts, the information becomes more credible to the recipient. Third, when the informer is one of the employees of the organization where a job is available, the job seeker is encouraged because of the possibility of working with his or her friend. The job seeker would certainly regard this as a "fringe benefit."

Employers benefit also from personal contact, since it is an inexpensive method of job information transmission (Rees, 1966). Through their past experiences, employers know that an employee referral is as dependable as the employee himself or herself. Thus, as long as employers are satisfied with the performance of employees, they are inclined to hire those referred by their own employees, which cuts their screening costs (Rees, 1966).

The two analytical foci, labor market segmentation and job information acquisition, combined together provide a comprehensive theoretical framework for the analysis of the structurally generated problems involved in the employment of immigrants in the United States.

In this chapter, we analyze the occupational experiences of the Los Angeles sample by the individual and structural approaches. In the analysis, we focus on various aspects of their occupational experiences such as occupational mobility, methods of job information acquisition used, objective conditions of work, and subjective response to work experiences. The general characteristics of their experiences in these areas reveals the structural conditions of their work in the American labor market.

In order to probe the role that the stock of human capital would play for the immigrant workers' occupational career, we examine their experience in these topics separately for the three groups categorized in Chapter 4: the noncollege graduates, Korean-college graduates, and American-college graduates. By formal education, the American-college graduates possess human capital most in the American labor market and the noncollege graduates possesses the least. As shown in Tables 4.3 and 4.7, the American-college graduates are also relatively most acculturated and the noncollege graduates are the least acculturated. By these two indicators of human capital stock (formal education and the degree of acculturation that includes English proficiency), we then rank the American-college graduates first, the Korean-college graduates second, and the noncollege graduates third.

It is also observed that among the male respondents, American-college graduates are ranked first by the total length of job experience in the United States (mean = 8 years, SD = 8.1), the Korean-college graduates second (mean = 4.8 years, SD = 3.2), and noncollege graduates third (mean = 3.6 years, SD = 2.0). Differences in the length of job experience are significant at the .001 level (F = 12.9, df = 2, 214). For the male respondents, we may then use the total length of job experience as another indicator of the stock of human capital.

Occupational Mobility of the Immigrants

Most of the male (220, 78.3%) and half of the female (172, 51.2%) respondents had job experience in Korea. Nine-tenths of these female respondents (120, 85.7%) were either professionals and semiprofessionals or clerical workers in Korea. A similar proportion of the male respondents who had job experience in Korea were in the following three categories of white-collar occupations in Korea: professionals and semiprofessionals (55, 25%), proprietors and managers (56, 25.5%), clerical-administrative or other white-collar workers (85, 38.6%).

In order to examine the occupational experiences of the respondents in the United States, their occupation is classified into the following five categories: (1) professionals and semiprofessionals, (2) proprietors and managers, (3) other white-collar workers, (4) skilled workers, and (5) semiskilled or unskilled workers.[1]

The majority of both employed male (118, 63.1%) and female (107, 57.1%) respondents had blue-collar occupations at the beginning of their career in the United States. When this distribution is compared with their preimmigration occupations, it is found that most of the respondents initially experienced a drastic downward mobility through immigration.

More than four-fifths of the male (241, 85.8%) and two-thirds of the female (214, 64.1%) respondents were employed at the time of their interview. Among them, most of the males were distributed into three occupations: proprietors and managers (34%), professionals and semiprofessionals (25.7%), and semiskilled and unskilled workers (19.9%), whereas most of the females were found in the four occupations: semi-skilled and unskilled workers (30.4%), proprietors (28.9%), professionals and semiprofessionals

(20.7%), and other white-collar workers (17.2%). (See Table 6.1).

This distribution indicates that more than two-thirds of the employed respondents were in white-collar occupations. This reveals that our respondents generally had experienced upward mobility, when their first and current occupations in the United States are compared. The distribution also indicates that proportionally more respondents were in blue-collar occupations than they were in Korea. In sum, the occupation of the respondents had not reached the level of their preimmigration occupation.

As shown in Table 4.2, the majority of the American-college graduates are currently in the professional and semiprofessional occupations; the majority of the Korean-college graduates are in the proprietary and managerial occupations, and the majority of the noncollege graduates are in the blue-collar occupations. This shows that the immigrants' stock of human capital is positively related to the prestige of their current occupation. This observation holds true for both male and female respondents, although among the females, the relationship between the two variables is not as strong as it is among the males.

Among the employed respondents, one-third of the males and one-fourth of the females are proprietors and man~~~~~~~ all of them are actually owners and/or managers of ~ This is a remarkable phenomenon in light of the fac portion of self-employed in retail trade does not ex of the total U.S. labor force (U.S. Dept. of Labor, 19

Moreover, the proportion of those who engage in s increases as time elapses. This is observed from th the total length of job experience in the United St the proportion of owners and/or managers of sn increases. Among those who have had job exper United States for three years or less, less than o 28.3% of the male respondents and 17, 18.9% of the fe dents) were small business owners and/or managers. However, among those who had job experience for six years or more, nearly half (30, 47.6% of the male respondents and 24, 45.3% of the female respondents) were engaged in small businesses.

A similar trend was observed by the length of residence in the United States. Thus, among those who had been in the United States for five years or more, about 40 percent were currently engaged in small business. However, among those who had been in the United States for eleven years or more, less than one-third of the employed male (8, 28.6%) and female (10, 31.3%) respondents were small business owners and/or managers. This is because in this category, the American-college graduates are heavily concentrated and mostly in professional or semiprofessional occupations.

Method of Job Information Acquisition

Information of job availabliity is a valuable resource for job seekers in finding employment and obtaining quality jobs. In order to examine the method of job information acquisition in the job search stage, we asked the following question: "Where did you find the job information which led you to your current job?" The majority of the employed respondents (191, 51.8%) obtained the information through personal contact, whereas others obtained job information by direct contact (30, 8.1%) or formal methods such as newspapers or other printed media (98, 26.6%), school or university placement services (12, 3.3%), employment agencies (13, 3.5%), or others (25, 6.7%).

Our further analysis of those who obtained job information through personal contact shows that they obtained the information from friends (90, 47.6%), kin (31, 16.4%), current or former work colleagues or business associates (12, 6.3%), church members (19, 10.1%), alumni (14, 7.4%), and others (23, 12.3%). The female respondents (105, 58%) used personal contact slightly more than the male respondents (86, 45.3%).

Nine-tenths of the "informers" (172, 90%) who passed job information to the respondents were Koreans. Thus, very few obtained job information from non-Koreans such as whites (12, 6.6%) or other Asians (6, 3.4%).

To the knowledge of the respondents, half of their informers originally obtained the job information from their own work organizations or the organizations with which they had some business contact (88, 48.6%). Nearly one-third of the informers learned the information from other Koreans (56, 30.9%). Some informers were in small businesses that eventually hired the respondents. Very few of the informers obtained the information from other sources (8, 4.5%)

With this analysis, we can construct a social structure of job information transmission. The ultimate source of job information is a variety of work organizations that create new jobs or have vacant positions to be filled. Information of job openings originate from these organizations and reach job seekers through various intermediaries.

The social structure of job information transmission available to the respondents is illustrated in Figure 7. The major inter-

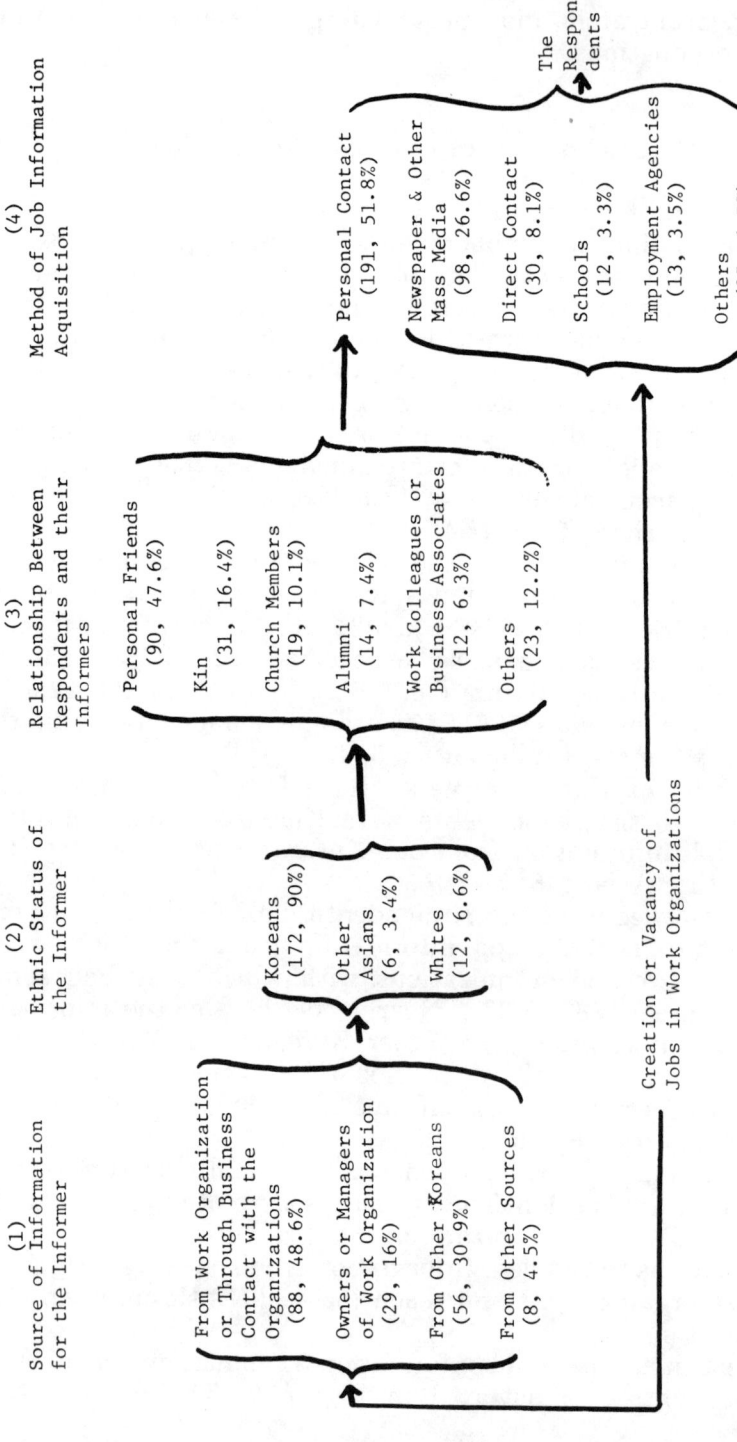

Figure 7. The Social Structure of Job Information Transmissions

mediaries for the respondents were mass media and personal contact through Korean friends, kin, church members, alumni, and others.

The method of job information acquisition used varies with the the occupation of the respondents. Professionals and semiprofessionals (32, 34.8%) used personal contact proportionally least, whereas semiskilled and unskilled workers (72, 65.5%) used the same method most in their job search behavior. The American-college graduates used the personal contact method proportionally least (10, 23.6%) and the noncollege graduates (72, 61%) used it the most.

Did personal contact introduce better jobs to the respondents than other methods of job information transmission? To answer this question, the respondents were divided into two categories: those who used the personal contact method and those who used other methods. Then, the relative effectiveness of the two methods was measured by the following three criteria: (1) the proportion of those who perceived that their current job had a good future prospect or gave them a good promotion chance, (2) the proportion of those who perceived that their current job gave them sufficient opportunity to use their ability acquired through their education or past job experiences, and (3) the proportion of those who made a high individual annual income (see Table 6.2).

As shown in Table 6.2, only one-third of those (52, 33.1%) who obtained job information through personal contact indicated that their current job had a promising future, whereas half of those who obtained job information through other methods (71, 49%) indicated a promising future. A similar difference is observed among those who preceived a sufficient opportunity to use their ability in their current job.

Proportionally, more of the respondents who obtained job information through other methods were found to belong to the two categories of high income ($17,000 or more) than those using personal contact (see Table 6.2). However, the reverse is true in the proportion of those who belong to the two categories of low income ($16,999 or less).

The preceding analysis shows that other methods have generally introduced better jobs to the immigrants than the personal contact method. In other words, the personal contact method is not found to have introduced better jobs than other methods among the Korean immigrants. A separate analysis for each occupational group confirms this observation. Thus, this observation holds true regardless of the respondents' occupations.

Objective Work Conditions

For an analysis of objective work conditions of the respondents, we asked the ethnic composition of their major work colleagues (or customers in the case of small business entrepreneurs). For about half of the respondents, the major work colleagues or customers (the numerical majority) were exclusively members of minority groups such as Koreans (21.7%), blacks (3.4%), Mexicans (7.5%), other Asians (2.4%), and various combinations of minority groups (14.3%). Only one-third of the respondents indicated whites as their major work colleagues or customers (37.9%) and one-tenth indicated a combination of whites and minority groups (12.3%). Since more than four-fifths of the workers in the United States are whites, excluding Mexican-Americans, this observation reveals a remarkable workplace segregation experienced by the respondents (U.S. Department of Commerce, 1976:24; Becker, 1978).

The male workers are more segregated from whites in their workplace than are the female workers as Table 6.3 indicates. The table also shows that, regardless of their current occupation, a high proportion of Korean immigrants are segregated in their workplace. But comparatively, the professionals and semiprofessionals are less segregated than those in other occupations. When sex and occupation of the respondents are combined, the female professionals and semiprofessionals are relatively less segregated.

Parallel to this finding, it is observed that regardless of sex, the American-college graduates are comparatively least segregated from whites in their workplace whereas the noncollege graduates are segregated most. Nearly half of the male American-college graduates (21, 46.7%) and three-fourths of the female American-college graduates (11, 73.4%) reported that their major work colleagues were whites. In contrast, less than one-third of both male (16, 29.1%) and female (19, 31.7%) non-college graduates indicate that their major work colleagues are whites. Thus, the respondents' stock of human capital is found to be directly related to the degree to which they are segregated in their workplace.

If we define stable employment as a continuous employment at the same workplace for three years or more (Miller and Form, 1964:543), it is found that most of the respondents except for the skilled workers did not have stable employment. Although half of the skilled workers (14, 48.3%) had been employed at their workplace for three years or more, about one-third of the respondents in other occupations had stable employment (38, 39.2% of professionals and semiprofessionals; 55, 39% of proprietors and managers; 15, 25.9% of other white-collar workers; 30, 30.3% of semiskilled or unskilled workers). As a whole, those who had been in the United States for more than six years tended to have stable employment in a greater proportion. Even among them, however, half (116, 50%) had not yet achieved such stability regardless of sex.

With respect to the respondents' work patterns, it is surprising to find that the majority of the employed immigrants worked on every Saturday or on certain Saturdays irrespective of sex and occupations (see Table 6.4). The proportion of those who worked on Saturdays was particularly high among the small business owners and/or managers. Some respondents even worked every Sunday (49, 12%) or on certain Sundays (60, 15%). Most of the workers in these categories were found to be either nurses or in small businesses.

About half (103, 47.5%) of the employed males worked eight hours a day and the other half (101, 46.5%) worked for more than eight hours a day. Among the female workers, slightly more than half (107, 56%) worked eight hours a day and nearly one-third (59, 30.9%) worked for more than eight hours a day.

In the proportion of those who worked for nine hours or more, occupational variations are observed. Small business owners and/or managers work exceptionally long hours. About 40 percent (32, 42.7%) of the male entrepreneurs worked for nine to ten hours, and 30 percent (22, 29.3%) worked for eleven hours or more a day. Of the female entrepreneurs 40 percent (25, 41.7%) worked nine to ten hours, and one-fourth (14, 23.3%) worked eleven hours or more. Only a few of the employed respondents (13, 6% of the males and 25, 13.1% of the females) worked for seven hours or less, and ten employed respondents were found to keep irregular work schedules. As a whole, the employed males worked considerably longer hours and also proportionally more on Saturdays than the employed females.

When annual individual incomes are divided into four categories, the employed males are widely spread into the four categories, whereas the employed females are heavily concentrated in the lowest income category (see Table 6.5). Regardless of sex however, two-thirds of the respondents had annual family incomes of $17,000 or more. The annual individual incomes for male and female respondents are significantly related to the prestige of their occupations. Among the males, small business people and professionals and semiprofessionals earned considerably more income than those in other occupations (see Table 6.6). Among the females, owners and/or managers of small business earned more income than professionals and semiprofessionals. Professionals and semiprofessionals in turn earned more than those in the remaining two categories of occupation (see Table 6.6).

In addition to occupation, ethnicity of work colleagues or customers is found to be related to annual individual incomes of both male and female respondents (excluding the males engaged in small business). The respondents who worked exclusively with whites earned substantially more than those who worked with minority members or with a combination of whites and minority members. This pattern is less pronounced among female workers than male workers. At the same time, the male respondents' individual incomes are positively related to two variables—the length of residence in the United States and the level of education.

In light of this observation, annual individual incomes of the male respondents are examined by these variables (time, jobs, ethnicity and education) on the basis of a statistical technique, multiple classification analysis (MCA). In the analysis, three variables—education, occupation, and ethnicity—are either nominal or ordinal variables, whereas the length of residence is an interval variable. (See Tables 6.7 and 6.8.) Analysis of the annual individual income is based on the original fourteen categories used in our interview schedule (see Appendix C, no. 39 E).

In the following two MCA tables (Tables 6.7 and 6.8), column A shows unadjusted income means of the categories of the variables expressed in terms of the category mean deviation from the grand mean. Column B indicates income of the categories of a variable controlled for other variables in the same column. Column C adds one more variable—the length of residence in the United States. Since the difference between columns B and C is the addition of one variable, the difference in the value of multiple R squared between the two columns reveals the proportion of income variations accounted for by the length of residence.

Table 6.7 shows multiple classification analysis of incomes of the male respondents who were employed in the occupations other than small business. Beta in column C indicates that education is a minor variable for their income variations and so is occupation another minor variable. In contrast, ethnicity of the respondents' work colleagues emerges as a *major* variable accounting for the variations in their individual incomes. Those who worked with whites earned considerably more income than those who worked with minority workers. The difference in the values of multiple R squared between columns B (.252) and C (.404) shows also that the length of residence in the United States is another important variable for their income variations.

As is evident in Table 6.8 (column C), for the men in small businesses, education is an important variable for their income variations, whereas the ethnicity of their customers is not. Among the small businessmen, American-college graduates earn more than Korean-college graduates. Korean-college graduates in turn earn more than noncollege graduates. Difference in the value of multiple R squared between columns B (.238) and C (.326) also demonstrates that the length of residence in the United States is another important variable for the small businessmen's income variations. Tables 6.7 and 6.8 reveal a common point—the male respondents earn more annually as their length of residence in the United States extends.

Since occupation and ethnicity are the variables related to annual individual incomes of the female respondents, only these two variables are used in the MCA analysis of the female workers' income. The MCA analysis reveals that occupation is a major variable accounted for the females' income variations, whereas ethnicity is not (see column B of Table 6.9). The results are similar whether the analysis is made for all employed females (I of Table 6.9) or only for those who are employed in occupations other than small businesses (II of Table 6.9).

Subjective Work Experiences

The preceding analysis focused on the objective work condition of the immigrants. Now our analysis is extended to their subjective work experiences. We first examined the immigrants' job satisfaction by asking the following question: "As a whole, how well are you satisfied with your present job?" The given response categories were "very much satisfied," "somewhat satisfied," "don't know," "somewhat dissatisfied," and "very much dissatisfied."

A great majority of the employed respondents were found to express "somewhat satisfied" (225, 53%) or "very much satisfied" (74, 17.4%). Their job satisfaction was also found to be related to the prestige of their current occupations. Regardless of sex, professionals and semiprofessionals (80, 84.2%) were proportionally most satisfied and semiskilled or unskilled workers (49, 53.6%) were least satisfied. The reverse was true in the proportion of those who expressed dissatisfaction with their current job. Job satisfaction of those in other occupations fell between the two extremes, with an exception of male other white-collar workers (20, 90.9%). It should be emphasized, however, that even among semiskilled or unskilled workers, the majority were satisfied with their current jobs.

With respect to levels of education, regardless of sex, the

American-college graduates (51, 83.6%) were relatively most satisfied with their current occupations, whereas the noncollege graduates (73, 65.2%) were relatively least satisfied. However, when we examine closely, the difference in the degree of job satisfiaction among the three groups of respondents is, significant only among the male respondents (statistically significant at the .05 level, chi-square = 7.48, $df = 2$).

For a further analysis of their job satisfaction, the following additional questions were asked: (1) Do you find your present job boring? (2) What are the future prospects of your present job or chances of promotion? (3) Is your income from the present job sufficient to support your family? (4) Is the knowledge and skill obtained through your past education and experience sufficiently utilized at your present job? (5) In your opinion, is your present income commensurate with your education (attained in Korea and in the United States)? (6) Is your occupation commensurate with your education? (7) Is your present income commensurate with the income of American workers who are doing similar jobs? (8) Since your immigration, do you think that everything has progressed as planned?[2]

Tables 6.10, 6.11, and 6.12 show the number and proportion of the respondents who answered these questions in the following manner: (1) My job is not boring. (2) I have good future prospects. (3) My income is sufficient for family support. (4) I have a fairly good chance to use my ability. (5) I feel congruence between my education and occupation. (6) I feel congruence between my education and income. (7) I feel congruence between my income and that of my American colleagues. (8) I think that everything has progressed as planned.

Table 6.10 shows that, as a whole, a majority of both sexes did not feel that their job was boring. They were, however, divided in the following aspects of their jobs: future prospects, perceived income sufficiency, and the chance to use their ability. They were also divided in two items of perceived status inconsistency: the degrees of congruence between their education and occupation and between their education and income. But they showed a high consensus on another item of perceived status inconsistency: a great majority felt that their current incomes were commensurate with the incomes of American workers who were doing similar jobs with them. This response reveals that the immigrants did not generally feel discriminated against. As a whole, the majority believed that everything had progressed as they had planned.

As Table 6.11 indicates, we observed some occupational variations in the respondents' subjective experiences at work. In one item, "I feel congruence between my income and that of my

American colleagues," little occupational variation is found. But in two items, "My job is not boring," and "I think that everything has progressed as planned," the occupational prestige is positively related to the proportion of those who agreed with these questions. Thus, professionals and semiprofessionals feel most proportionally that everything has progressed as planned and do not feel that their job is boring. The reverse is true for blue-collar workers.

Those who worked in small businesses agreed proportionally more than those in other occupations with the following three items: "I have good future prospects," "My income is sufficient for family support," and "I feel congruence between my education and income." With the remaining two items, "I feel congruence between my education and occupation," and "I have a good chance to use my ability," the professionals and semiprofessionals agreed most proportionally.

Among the female respondents, those with a higher stock of human capital felt more proportionally that they had a good chance to use their ability and that everything had progressed as planned. Among the male respondents, those with a higher stock of human capital were most likely to agree with the following four items: "My job is not boring," "I have a good chance to use my ability," "I feel congruence between my education and occupation," and "Everything has progressed as planned" (see Table 6.12).

Most of the respondents also felt that their occupational opportunity was severely limited. To the question, "In what areas do you think that Koreans in the United States can be successful?" most of the respondents mentioned either self-employed business (373, 52%) or highly technical or professional fields (278, 39%). They knew that they needed a high level of academic degree or professional license to enter the latter. Since most of them did not have such academic or professional credentials, technical or professional fields were not available to them. What is left is self-employed business.

Along with their perception of limited opportunity in the United States, most of the respondents have experienced a serious problem of communication. To the following open-ended question, "Generally, what have been the major difficult problems in your immigrant life in the United States?", virtually all of those who responded to this question (475, 94%) mentioned English as their major problem. This language problem deeply affects their perception of their own job experiences in the United States. To another open-ended question, "Because you are a Korean or a member of a minority group, have you had difficulties in getting a job," 70 percent of those (88) who responded to this question mentioned their experiences of difficulty in getting a job as a result of their own English problem rather than racial discrimination in the labor market.

Summary and Conclusions

Through immigration, the respondents have generally experienced both downward and upward mobility in the United States. In general, however, their current occupations have not reached the level of their preimmigration occupation. The respondents were widely spread into various occupations, ranging from professional to blue-collar occupations.

From the analysis of their occupations, two distinct features emerge. First, a high proportion of them are concentrated in small businesses, and the proportion of those who engage in small business increases as time elapses. Second, the majority of the employed respondents are segregated from whites in their workplace. This is generally true cross-occupationally. These two points reveal some structural conditions of their employment in their new country.

Becker (1978) makes a distinction between two types of employment segregation: (1) the disproportional concentration of minority workers in certain occupational categories, and (2) segregation of whites and minority workers in the same occupation across different places of employment. We call the former the occupational segregation and the latter, the workplace segregation. From our analysis of the respondents, we observed both types of segregation among Korean workers. The concentration of the respondents in the area of small business shows the occupational segregation; their segregation from whites in the place of employment demonstrates the workplace segregation.

Even though small business owners and/or managers are generally self-employed entrepreneurs, they work for extremely long hours. This demonstrates that the Korean immigrants' small business is a labor-intensive enterprise. Korean small businesses are also heavily concentrated in retail or service business as noted in this chapter (see note 1).

In light of this fact, Bonachich (1978 and 1979) characterizes the Korean immigrant business as a cheap form of labor or as a variant of the split labor market. This type of small business is under a constant pressure to lower its labor cost in order to survive competition with other small businesses. This struggle to reduce labor cost tends to produce relatively unfavorable work conditions, and such unfavorable work conditions are further aggravated by slow business turnover, high poverty, crime, and credit problems of difficult market in Bonacich and Jung's terms (Bonacich and Jung, 1979).

The majority of the male respondents who were employed in nonsmall business occupations worked in segregated workplaces. Moreover, they were found to earn less than those who worked with white workers. This indicates that the majority of nonsmall business males are employed under relatively unfavorable work conditions. The situation is consistent with that of other immigrant groups. Based on their study on Mexican and Cuban immigrants, Portes and Bach (1980) report that ethnicity of work colleagues is the single most important predictor of earnings of the immigrants. In this respect, Portes and Bach contend that an important factor for earnings is not past education or occupational skills but the manner in which the immigrants become incorporated into the U.S. labor market.

From the foregoing discussions, two pervasive features of the male respondents' labor market experiences in the United States emerge: (1) occupational or workplace segregation and (2) employment under unfavorable work conditions. These two points lend support to the theoretical perspective of the labor market segmentation approach.

A high proportion of the female respondents were found to be owners and/or managers of small businesses. Their labor market position appears to be similar to that of their male counterparts in terms of hours of work, earnings, and the kind of small business that they manage, although the educational level of the small-business women was not related to their income.

Among the female workers who were employed in occupations other than small business, ethnicity of their work colleagues made no difference in their individual incomes. In this respect, the female immigrants' labor market experience is different from their male counterparts. This may derive from the fact that female workers in general are segregated in their employment regardless of race and ethnic differences (Blau, 1978; Freedman, 1976). Under this condition of sex segregation in the American labor market, Korean female workers are likely to work with other female workers, and white female workers are not much more advantaged in the labor market than minority female workers. Therefore, Korean female workers who work with white female workers do not earn more than those Korean females who work with minority female workers.

We have observed that personal contact is the most frequently used method of job information acquisition among the immigrants. But ethnicity of the informers shows that most of the informers were members of the same ethnic group (Koreans). Very few of the respondents indicate that they have obtained job information from whites.

Since whites are structurally better placed in the American labor market to introduce better jobs than minority workers (Crain, 1970; Freedman, 1976), this observation indicates that the Korean immigrants have been deprived of better job information. In this chapter, the following attests to this point: contrary to the findings of other studies, the personal contact method has failed to introduce better jobs to our respondents than other methods.

It seems that as immigrants themselves, most of the job informers for the respondents are employed in the easily accessible, but relatively unfavorable workplaces (the secondary labor market). This would limit their access to information about better jobs. Thus, when the informers passed job information on to the respondents, the information of the jobs turned out to be no better than that of the jobs that others obtained through formal method or direct method. When placed in the context of Korean immigrants, this information deprivation would mean that the respondents have had little chance for employment in the labor market where job information is substantially controlled and compartmentalized by whites.

Freedman characterizes the concept of "work establishment" by (1) attachment to an occupation or an organization, (2) stability of employment and minimum protection against risk, and (3) earnings sufficient to support a worker and his dependents according to accepted standards of health and decency (1969:5). She notes that most American workers achieve their work establishment between the ages of twenty-five and thirty-five. This age range is, however, exactly the one at which the majority of our respondents immigrated to the United States and began to search for a new occupation. This demonstrates that the beginning of the process of the Korean immigrants' work establishment in the United States is late as compared with members of the majority group. In addition, the respondents have been facing job information deprivation.

In this chapter, we have also observed that among the male small business entrepreneurs, the American-college graduates earned more than the Korean-college graduates, whereas the Korean-college graduates earned more than the noncollege graduates. This indicates that the human capital theory is also a useful approach to explain the Korean immigrants' relative earnings. The usefulness of the human capital theory is further enhanced by the fact that academic credentials of the Korean-college graduates are not generally recognized in the American labor market. Thus, the immigrants cannot fully take advantage of the certification effect of their Korean college degrees. In spite of this limitation, the Korean-college graduates earn more than the noncollege graduates.

As immigrants, the majority of our female respondents are currently employed. Economic contributions of the female workers may be substantial to their families. The Korean female workers appear, however, to be "secondary workers." According to Wilcox (1957:167), major features of the secondary workers include primary attachment to nonlabor force activity and leeway in deciding on labor participation.

Both male and female respondents express that it is primarily the female's responsibility to perform such household tasks as grocery shopping, dishwashing, cleaning the house, and laundry (see Chapter 7). Thus, the female respondents in our study are generally secondary workers in their families.

The females' labor participation is also considerably less than the males' in terms of the proportion of those who work and the hours they work. This suggests that the Korean females have more leeway in deciding on their labor participation than the Korean males who may have to work for family support.

As secondary workers, the female immigrants' primary attachment to the nonlabor force activity may have detracted them from developing a career or maintaining steady employment. Taking advantage of this situation, employers might possibly ignore the level of the female workers' education and pay them at a uniformly low level.

We now examine the immigrants' subjective work experiences. As mentioned, a great majority of our respondents were satisfied with their jobs regardless of their occupations, but they generally worked under conditions of an unfavorable labor market. This reveals a sharp discrepancy between their objective work conditions and their subjective experiences at work. A discrepancy is also noticed between their job satisfaction and other aspects of their subjective experiences at work. Most of the immigrants are acutely aware of the limited job opportunities available to them in the United States. A high proportion of the immigrants see no future at their current jobs and do not feel that their income is sufficient for family support, except those who are in small business.

Job satisfaction of workers results basically from their *judgment* of their job experiences as attaining or blocking the rewards sought at work. Since job satisfaction is based on such judgment, a crucial point in the study of job satisfaction is to understand the *standard of judgment* that the workers use in their evaluation of their job experiences. If they have a low standard of judgment, they can be satisfied with the relatively low level of rewards received.

Two theories provide a useful framework to ascertain workers' standard of judgment: the equity theory and the idea of comparison level (CL). The equity theory explains the standard of judgment in terms of relative inputs and outputs (Adams, 1963a, 1963b, and 1965; Homans, 1961; Lawler, 1977). If workers feel that their inputs (e.g., skill, effort, training, experiences, age, and education) are higher than those of their significant others, they feel that they should receive a greater amount of reward (expected output). Thibault and Kelley argue that the comparison level is an actor's standard of judgment of what he/she deserves. The level is determined by "some model or average value of all known outcomes, each outcome weighed by its salience or strength of instigation..." (1967:21). The authors state that an actor comes to know the outcomes available to him or her through his or her own experiences and those of others who are in a similar situation.

As already mentioned, an overwhelming majority of the immigrants stated that the language problem was one of their major difficulties. This problem so deeply affected their outlook in the United States that they tended to blame themselves when they encountered problems at the workplace. This tendency of self-blaming would definitely suppress their sense of discrimination. The same language problem and other problems associated with it would deflate their standard of judgment in the evaluation of their job experiences. As a medium of communication, language is a crucial component of the inputs at work. Thus, when the immigrants acutely feel that they have a language problem, they would think that their inputs are something less than those of the native-born workers. According to the equity theory, when workers' inputs are lower than others, the worker's expected outputs or standard of judgment are correspondingly low.

The immigrants' low standard of judgment would be reinforced by their ethnic confinement in the intimate social relations and employment segregation. Such structural confinement limits their perception of alternative opportunities available and would keep their comparison level low. This low level of comparison, in turn, keeps the level of their job satisfaction relatively high.

Their low standard of judgment could also explain why most of the respondents believed that since their immigration everything had progressed as planned. With a low standard of judgment, it is relatively easy to come to the conclusion that everything is going well, even though the respondents were objectively placed in the unfavorable labor market.

The relative job satisfaction among the respondents, however, might be explained by the degree to which they were rewarded or perceived themselves as being rewarded. Both male and female respondents showed that those who held more prestigious occupations earned more income measured by their annual individual incomes. At the same time, those with more prestigious occupations perceived themselves as being more rewarded in terms of the chance to use their ability at work, earning of income for family support, future prospects, and congruence between their education and occupation (with some exceptions from small businessmen or other white-collar workers). Under these circumstances, the occupational prestige is positively related to the degree of job satisfaction (with one exception of other white-collar workers). This observation shows that the relative job satisfaction among the respondents generally reflected their actual experiences of reward or perception of such experiences.

Notes

1. Among the currently employed respondents, professionals and semiprofessionals include physicians, dentists, nurses, medical technicians, pharmacists, engineers, research staffs, chemists, computer programers, CPAs, financial planners, professors, teachers, teacher's aids, social workers, counselors, clergymen, announcers, painters, musicians, and Tae-Kwon Do instructors. Proprietors and managers include those who are employed as managerial or administrative staffs of industries, business firms, and other large scale organizations (e.g., government agencies). Most of the proprietors and managers are, however, owners and/or managers of small businesses with their collaborating spouses.

Their small businesses include the following types: grocery, restaurant, coffee shop, donut shop, ice cream shop, candy shop, other food-related business, liquor store, janitorial service, painting shop, sewing shop, gas station, automobile service, auto body shop, various repair shops, gift shop, variety shop, wig shop, clothing store, security service, nursery, drugstore, jewelry or watch shop, floral shop, beauty salon, locksmith, music store, hotel or motel, bookstore, gallery, nursing home, laundry, travel service, real estate, and shoe store, and other small businesses.

Other white-collar workers are the white-collar workers who are not included in the aforementioned two categories. Such workers include secretaries, typists, cashiers, salesmen, accountants, clerks, other office workers, and airplane attendents. Skilled workers included car mechanics, carpenters, cooks, beauticians, sample makers, gardeners, plumbers, repairmen, bartenders, skilled machine operators, and supervisors. All other blue-collar and service workers are classified as semiskilled or unskilled workers. They include assembly linemen, machinists, sewing machine operators, other factory or manual workers, dishwashers, waiters, key punchers, nurse's aids, janitors, laborers of small businesses or warehouses, and truck drivers.

2. For a detailed description, see Appendix C.

7
Family Role Adjustment: Persistence and Change in the Traditional Role

In this chapter, the major focus is shifted to the families of the respondents. The family may be considered as an emotional unit as well as a task unit; the concern of this chapter is with the family as a task unit. The family has a number of tasks that should be performed by family members for its maintenance and for the survival of its members. Two of such tasks are the earning of income for family support and the performance of household tasks. A crucial question regarding these tasks is which family members perform them and to what extent.

In the United States, the question of earning income is usually a matter of employment outside the family. As reviewed in the preceeding chapter, a high proportion of our respondents were employed. It is particularly noted that more female respondents were employed in the United States than when they were in Korea. This observation leads to the question of how Korean immigrants divide household tasks in their families.

This chapter focuses on this issue, and our analysis is guided by three hypotheses advanced by Stafford, Backman, and Dibona (1977): socialization-ideology, time availability, and power-authority. The socialization-ideology hypothesis states that "women are socialized to believe that their major role should be that of homemaker" (1977:46). Because of this socialization, the present attitude (ideology) of women is that they should assume major responsibility for household tasks. Implied in the hypothesis is that men are socialized to believe also the same idea, namely, wives should bear most of the burden of performing household tasks.

Assuming that "husbands and wives allocate tasks in response to the availability of time," the time-availability hypothesis suggests that household task performance is divided primarily in response to the employment status of spouses (1977:46–47).

However, in light of the overwhelming evidence that working wives still bear most of the burden of performing household tasks, Stafford, Backman, and Dibona point out that the time-availability hypothesis does not imply a complete equality of performance and responsibility. It rather suggests that the working wives bear less responsibility than otherwise.

The basic premise of the power-authority hypothesis is that "men hold more power and authority in the marital dyad and call the tune" (1977:45). Since household tasks are "inherently distasteful and personally demaning," the hypothesis suggests that husbands would perform household tasks only to the extent that they feel obliged to or perhaps even less than they feel obliged. This would force their wives to perform household tasks more frequently than the wives feel obliged to do.

In the traditional Korean family, the wife is confined to the home and bears the major responsibility of performing household tasks, whereas the husband is expected to be the breadwinner. Hence, the socialization-ideology hypothesis is suitable to test whether the traditional division of labor is followed in the Korean immigrant families. If the hypothesis is confirmed, the following are expected to be observed: (1) the wife heavily performs household tasks, and (2) both the wife and the husband believe that it is the wife's responsibility to do so.

As already noted, a high proportion of the immigrant wives were employed. Employment of the wife is, however, a sharp break from the traditional Korean marital role. We may then ask: When the wife shares the role of a breadwinner, will her husband share the role of a homemaker?

The time-availability hypothesis tests this issue. If the Korean immigrant families divide household tasks in response to (relative) time availability among family members, the employed wives will perform household tasks less than before because of their limited time available for home work. This would compel their husbands to perform household tasks more than before. Under this condition, the time-availability hypothesis contends that comparatively, (1) the employed wives perform household tasks less than the nonemployed wives, and (2) husbands of the employed wives perform household tasks more than husbands of the nonemployed wives. Needless to say, this contention assumes that husbands of the two types of families are currently employed.

In the traditional Korean family, the husband is expected to exercise the final authority in his family legitimized by the patriarchal culture. Thus, if this traditional system persists in the Korean immigrant families, the power-authority hypothesis suggests that many husbands perform household tasks even less than they feel obliged to. This would compel their wives to perform more than they feel obliged.

Employment and Division of Labor

Since we are concerned with family relations, this chapter analyzes only the married respondents ($N = 483$). In the majority (261, 54%) of the respondents' families, both husbands and wives were employed. One-third of the married respondents indicated that only the husband was employed (155, 32.1%). These two types of families account for more than four-fifths of the families of the married respondents (86.1%); the rest include such categories as "wife alone employed" (0.8%), "husband, wife, and others" (0.8%), "unmarried children only" (0.4%), "children and one parent" (3.2%), and "none of the family members employed" (7.7%).

Annual income of husbands is negatively related to the proportion of their wives who are employed—the lower the income of husbands, the higher is the proportion of wives who are employed. The relationship is significant at the .01 level (chi-square value = 11.99, $df = 3$). The wife's employment is thus definitely related to the husband's income.

As expected, when both the husband and wife are employed, their combined annual family income is significantly higher than that of the families in which only the husband is employed (chi-square value = 11.99, $df = 3$, significant at .01). About half of the two-income families (112, 45.5%) reported that their annual income was $25,000 or more, whereas only one-third (32, 32%) of the one-income families indicated an income of this level.

Division of household tasks was examined by the following two questions: (1) Among your family members, how do you divide household tasks? (2) In your opinion, how should the household tasks be divided in principle? For the response, these six items of household tasks were given: grocery shopping, housekeeping, doing the laundry, dishwashing, disposing of garbage, and managing the family budget.

The respondents were then asked to rank their family members in terms of their relative performance of each of these items. Of the two questions asked, the first deals with role behavior of family members—their performance of household tasks by virtue of their position in the family. The second question deals with role expectation—their normative standard concerning division of household tasks in the family.

The respondents revealed various types of division of household tasks in their families, which can be classified into six categories. The first three categories (A, B, and C) include the performance types in which only husbands and/or wives perform. Category A refers to a combination of the performance types, "wife alone performs" and "wife performs more than husband." Category B refers to "husband and wife perform equally." Category C refers to a combination of the performance types, "husband alone performs" and "husband performs more than wife." Category D refers to the performance type which involves the performance of children. In this case, however, children perform less than their parent(s). Category E refers to a combination of two performance types, "children alone perform" and "children perform more than parent(s)." Category F refers to a combination of performance by other family members such as mother or mother-in-law of the respondents or their unmarried sister or brother, along with husband, wife, and/or children.

Table 7.1 shows the distribution of the respondents' families by the six categories of performance. Across the six task items, the three categories, A, B, and C, account for at least two-thirds of the families for both role behavior and expectation. This means that in most of the immigrant families, husbands and/or wives mainly perform household tasks. Only in a limited proportion of the families do children make some contribution. Even in a smaller proportion of the families are other family members involved in tasks performance.

An examination of Table 7.1 shows that in one-half or more of the families, it is the wife who actually bears the heavy burden of performing four items: grocery shopping, housekeeping, doing laundry, and dishwashing. In a similar proportion of the families, the wife is also *expected* to perform these tasks mainly. Only in a small proportion of the families does the husband mainly perform household tasks or is expected to do so. In two task items, disposing of garbage and managing the family budget, the burden of performance is generally distributed evenly between the husband and the wife, although the wives were not so expected, especially in the handling of family budget.

For a more detailed analysis, we first focus our attention on the two types of families in which (1) only the husband is employed, and (2) both the husband and the wife are employed. Because the presence of children may affect the division of labor in the family, the two types of families are further divided into another two groups: families with children ($N = 346$) and those without children ($N = 70$). The categories of task performance in Table 7.1 are also rearranged: whereas category A remains the same, categories B and C are combined into a single category. The former (A) is referred to as "wife performs predominantly" and the latter (B and C) are referred to as "husband performs substantially." The remaining three categories, D, E, and F, are combined into a single category, which is referred to as "children or other family members are involved."

Among the families without children, most of the wives are found to perform predominantly four of the task items: grocery shopping, housekeeping, doing laundry, and dishwashing. In the majority of these families, wives are also *expected* to perform these tasks. In this respect, employment of the wife makes no difference; she bears the major responsibility of performing household tasks whether she is currently employed or not.

Under this condition, it is natural that only a small proportion of the husbands in families without children perform the four items to a substantial degree. Moreover, a considerable proportion of husbands perform the six items even less than they feel obliged to (see Columns 1 and 2 of Table 7.2). In correspondence to this situation, a substantial proportion of wives perform the tasks more than they feel obliged to. Again, employment of the wife makes little difference in this discrepancy with the exception of two items: dishwashing and disposing of garbage.

In the families with children, employment of the wife makes a difference in the division of household tasks. Most of the nonemployed wives were found to perform the four items proportionally more than employed wives (see Table 7.3), and were generally so expected by both male and female respondents (wives and husbands). Husbands of the employed wives, however, did not perform the tasks proportionally more than the husbands of the nonemployed wives. As shown in Table 7.3, the proportion of husbands who performed the tasks substantially remains unchanged with few exceptions, whether their wives were employed or not (see Table 7.3). Furthermore, husbands of the employed wives were not expected to perform more tasks than the husbands of the nonemployed wives (see Table 7.4).

Whereas husbands of the employed wives do not increase their relative share of task performance, their children or other family members are proportionally more involved in task performance (see Table 7.3 and 7.4). This means that when wives are employed, the burden of performing household tasks is shared with their children or other family members, but not with their husbands.

The sharing of tasks is also confirmed in the analysis of discrepancy between role expectation and behavior. Whether their wives are employed or not, a similar proportion of husbands underperform the tasks judged by their own standard (see Columns 5 & 6 of Table 7.2). Under this condition, a substantial proportion of the nonemployed wives reported that they overperformed tasks in terms of their own expectations (see Columns 3 and 4 of Table 7.2). But very few of the employed wives reported this. Instead, a substantial proportion of the employed wives indicated that their children or other family members overperformed household tasks by the standard of the employed wives (see Columns 7 and 8 of Table 7.2). In other words, from the perspective of the employed wives, the burden of overperformance was shifted from them to their children or to other family members.

Only in the families with children is the number of respondents large enough to warrant a separate analysis by the respondents' sex. The male and female respondents in these families generally show no sex difference in their perception of relative performance of household tasks or their own role expectation.

Summary and Discussion

It has been observed that in most of the respondents' families, the wives predominantly performed four of the household task items, grocery shopping, housekeeping, doing laundry, and dishwashing. Wives were also expected to perform such tasks by most of the husbands and wives in this study. This confirms the socialization-ideology hypothesis, revealing that the Korean traditional division of labor persists in these four task items.

In the remaining two household task items—managing the family budget and disposing of garbage—Korean immigrant husbands were substantially involved. The reasons for this are not hard to speculate: managing the family budget requires bookkeeping, planning of family spending, and other financial decisions that are compatible with the husbands' role as the main breadwinner in the family. Garbage disposal is a simple task that neither takes much time nor effort in comparison with the four main household tasks performed predominantly by wives.

An exception to these patterns of division of labor is found when employed wives can share their tasks with their children and/or other family members. This confirms the time-availability hypothesis, but in a modified way. Because of the employed wife's time constraint, her household tasks are shared with her children and other family members; however, even in this situation, the husband's sharing is limited to his traditional sex role in the family. In short, the time-availability hypothesis affects husbands in a limited way. This is another indication of the persistence of the traditional division of labor in the Korean immigrant families.

Under the pervasive influence of the traditional system, the power-authority hypothesis is also confirmed by the following fact: a substantial proportion of the Korean immigrant husbands were found to perform household tasks even less than they felt obliged to irrespective of the employment of their wives or the presence of children in their families. Under this condition, a considerable proportion of wives perform the tasks more than they feel obliged to unless the wives shift the burden of over-performance to their children or other family members.

This analysis leads us to question why the traditional division of household tasks persists so pervasively in the Korean immigrant families. Obviously, the past socialization or indoctrination of the respondents may be a major factor, as the socialization-ideology hypothesis contends. This is supported by the fact that a great majority of *both* husbands and wives adhere to the traditional patterns of role expectations regarding the division of labor in their families. In short, wives in the Korean immigrant families are no less traditional in their conception of marital roles than their husbands.

The traditional attitudes of the respondents might have been reinforced by the racial-ethnic structure and labor market conditions in the United States. Because of racial and ethnic segregation inherent in the American social structure, Koreans are not well accepted socially by the dominant group as previously discussed. As a result, Korean immigrants in the United States mostly associate with members of their own ethnic group. This strong ethnic attachment has undoubtedly provided a social structural base for the immigrants' adhesive mode of adaptation.

Furthermore, most of the husbands in this study were employed in jobs that required or necessitated working for unusually long hours and some of them even worked on Saturdays as analyzed in the preceding chapter. Such work would exhaust them physically and mentally. This situation can hardly encourage the Korean immigrant husbands to be more involved in performing household tasks at home.

As also mentioned earlier, a great majority of the employed wives were blue-collar workers or owners and/or managers of small businesses. In these jobs, they were unlikely to experience intrinsic job satisfaction (e.g., self-growth) or to expect good future career prospects. For them, the job is a necessity for family support or for saving money for a future business. As soon as financial pressure is alleviated, the women might prefer to stay home and be full-time homemakers. Thus, their current life conditions in the United States could hardly given them any incentive to revise basically the traditional division of labor and to develop their own occupational careers.

8
Religious Participation: Ethnic Roles of the Korean Church

Compared with Chinese and Japanese immigrants, Korean immigrants have been known as "churchgoers." Bok-Lim Kim's recent study on Asian-Americans in the Chicago area reveals that the Korean immigrants' religious involvement (church participation) is greater than that of any other Asian group except the Filipinos (1978:178). Our study on ethnic roles of the Korean church in the Chicago area is supportive of Kim's findings (Kim, Kim, and Hurh, 1978).

There were 264 Korean churches throughout the United States in 1976, but the number jumped to over 400 in late 1977 (*Dong-A Ilbo*, January 10, 1978). In Southern California alone, where the heaviest concentration of Korean residents has been taking place, the number of Korean ethnic churches has increased 20 times during the past 14 years—from 11 churches in 1965 to 215 in 1979 (*Hankuk Ilbo*, May 18, 1979).

Religious participation thus appears to be one of the integral parts of the Korean immigrants' adaptation in the United States. In this chapter, we discuss the behavioral and motivational patterns of religious involvement of the Korean immigrants primarily based on our Los Angeles data. Since only nine Buddhists (1.5% of the total sample) were included in our sample, our data mostly concern Christians.

First, we describe the extent of, and expressed reasons for, the Korean immigrants' church participation in the United States. Next, major structural and subjective variables are cross-analyzed for theoretical and practical relevance.

Church Affiliation in Korea and the United States

Prior to their emigration from Korea, about half (316, 51.3%) of our respondents were already affiliated with Christian churches, but the proportion has significantly increased since their arrival in the United States—almost 70 percent of our respondents were affiliated with Korean ethnic churches in the United States (430, 69.9%). These proportions of church affiliation among our respondents are surprisingly higher than that among the national population in Korea where only an estimated 12 percent of the total population is church affiliated (*Korea Week*, February 1978).

In terms of denominational distributions, 10 percent of the church affiliates belonged to the Roman Catholic church and the rest were affiliated with various Protestant denominations (Presbyterian, 52.8%; Methodist, 9.1%; Baptist, 4.9%; Seventh-Day Adventist, 4.4%; Holiness, 1.4%; Nondenominational, 3.9%; Evangelical, 1.6%; other, 11.9%).

Involvement in the Church

A vast majority (359, 83.5%) of the church affiliates attended church at least once a week. Besides attending Sunday services (and masses), their activities in the church included Sunday School, choir, evangelical services, youth group, clerical, financial, and other related matters. Approximately one-fourth (111, 25.8%) of the Korean church affiliates held staff positions, such as elder, deacon, and exhorter.

In order to assess the motivational aspect of religious involvement, we asked our respondents: "Which of the reasons listed below is the main reason for you to attend church? If more than one, please rank the reasons." Table 8.1 summarizes the respondents' foremost reasons for attending church. Their ranked reasons by sex are also shown in Table 8.2.

As Table 8.2 reveals, a great majority of both male and female respondents expressed their primary motives for attending church as religious (worship of God, salvation, sermon, and believer's obligation). A moderate proportion of the respondents identified their secondary motives for attending church as psychological in nature (peace of mind). Only a small portion of the respondents expressed social motives (friendship, social obligation, and reciprocity) as their major reasons for attending church. Intrinsic reasons thus appear to predominate over extrinsic reasons for our respondent's church participation.

We asked another question that concerns the function of the ethnic church and also serves to check the reliability of the previous question: "What would be the advantages and disadvantages of attending church?"[1] The results of our content analysis of the most advantageous and disadvantageous aspects in order of frequency are shown in Table 8.3.

Comparing these responses with the ranked motives for attending church (Table 8.2), we noticed discrepant patterns. The religious motive predominates over all other reasons for attending church but not in terms of the benefit or advantage gained by attending church. The psychological motive ("peace of mind") was the second important reason for attending church but is the foremost advantageous aspect of attending church. Interestingly, the least important motive for attending church—the social motive ("meeting people")—turns out to be the second important advantage gained by attending church.

In short, "peace of mind" is undoubtedly the most reliable variable significantly related to the respondents' church participation. However, how do we account for the discrepant patterns in the religious and social dimensions? We conjecture that the discrepancies derive mainly from semantic problems embedded in the questionnaire. The majority of our respondents may have perceived the last question ("What would be the advantages and disadvantages of attending church?") in a strictly secular sense. In other words, they may have understood the question to the effect: "In addition to religious service, what kinds of things would you benefit from attending church?" Table 8.4 confirms our conjecture. The majority (61%) of those who indicated "meeting people" as the main advantage of attending church are the ones who also indicated the religious motive as their primary reason for church participation. What emerges out of this descriptive analysis is a profile: Korean immigrants attend church primarily for religious reasons, secondly for psychological comfort, and thirdly for social needs.

A descriptive summary of the Korean immigrants' behavioral and motivational patterns of religious (church) involvement is as follows. In contrast to Chinese and Japanese immigrants, a great majority (69.9%) of our respondents are affiliated with Christian churches.[2] The church participation of our respondents substantially increased after their arrival in the United States—an increase of 36 percent. Koreans are also found to be active Christians: about 84 percent of the church affiliates attend church at least once a week, and one-third of them hold staff positions in the church.[3] Their expressed *motives for attending* church are primarily religious in nature, and "peace of mind" and "meeting people" seem to be the main *advantages in attending* church. These patterns are somewhat similar to those of our previous study on the ethnic roles of the Korean church in the Chicago area (Kim, Hurh, and Kim, 1978). The vast majority (86%) of our

Chicago sample reported that their church involvement was primarily religious, and nearly all of them (96%) identified communality (sociability) as their secondary reason for participating in church activities.

A number of questions can be raised from this profile. Why is there such a heightened interest in church among the Korean immigrants? Since the overwhelming majority of the respondents indicated that their foremost reason for church attendance was religious in nature, is their church participation really based on some factors *intrinsic* to religious beliefs and practices or is it attributable rather to some secular factors *extrinsic* to religion, such as the new immigrants' intensified needs for phychological comfort and sociability in a "strange land"? Would the immigrants' church participation become less if their length of residence in the United States extends, their socioeconomic conditions improve, and their acculturation and assimilation to the American life become extensive? Would the immigrants' ethnic attachment (attitudinal and behavioral) to the Korean culture and society have anything to do with their church involvement? And finally, what would be the primary functions of the Korean ethnic church? A cross-analysis of major structural, behavioral, and attitudinal variables is necessary to answer these questions.

Structural Variables and Religious Participation

In an attempt to answer the foregoing questions, the relationships among the immigrants' structural, situational, and religious participation variables are cross-analyzed; for instance, socioeconomic status, length of residence in the United States, and church attendance. To our surprise, our cross-analyses reveal that the Korean immigrants' religious (church) involvement is *not* related to any of their major structural and situational variables, such as socioeconomic status (education and occupation), length of residence, acculturation, assimilation, and ethnic attachment. In short, the immigrants' religious participation is independent from their individual life conditions and experiences in the new country. For the majority of our respondents, whether newcomer or old-timer, poor or rich, church attendance appears to have become a pervasive modus vivendi in the United States.

How can we explain this pervasive religious participation among the Korean immigrants when the individual immigrants' backgrounds and current life conditions are largely unrelated to the patterns of their religious involvement? One needs to go beyond correlational analysis to understand the phenomenon.

Function of the Korean Ethnic Church

The functions of the Korean ethnic church can be better understood when the *dynamic* aspect of the immigrants' subjective experiences are analyzed in relation to the changes taking place in their objective existential conditions. Immigration is a process, and like many other social processes, the adaptation process of the first-generation immigrants can be studied from two fundamental perspectives: continuity and discontinuity in the individual's sociocultural world. The individual's sociocultural world includes one's social network, cultural traits, historical heritage, and sense of collective identity (cf. Schütz, 1967). Some of these elements continue to be integral parts of the immigrant's life in the new country; however, others may no longer be with the immigrant, and the void must be filled. For instance, such core cultural elements as language, religious beliefs, and food habits tend to persist despite migration, whereas intimate communal (*Gemeinschaft*) and extensive associational (*Gesellschaft*) bonds with the people "back home" are broken and must be reestablished in the strange land.

Past theories on the ethnic role of immigration churches have thus generally emphasized this communal function (Francis, 1945, 1948; Herberg, 1955; Sklare, 1955; Greeley, 1972). For instance, Greeley elucidates this point well:

> If one tries to define ethnicity, one finds a communal bond, which is an attempt to replace the *Gemeinschaft* relationships of the village or neighborhood left behind when an immigrant came to the industrial New World. Often language or nationality become the focal point for an ethnic group which in their country of origin would have centered around an area or village. In the United States, the churches came to serve an ethnic role; they helped sort out "who one was" in a bewildering complex society. As a result, the various denominations have been immeasurably strengthened, as they serve not only a religious need, but a social one as well. (1972:125)

Among many immigrant groups in the United States, it is commonly observed that the language used in sermons, liturgy, or hymns is often the one spoken in the homeland; that certain rites and holidays are observed which are celebrated only by members of the special ethnic group; and that quite often celebrations commemorate events unique to the history of the group. The ethnic church commonly has special educational programs designed to teach its youth those special loyalties necessary for the survival of the group. This frequently includes instructions in the history and language of the homeland.

Historical documents reveal that the Korean ethnic church has also performed social functions similar to these including nationalistic movements against Japanese colonialism in Korea (Adams, 1937: 188; Warren Kim, 1971; Choy, 1979:253-274). The ethnic church has indeed become an important way of life for the survival of the Korean ethnic group by providing fellowship with communal bonds—an ethnic fellowship. An ethnic fellowship could, however, also be provided by other ethnic voluntary associations such as alumni clubs, regional associations of Korean residents, language schools, and Korean cultural centers. Why then particularly the church?

There seem to be three major reasons why the ethnic church has become a focal point of Korean immigrants' social interaction in the United States. First, the immigrants' need for a religious or spiritual (Christian) fellowship. As mentioned earlier, more than half of our respondents were already church affiliates prior to their emigration from Korea, and undoubtedly they would like to continue a Christian fellowship in the new country. Their need for spiritual fellowship may have been even more intensified because of the marginal situation they faced as immigrants. Lee (1980:37-38) expresses this aptly:

> We came here, of course, for our own personal and very human reasons—for a better education, for financial well-being, for greater career opportunities and the like. But we now find that we do not wholly control our circumstances by ourselves. We find ourselves in a wilderness, living as aliens and strangers. And the inescapable question arises from the depth of our being: What is the real meaning of our immigrant existence in America? What is the spiritual meaning of our alien status?

For a similar quest for one's existential meaning, many non-Christians may have joined the ethnic church in addition to their need for an ethnic fellowship. Among the immigrants, the social, psychological, and religious motives for attending the ethnic church are, therefore, intertwined because of their marginal existential conditions in "the strange land" (e.g., "I attend church and pray because I am lonely and seek peace of mind").

The Korean immigrants appear, therefore, to crave both types of fellowship—spiritual (Christian) fellowship *and* ethnic fellowship (cf. Hae-Jong Kim, 1979). The Korean ethnic church provides best both fellowships for the immigrant as shown in the following chart:

		Christian Fellowship	
		Yes	No
Ethnic Fellowship	Yes	Korean Ethnic Church	Korean Voluntary Association
	No	American Church	American Voluntary Association

The second reason for the immigrants' pervasive participation in the ethnic church is the inclusive nature of the church as a social institution. Regardless of sex, age, or socioeconomic status, every Korean immigrant is invited (or even solicited) to join the ethnic church whereas other voluntary ethnic associations have specific requirements for membership such as age, school, and locality. As compared with other ethnic associations, the ethnic church also provides the immigrants with frequent and regular opportunities (at least once a week) for primary-group *and* secondary-group interactions. The ethnic church usually provides not only a communal bond (the primary group) but also a *Gesellschaft* (the secondary group), which the immigrant also left behind. In other words, the immigrants are drawn together in the ethnic church not only to meet intimate friends but also to see "new faces" other than their family members, relatives, and close friends. In short, they miss both the informal and formal aspects of the Korean society back home, and the ethnic church seems to provide a microcosm of both. Past studies on the ethnic role of immigrant churches have largely neglected immigrants' secondary-group needs, such as social status, prestige, power, and recognition within the immigrant community. These needs would be particularly strong for those immigrant groups who cannot penetrate into the mainstream of the dominant group's social structure. In other words, the immigrants are not necessarily always looking for a small intimate church for affective personal relations but are often attracted to large formal churches. There are fifteen large churches in the Los Angeles area with more than 200 members. The *Yongnak* church is the largest with more than 1,000 members (*Hankuk Ilbo*, May 18, 1979). Such a large church performs associational functions similar to those performed by the Korean society at large in Korea. In this sense, geograpical propinquity (neighborhood church) seems to have very little to do with what church one attends. Often some immigrants drive more than ten miles to their churches (cf. Hae-Jong Kim, 1979).

The third major reason for the immigrant's gravitation to their ethnic church deals with the idea and practice of religious pluralism inherent in the American society. As Herberg points out:

> In American religious pluralism is thus not merely a historical and political fact: it is, in the mind of the American, the primordial condition of things, an essential aspect of the American Way of Life, and therefore, in itself, an aspect of religious belief. Americans, in other words, believe that the plurality of religious groups is a proper and legitimate condition. (1955:85)

Since racial and ethnic separatism (as expressed in the form of secular organization exclusively for a particular racial or ethnic group) is not officially encouraged in American culture, but religious distinctiveness is, ethnic churches in the United States have been found to be the most convenient vehicle for enhancing and preserving ethnic culture and identity (Sklare, 1955). In short, the proliferation of Korean ethnic churches and the immigrants' pervasive involvement in them are in a way encouraged by the host society. It is not uncommon to observe that many American churches help to establish Korean ethnic churches in their districts, often even within their own church buildings.

Theoretical Implications

Korean immigrants' extensive involvement in the ethnic church has become an important "way of life" of the immigrants in America. They seem to have a composite reason for such a modus vivendi: to pray, to seek peace of mind, to meet friends, to see new faces, to be recognized, and simply to be with a large group of Koreans without particular obligation, threat, demand, or attachment—"a little Korea" in America. The ethnic church thus functions to provide the immigrants with a fellowship that is both religious (Christian) and ethnic (Korean).

The theoretical implications of our findings are summarized as follows: (1) the conceptual distinction between the religious, the psychological, and the social is not heuristically clear in the study of immigrants' religious involvement; (2) the secondary-group needs of immigrants are as important as the primary-group needs in their involvement in the ethnic church; (3) the proliferation of ethnic churches in the United States is encouraged by religious pluralism inherent in the American society; (4) the first-generation immigrants' gravitation to the ethnic church reflects their adhesive mode of adaptation—persisting importance of an ethnic fellowship as well as a Christian fellowship; and (5) the ethnic church will survive or even flourish throughout the successive generations of the immigrants as long as their adhesive adaptation persists in the form of a bilingual church.

Notes

1. Literal Korean translation of this question: "What are the good points and bad points you would gain by attending church?"
2. According to Bok-Lim Kim's study (1978), 32 percent of her Chinese sample and 28 percent of the Japanese sample are affiliated with Christian churches in the Chicago area. Comparative data on the Chinese and Japanese immigrants in the Los Angeles area are not available.
3. According to the recent Gallup opinion poll, 40 percent of adults in the United States attended church or synagogue in a typical week of 1979 (Gallup, 1980: 291–92).

9
Life Satisfaction: Shrinking Aspirations and Contentment

In this chapter, we discuss the Korean immigrants' subjective perception of their general life satisfaction in the United States. The immigrants' "successful" adaptation would ultimately have to include psychological satisfaction as well as socioeconomic achievement in the new country. In general, one's life satisfaction or dissatisfaction is heavily influenced by one's cognitive frame of reference or standard of comparison. As Campbell, Converse, and Rodgers (1976:14) point out, such a cognitive frame of reference includes aspiration levels (what one hopes to attain in the long run), expectation levels (what one is likely to attain in the immediate future), equity levels (what one is entitled to attain), reference group levels (what one's reference others have already attained), personal needs (what one thinks he or she personally requires), and personal values (one's enduring beliefs and preferences such as freedom, equality, and the like). These researchers make a useful distinction between a satisfaction associated with rising expectations (success) and one which is associated with declining expectations (resignation). Among these critieria, particularly relevant to our present study are the immigrant's aspiration levels and their reference groups seen later in our analyses.

Regardless of which criteria each immigrant may include in his or her cognitive frame of reference, the general pattern of the immigrants' life satisfaction would largely reflect the degree of the immigrants' adaptive capacities and the extent of the host society's openness in its socioeconomic and psychological structure. As Eisenstadt aptly put it, "the degree of adaptation is determined by the relation between the immigrants' level of aspiration and the degree of their realizability in the new setting" (1951:259). In this sense, the life-satisfaction study of Korean immigrants in particular and of nonwhite minorities in general may be a crucial approach toward an understanding of their adaptation problems as well as in examining the structural problems that are inherent in the American society. Unfortunately, however, past studies on life satisfaction (life quality, well-being, or happiness) in the United States have largely been limited to white Americans (cf. Campbell, Converse, and Rodgers, 1976:446; J. Freedman, 1978:6).

As an exploratory study on the ethnic minority's life satisfaction, this chapter focuses on the Korean immigrants' subjective perception of their overall life satisfaction in relation to the length of their residence in the United States and other significant variables such as sex, age, marital status, socioeconomic status, acculturation, social assimilation, and ethnic attachment.

Length of Residence and Life Satisfaction

As our analyses revealed in the preceding chapters, length of residence is a crucial variable that is pervasively related to many adaptation variables. For instance, the longer the immigrants stay in the United States, the higher the degree of their socioeconomic status and acculturation becomes. Can we assume, then, that the degree of the immigrants' life satisfaction would also become higher as the lengths of their sojourn in their new country extend?

Prior to our Los Angeles study, we had suspected that there might be a limit to the degree of life satisfaction among the Korean immigrants in spite of their progressive acculturation and relatively improved economic conditions as time elapsed (cf. Glazer, 1954; Becker, 1968; Cha, 1975; Hurh, 1977a). In other words, the process of adaptation (especially social and psychological) may be progressive up to a certain point, parallel with the initial period of adjustment and subsequent occupational advancement. But we wondered if the process might not continue further, as in the case of the inverted U-curve pattern of adjustment and attitudinal changes among the foreign students from developing countries (Becker, 1968).

1. A Hypothetical Model of Psychological Adaptation

As Korean immigrants move up the occupational ladder (especially in the professions), they may tend to compare their life conditions to those of their WASP peers, rather than to their pre-emigration status or to other Korean immigrants (cf. Hyman and Singer, 1968). When and if this transfer or shifting of reference group occurs, the immigrants would begin to "discover" an immutable barrier (race) which blocks their way toward further mobility. Simply put, the more closely Korean immigrants identify themselves with their WASP peers, the more they will experience heightened feelings of relative deprivation, social alienation, and identity ambivalence. At this point, the degree of the immigrant's life satisfaction (psychological adaptation) and their desire for assimilation (sociocultural adaptation) may start to decline. To mitigate the problematic situation, some immigrants may shift their reference group back to their own ethnic group (Koreans) or some may seek their identity and reference group elsewhere (Hansen, 1940). If this is true, the relationship between the length of sojourn and the degree of adaptation (life satisfaction) may not be linear but rather quasicurvilinear as shown in Figure 8.

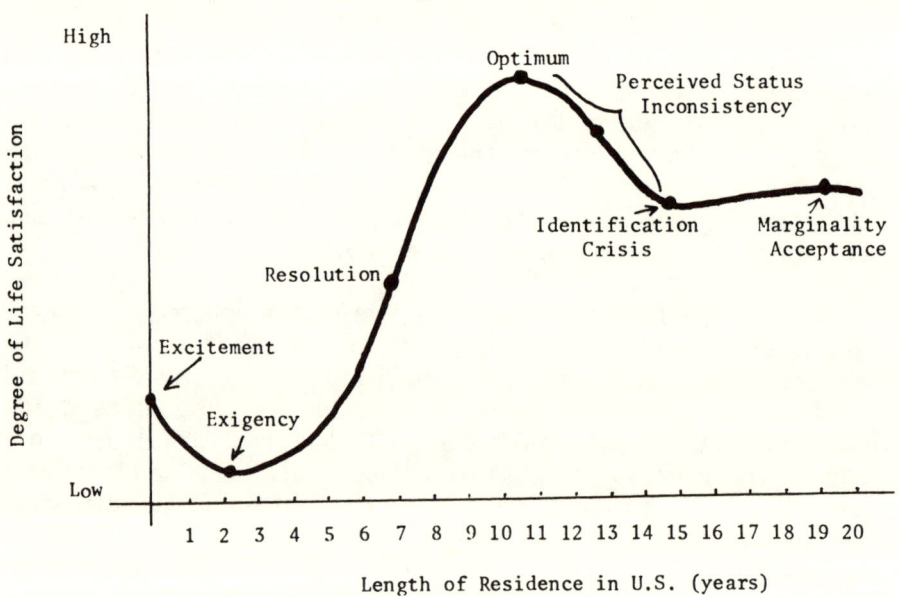

Figure 8. Length of Residence and Life Satisfaction: A Hypothetical Model

The six adaptive stages (or phases) included in this model require explanation. Upon their arrival in the United States, some Korean immigrants may experience a set of elated feelings such as feelings of relief that they have finally "made it" safely to the country they had aspired to settle in and excitement over reunion with their families, relatives, and friends who have already settled in the United States. However, most of the immigrants would confront a harsh reality soon after their arrival. The first one or two years of the initial adaptive stage may be called "exigency" characterized by problems of (1) the language barrier, (2) unemployment or underemployment, (3) social isolation (loneliness for the elderly especially), and (4) culture shock in general. At this stage, the immigrants would most likely doubt whether they could really "make it." Some may regret that they had left "home" for a strange land and yearn to return to their familiar milieu. This may be the most critical phase in the entire adaptation process, especially for those who are relatively older and had high pre-immigration occupational statuses. In other words, the disjuncture between one's high expectations and one's perceptions of the limited ability and opportunity may lead to a condition of cognitive ambivalence and exigency. The degree of exigency may be the highest among recent Korean immigrants in comparison with immigrants from other countries because of the very high preimmigration socioeconomic status of Koreans, as mentioned earlier.

As time goes on, acculturation starts, and exigency is redressed eventually through the resolution phase. At this stage, immigrants are now employed (even if underemployed), their English is improving, and their incomes are stable. Although some of their initial disillusionment may still linger on, immigrants have now developed a taste for material affluence, gained self-confidence, and by approximately the tenth year, their past aspirations "in the land of opportunity" may be revitalized. Approximately 18 percent of our Chicago sample were already residing in their own homes in 1975 (the average length of sojourn in the United States was 4.2 years), and 37 percent of our Los Angeles sample owned their own homes in 1979 (their average length of sojourn in the United States was 6.5 years). Hence, at this stage the immigrants' life satisfaction and desire for Anglo-conformity may reach its peak, and we would see a number of Korean immigrants becoming naturalized, their names becoming Anglicized, and social interaction with their WASP peers becoming more frequent, although the majority of immigrants' reference groups are still Koreans in Korea and/or in America.

Revitalization and accentuation of aspirations for "success" may, however, lead to another crisis, if and when such process involves the shifting of the immigrants' reference group—from the minority group (Koreans) to the dominant (white Americans). This crisis is characterized by feelings of relative deprivation, status inconsistency, perceptions of limited assimilation, and social marginality. The feelings of status inconsistency at this stage are quite different from that of the exigency stage: the immigrants would now compare their life condition to that of white Americans, not to their preemigration status or to their fellow Korean immigrants. The more closely they identified themselves with their WASP peers, the higher their feelings of relative deprivation and social marginality would become.

Thus, identification crisis would follow the third stage. The immigrants would begin to discover an immutable barrier (race) that blocks their way toward structural assimilation and over which they have no control. As other racial minorities have often experienced in the past, Korean immigrants too would painfully realize that the United States is not a "melting-pot" society for them. The question of "Who am I?" is hence intensely problematic at the fifth stage.

This existential limbo may lead to the last stage—the immigrants' creating and joining a new ethnic community (the Korean-American identity) or passive acceptance of their precarious place as the Korean minority in America (marginality acceptance).

These various stages are ideal types for heuristic purposes and deviations from this model may occur. For instance, some immigrants may skip a certain stage (or stages), whereas others may stop proceeding further or may even regress. The time length associated with each stage also needs to be interpreted as strictly hypothetical—some may attain the optimum within five years, others may take twenty years. One has to take many diverse factors into consideration—structural, interactional, and personality variables. In the absence of any significant empirical research on the subject, we had to choose an arbitrary benchmark based on commonsense observation. For instance, Marn J. Cha (1975) adopted the fifth year as a benchmark to divide his Korean respondents in Los Angeles into the newcomer and old-tmer categories. Through our previous study in the Chicago area, we learned that our respondents' resolution stage seemed to last longer than five years. Based on the noticeable changes taking place from the ninth year in the perceived status inconsistency scores, we tentatively estimated the optimal length of sojourn for a high degree of life satisfaction at the tenth year.

From this conjecture and theoretical base, we developed the following hypothesis to be tested on the Los Angeles sample.

> Among Korean immigrants (or nonwhite immigrants in general), the relationship between the length of residence in the United States and the degree of life satisfaction is quasi-curvilinear.

2. Hypothesis Testing

Our hypothetical model predicts the inverted U-curve pattern of life satisfaction of Korean immigrants in spite of their progressive cultural and socioeconomic adaptation. In order to test the model, the following major variables are examined in relation to the length of residence: acculturation, social assimilation, economic improvements, comparative reference group, and general life satisfaction.

As revealed in Chapters 4 and 5, the degrees of acculturation and social assimilation are positively related to the length of residence in the United States. It must be pointed out, however, that our inference derives from cross-sectional data on different groups of individuals in terms of their length of residence, rather than from panel (or longitudinal) data from the same group of individuals over different time periods. The panel study would certainly be the best method for testing our process model, but it was not possible because of various reasons. The time factor is obviously the most difficult problem (one has to wait ten or more years to test our model), but another serious problem deals with the protection of human subjects—anonymity and confidentiality of personal data.

Table 9.1 shows changes in two other adaptation variables in relation to the length of residence: economic improvement and selection of comparative reference group. The economic improvement (or adaptation) is measured by (1) the proportion of respondents in white-collar occupations, (2) the proportion of those who earn relatively high incomes ($17,000 or more annually), and (3) the proportion of those who own their own homes. As can be seen in Table 9.1 (A, B, and C), the respondents' economic conditions improve as their length of residence increases, especially in the period between the seventh and tenth year.

The respondents' *comparative* reference group is ascertained by responses to the following questions (cf. Hyman and Singer, 1968:149; Schmitt, 1972:64–66): "In assessing your achievement in the United States, from what group of people do you get your standard for comparison?" Nine response categories for this question are provided: Koreans in Korea, Koreans in America, White Americans, Black Americans, Mexican-Americans, Asian-Americans (other than Koreans), Don't Know, None, and Other.

As Table 9.1 (D) reveals, up to the sixth year of residence, little changes are observed in the proportion of our respondents who choose white Americans as their comparative reference group; however, the proportion increases markedly thereafter (from 20% to 47%).

In sum, the longer the length of residence, the more immigrants are acculturated, socially assimilated (although limited to certain dimensions), economically improving, and choosing white Americans as their reference group as predicted in our model. How about life satisfaction (the psychological dimension of adaptation)?

In order to construct a scale for measuring the degree of life satisfaction, the following six five-point scale questionnaire items are factor-analyzed. These items are considered most relevant to the general life experiences of Korean immigrants in the United States based on our previous study in the Chicago area (Hurh, Kim, and Kim, 1978):

(1) Do you regret that you came to the United States? (*regret*)
(2) Since your immigration, do you think that everything has progressed as you planned? (*progress*)
(3) How well are you generally satisfied with your immigrant life? (*general life satisfaction*)
(4) How strongly do you feel about the following statements?
   a. Since immigration, I feel more lonely than ever. (*loneliness*)
   b. One thing that I have learned through immigrant life for sure is that one should employ whatever means in order to survive. (*normlessness*)
   c. Since the world is run by a few people, Korean immigrants' influence on the American society is negligible. (*powerlessness*)[1]

Table 9.2 shows the results of factor analysis of the six items by varimax rotation. Two factors are identified. Factor 1 is associated with four items (regret, progress, general life satisfaction, and loneliness), and Factor 2 is associated with two items (powerlessness and normlessness).

Since the remaining items in each factor show such low loadings, the high loading items for both factors are clearly not overlapping. This means "powerlessness" and "normlessness" items constitute clearly a separate factor (alienation) from Factor 1, which involves the life satisfaction item as the highest loading item and three other items dealing with subjective dimensions of the immigrants' life experience (regret, progress, loneliness). By adding the scores of the four high loading items for Factor 1, a life satisfaction scale (a minimum of 4 to a maximum of 20 points) is thus constructed. In terms of interitem correlation, our scale is found to have a high Alpha-reliability correlation coefficient of 0.71 (cf. McKennel, 1977).[2] Correlation of the life-satisfaction scale with the alienation scale is, however, very low ($r = .01$).

In order to examine the validity of our scale, the relationship

Shrinking Aspirations and Contentment   145

between the degree of life satisfaction and the degree of job satisfaction of the respondents is analyzed. It has generally been found that these two variables are positively related (Andrews and Withy, 1974). As Table 9.3 demonstrates, our data bear out the positive relationship suggesting the strength of the validity of our scale.

The life satisfaction scores in relation to the length of residence are shown in Table 9.4. For female respondents, the two variables are positively related to one another. This means the longer the female respondents stay in the United States, the higher their level of life satisfaction becomes. For male respondents, a similar positive relationship is also observed but with a slight deviation among those who have resided in the United States for eleven years or more. Moreover, the positive relationship for males is on the whole less conspicuous than it is for females. In other words, the male respondents' degree of life satisfaction increases as their length of sojourn extends up to the tenth year, but not further thereafter.

Therefore, this pattern for males is certainly not curvilinear. A curvilinear pattern of relationship between the length of residence and the degree of life satisfaction is observed among male professionals and semiprofessionals (see Table 9.5). Their life satisfaction reaches its peak during the period between the seventh and eighth years, and declines gradually thereafter (see Figure 9).

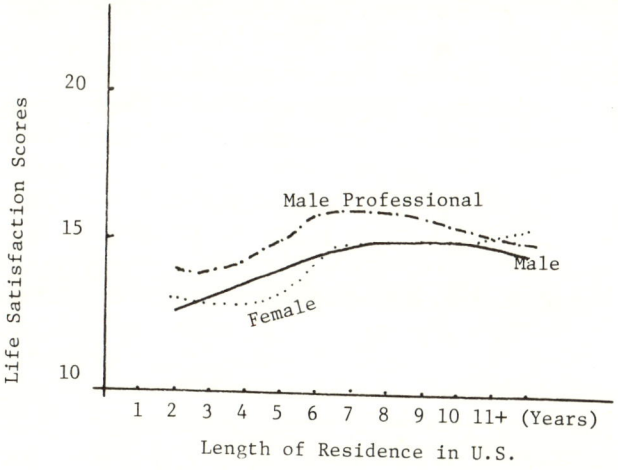

Figure 9. Degree of Life Satisfaction in Relation to Length of Residence (Male, Female, and Male Professional)

The foregoing analyses lead us, therefore, to reject our hypothesis except for male professionals and semiprofessionals. How do we interpret these findings? Assuming that methodological errors are negligible, what might have been the main theoretical errors or problems in constructing our original hypothetical model? We suspect the key problem dwells in the ambiguity inherent in the reference group concept, and, therefore, in the inconsistency between objective and subjective (relative) deprivation. Our theoretical conjecture about the curvilinear relationship between the length of residence and life satisfaction was predicated upon the following hypothetical process in which *reference-group shifting* would play a crucial role for the downturn of life satisfaction as illustrated:

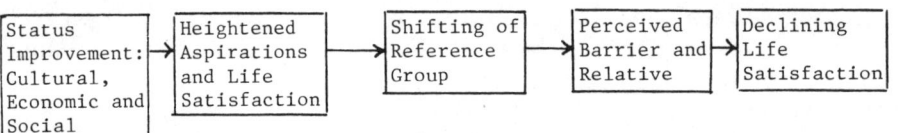

In reality, however, Korean immigrants do not seem to *shift* their comparative reference group from Koreans to white Americans. If "shifting" were meant to reject the old reference relationships with Koreans altogether and to embrace new reference relationships with white Americans in their entirety, those who "shifted" should have indicated decreasing ethnic attachment to the Korean immigrant community and increasing social participation in the white American society. As our data indicate, however, the immigrants' strong and pervasive ethnic attachment is unaffected by their choice of white reference groups and their length of residence. This pattern confirms the adhesive mode of sociocultural adaptation of the immigrants discussed in Chapters 4 and 5. At the same time, social participation of the immigrants in the white society continues to be limited in its scope and intensity as mentioned earlier. Apparently, white Americans are therefore "nonmembership reference other" and are only segmentally relevant to the immigrants' social world (Schmitt, 1972:4–5; Turner, 1955). In this sense, even those immigrants who never participate directly in the white American society may adopt certain selected values and norms of the dominant group as an ideal frame of reference or aspiration goal (Shibutani, 1961:256; Williams, 1970).

As an ideal normative reference category, white Americans are thus *added* to the immigrants' reference set (adhesive reference group), and their real comparative group is still Koreans in Korea and/or in America. In other words, "what is ultimately desirable to attain in the future" is added on to "what is realistically possible and comparable now." Despite the fact that the proportion of our respondents who chose whites as their reference group generally increases as the length of residence extends, the degree of their strong ethnic attachment remains constant (see Chapters 4 and 5).

The vast majority of our respondents interacted primarily with their fellow Koreans regardless of the length of their residence and their choice of white reference groups. Hence, the inclusion of the white American model as an abstract aspiration goal in the immigrants' frame of reference would not necessarily produce feelings of relative deprivation or lower the level of their life satisfaction. On the contrary, those who chose white Americans as their reference group showed higher life-satisfaction scores (Mean = 14.33, SD = 3.38) than those who chose their fellow Koreans as their reference group (Mean = 13.67, SD = 3.40). The difference between the two scores is significant at .05 level by t test (t = 1.97, df = 439). In fact, choosing a white reference group may even be an effect rather than the cause of life satisfaction. In other words, white Americans are chosen not for a standard for self-evaluation but for an aspiration goal to further life satisfaction.

Certainly the conventional sense of relative deprivation as a result of reference-group shifting does not seem to apply in our study (cf. Hyman and Singer, 1968; Merton and Kitt, 1950; Form and Geschwender, 1962). Among our respondents, the choice of white reference groups and strong ethnic attachment is not mutually exclusive. Our theoretical oversight thus stems from the ambiguity in the reference-group concept (abstract versus concrete, primary versus secondary, ideal versus real comparative reference group), multiplicity in the choice (shifting versus adding), and also differential effects of the diversity on the degree of life satisfaction.

To conclude our data analysis, for the majority of our respondents, the length of residence, status improvement, status aspiration, and choice of white reference groups are all positively related to the degree of life satisfaction. One question, however, still remains: What accounts for the curvilinear pattern of life satisfaction among male professionals and semiprofessionals?

Two answers may be plausible for this question. First, still in line with our initial theorizing, male professionals and semiprofessionals do *shift* their *real* comparative reference group from Koreans to white Americans, and as a result, they feel relatively deprived at a certain point in time (the ninth- and tenth-year period). Second, their choice of white reference groups continues to be irrelevant but some other factors affect the downturn of life satisfaction. Because of the small N for male professionals and semiprofessionals, neither of these answers can be varified by this study.

3. Adhesive Reference Group, Ethnic Attachment, and Contentment

In this chapter, we hypothesized that the relationship between the length of residence and the degree of life satisfaction would be curvilinear among Korean immigrants in the Los Angeles area. This hypothesis was derived from a general model of immigrants' adaptation in which the immigrants' shifting of their comparative reference group from Koreans to white Americans (the dominant group) was considered as the major cause for producing feelings of relative deprivation. As we analyzed, our data do not, however, lend themselves to support the hypothesis except for male professionals and semiprofessionals. Among the majority of our respondents, it has been found that *shifting* of their reference group did not occur. Instead, white Americans were *added* to the immigrants' reference set as an abstract aspiration category. The immigrants' strong and persisting ethnic attachment, especially within the well-established Korean community in Los Angeles, seems to have prevented them from shifting their primary and concrete reference other. The Korean immigrants in such a large ethnic community appear to have two major reference others: one is concrete (Koreans) and the other is abstract (white Americans). As long as the latter remains as an abstract aspiration group, feelings of discrimination, marginality, and relative deprivation would not enter the minds of the immigrants (cf. Shibutani, 1955, 1961:256). In this sense, strong ethnic attachment and choice of the dominant group as an abstract reference category are not necessarily mutually exclusive (cf. Turner, 1955; Williams, 1970). In the long run, such a cognitive segmentation (aspiration versus realizability) may tend to perpetuate ethnic segregation, but in the short run, it serves to lower the dissatisfaction level of immigrants (cf. Eisenstadt, 1951). No wonder the majority of our respondents show a relatively high degree of life satisfaction regardless of their pre- and postimmigration status inconsistency.

In two situations, however, adding of the dominant group as a reference category becomes problematic: (1) when such a reference category becomes a concrete comparative reference group, and (2) if one's ethnic attachment is weak. In both instances, feelings of relative deprivation and social marginality would be high, and hence low life satisfaction would occur. An example for the first situation may be male professionals and semiprofessionals in our study, and for the second situation, it would be the second-generation Koreans living detached from the Korean ethnic community. To conclude, the relationship between the length of residence and the degree of life satisfaction is still largely affected by reference group but is dependent on three major pairs of variables: concreteness versus abstractness, shifting versus adding, and strong versus weak ethnic attachment (see Table 9.6).

Other Major Variables and Life Satisfaction

The second objective of this chapter is to study the relationship between the immigrants' life satisfaction and major adaptation variables, such as demographic, socioeconomic, acculturation, assimilation, and ethnic attachment variables.

1. Demographic Variables and Life Satisfaction

In general, male and female respondents show little difference in their overall mean scores of life satisfaction (13.90 for males and 13.89 for females). However, some notable differences emerge when other specific variables are introduced. We therefore control sex for all of our further analyses on the life satisfaction of our Los Angeles sample.

The degree of life satisfaction is significantly related to age for both male and female respondents. The oldest age category (51 or more) is found to be the most satisfied, the next is the youngest age category (30 or less), and the least satisfied group is the middle-age category (31-50). This pattern is somewhat similar to that of the U.S. national sample for Freedman's "happiness" study (1978). In terms of sex difference, the oldest females are the most satisfied group (Mean = 15.41), and the early middle-age males (age, 31-40) are the least satisfied group (Mean = 13.21).

Marital status does not seem to have significant bearing on the female respondents' life satisfaction, but among the male respondents, bachelors are the most satisfied group (Mean = 14.31) and the postmarital singles (widowers, divorced, and separated) are the least satisfied (Mean = 8.40). This pattern deviates a great deal from that of the U.S. national sample. In terms of marital status, the most satisfied are those who are married, regardless of sex (Freedman, 1978; Campbell, Converse, and Rodgers, 1976; Andrews and Withey, 1976).

2. Socioeconomic Variables and Life Satisfaction

In general, the level of education is positively related to the degree of life satisfaction of both male and female respondents: the higher the level of education, the higher is the degree of life satisfaction. The relationship between the two variables is significant for both male ($F = 8.72$, $df = 2, 245$) and female respondents ($F = 6.85$, $df = 2, 287$) at the .001 level by one-way analysis of variance. There is, however, an exception. Those females who graduated only from Korean colleges are the least satisfied group (Mean = 13.17) among all female respondents, although they constitute a majority among our female sample.

Employment status does not seem to have any significant effect on the male respondents' life satisfaction, but among females, those who are employed are relatively less satisfied with life (Mean = 13.33) than those who are not employed (Mean = 14.70). The difference in their life-satisfaction scores is significant at the .01 level by one-way analysis of variance ($F = 13.34$, $df = 1, 332$). This finding is exactly contrary to Freedman's findings (1978) on American women. Would the Korean traditional sex role have anything to do with this difference? We defer our discussion on this matter until later.

The sex difference is more pronounced in the relationships between other socioeconomic variables and life satisfaction. Occupational statuses and annual incomes (both individual and family) are positively related to the degree of life satisfaction for male respondents but not to that of female respondents. In other words, the higher the occupational prestige and incomes, the higher is the degree of the male immigrants' life satisfaction. On the other hand, there is no significant difference in the degree of life satisfaction for female immigrants in terms of their occupational categories and incomes, e.g., female professionals are not any more satisfied than women employed in some other occupational categories. These findings would suggest that the Korean female immigrants' life satisfaction is largely dependent on factors other than occupation and income.

As expected, homeowners are significantly more satisfied with their life than nonhomeowners. No sex difference is found in this regard.

3. Sociocultural Assimilation Variables and Life Satisfaction

In order to examine whether the immigrants' life satisfaction is affected by the degree of their Americanization, two social assimilation variables and four acculturation variables were analyzed in relation to the degree of life satisfaction: for social assimilation, interaction with white friends and participation in American voluntary associations; and for acculturation, subscriptions to American newspapers and American magazines, Anglicization of Korean names, and proficiency in English.

The degree of social assimilation is not related to the degree of life satisfaction for both male and female respondents. For male respondents, all of the acculturation variables except one (subscriptions to American magazines) are positively related to life satisfaction. The correlation coefficient between English proficiency and life satisfaction is .21 ($N = 281$, $p = .05$).

However, for female respondents, *none* of these variables is related to life satisfaction. Again, the source of the female immigrants' life satisfaction cannot be ascertained by studying Americanization variables.

Both male and female respondents show their subjective perception of social acceptance by whites as positively related to their life satisfaction.[3] The correlation coefficient between the respondents' perceived social acceptance by whites and life satisfaction is .28 for the male respondents ($N = 281$) and .21 for the female respondents ($N = 334$). Although these values are not high, they are significant at the .001 level. Implications of this finding are elaborated on later.

4. Ethnic Attachment Variables and Life Satisfaction

For both male and female respondents, having relatives in the Los Angeles area made no difference in their life satisfaction.

For male respondents, those who participated in Korean voluntary associations showed a relatively higher degree of life satisfaction than those who did not participate. Likewise, among the male respondents, the Korean ethnic church affiliates showed a higher degree of life satisfaction than the nonchurch affiliates. Furthermore, among the male church affiliates, those who attended church more frequently are found to be significantly most satisfied with life than those who attended church less frequently.

However, curiously enough again, neither the Korean voluntary association nor the Korean ethnic church is related to the degree of the female respondents' life satisfaction. In fact, we have not found any significant variable uniquely related to the female respondents' life satisfaction with one exception (employment status). To summarize our findings, the major significant variables related to a *relatively* high degree of life satisfaction by sex are shown in Table 9.7.

As in most cases of the life-satisfaction study, caution is needed in interpreting this table for the following reasons: (1) the table merely describes a crude profile of *objective conditions* in relation to life satisfaction, and, therefore, the conditions, whether in part or as a whole, may not be necessary nor sufficient to "produce" or "ensure" every immigrant's life satisfaction; (2) the variations in the life satisfaction scores are not generally great (see Tables 9.4 and 9.5); (3) more importantly, the general level of life satisfaction for Korean immigrants is rather high (a mean score of 13.9 in a 20-point scale)[4]; and hence (4) the table does not *explain* why certain individuals are subjectively dissatisfied in spite of the favorable conditions or satisfied despite unfavorable conditions. To understand what these findings mean, we now turn to the last objective of this chapter—theoretical inferences and practical implications.

5. Theoretical Inferences and Practical Implications

In order to draw some meaningful inferences, one needs first to examine the structural and situational conditions of the Korean immigrants' adaptation in the United States as a whole. As mentioned earlier, the degree of life satisfaction is largely dependent on the immigrants' levels of aspirations and the possibility of attaining them in the new country. The levels of aspirations are determined by the immigrants' capacity to modify their traditional social roles that are inherent in the Korean society and adaptable to the new setting, and also by the degree of openness in the American socioeconomic structure. In this sense, four factors are deeply implicated in the immigrants' subjective perception of their well-being: *the American social structure* and the *immigrants' adaptive capacity* jointly determine the levels of their *socioeconomic status* and *expectations* (aspirations). For instance, limited opportunity and limited ability (e.g., in English) would lead to a lower socioeconomic status, and thus also may shrink further aspirations. Figure 10 illustrates this relationship.

As shown in Figure 10, the American social structure of ethnic confinement (social and employment segregation) limits the range of the immigrants' socioeconomic opportunities, and the immigrants' perception of such structural limitations (including their own cultural handicap) would tend to lower the levels of their aspirations. As a consequence, they may feel relatively satisfied with their immigrant life in spite of the objectively apparent status inconsistency in the new country (see Chapter 6). No wonder the general level of Korean immigrants' life satisfaction is rather high in spite of their unfavorable labor market conditions

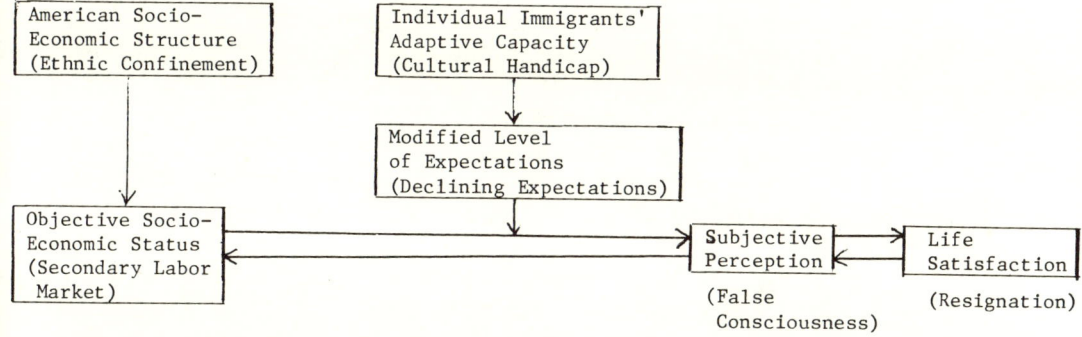

Figure 10. Relationships Among Variables Related to Korean Immigrants' Life Satisfaction

and social marginality (cf. Hurh and Kim, 1979b; Kim and Hurh, 1980c).

To be more specific, the employed immigrants' job satisfaction level is high despite the fact that the majority of them work in the secondary labor market (see Chapter 6). Perceiving limited opportunity and ability, but having little power and means to change the situation, the immigrants seem to lower their expectation levels in order to minimize their feelings of relative deprivation and discontentment. Thus, the lower aspiration levels serve as "shock absorbers" to cope with change (Campbell, Converse, and Rodgers, 1976:208). For instance, the majority of employed immigrants do not expect significant upward mobility in their occupational career in the foreseeable future, and most of the immigrants consider small businesses to be the most successful area for Koreans in the United States (see Chapter 6). The immigrant workers' comparative reference groups for measuring their "success" seem to be predominantly Koreans either in America or in Korea.

Another example that is relevant to the disparity between the objective conditions and the subjective definition of the situation is the fact that the Korean immigrants' perceived social acceptance by white Americans is found to be a universal correlate of life satisfaction among the majority of Korean immigrants in spite of their *limited* social interaction with white Americans (cf. Chapter 5). This phenomenon may be attributed to the pervasiveness of social segregation of the nonwhite minorities from the dominant group in the United States. Under such conditions of pervasive ethnic segregation, even a slight degree of social interaction with members of the dominant group would give the immigrants a sense of social acceptance, and hence also a feeling of contentment. In other words, precisely because ethnic confinement of the Korean minority is expected as "normal," social interaction with the dominant group, even in its limited scope and intensity, would be particularly rewarding to the majority of Korean immigrants.

Under such circumstances of contained aspirations, it is not difficult to understand why the male immigrants would be relatively satisfied with their immigrant life as long as they have jobs with stable incomes, become acculturated, feel socially accepted by the dominant group to a certain extent, and can maintain close social ties with their fellow Koreans. Traditional male sex roles appear to be implicated in these correlates—job, income, activities, and friends outside home.

As to the source of the female immigrants' life satisfaction, no plausible inferences can be drawn at the present stage of our analysis. As mentioned earlier, none of the acculturation, assimilation, and ethnic attachment variables are related to the female immigrants' life satisfaction. Neither is occupation or income related to their life satisfaction. Only five structural variables (length of residence, age, employment, type of residence, and education) and two subjective variables (job satisfaction and perception of social acceptance by Americans) are related to the female immigrants' life satisfaction; however, these variables are *not unique* to the female immigrants except employment. In short, fewer numbers of correlates of life satisfaction are identified for the female immigrants than for the male immigrants.

These observations suggest that either (1) the female immigrant's aspirations would be even more limited than that of the male immigrants' (job, income, social status, and social participation are irrelevant to life satisfaction), or (2) the female immigrants' frame of reference for judging a "satisfactory life" may be more diverse and complex than that of the male immigrants; therefore, there is a lack of consensus as to certain definitive criteria.

Regardless of the validity of these conjectures, *both male and female immigrants do perceive generally a relatively high degree of life satisfaction despite their objective conditions of socioeconomic and cultural marginality in their new country.* Our theoretical inference is thus that objective structural variables do not exert a direct influence on the degree of life satisfaction unless they are translated into subjective symbolic variables (the subjective definition of the situation). Moreover, one of the most important factors affecting the immigrants' subjective definition is their aspiration (or expectation) levels.

To conclude this chapter, the general pattern of the Korean

immigrants' life satisfaction may be characterized by "a satisfaction which is associated with an experience of declining expectations" (resignation), rather than "one which is associated with rising expectations" (Campbell, Converse, and Rodgers, 1976:10). Such a mode of psychological adaptation may serve to lower the levels of the immigrants' frustration and disappointment in the short run, but it tends to perpetuate ethnic confinement in the long run, as briefly mentioned earlier in this chapter. Such a false sense of satisfaction or even "success" within the confines of Korean "ethnic islands" will have a more profound and serious effect upon the second and third generation Korean-Americans than on the first generation (Hurh, 1980). Several theoretical propositions are advanced in the concluding chapter of this book.

Notes

1. Each of these six items has five response categories ranging from the most positive to the most negative responses (e.g., "strongly agree," "agree," "don't know," "disagree," and "strongly disagree").

2. Alpha = $\dfrac{m \bar{r}ij}{1 + (m - 1\, \bar{r}ij)}$

   m = the number of separate items in the text
   $\bar{r}ij$ = the average of all the interitem correlations

3. The index for perceived social acceptance by whites is constructed by adding the immigrants' responses to the following three five-point scale items: (1) Do you think that it is generally difficult to make friends with Americans? (2) When I am with Americans, I often feel "left out" or isolated. (3) Most of the Americans whom I personally know do not seem to understand how I feel about things.

4. A high level of life satisfaction is not a phenomenon unique to Korean immigrants. According to Andrews and Withey (1976:311), two-thirds of American adults are satisfied with life-as-a-whole.

Conclusion: Structural Roots of Ethnic Confinement and Adhesive Adaptation

On January 13, 1903, the first shipload of 101 Korean immigrants arrived in Honolulu, Hawaii. Seventy-seven years later, approximately three hundred and fifty-five thousand Koreans reside in the United States. About two-thirds of these are "new immigrants" who came to America after 1970. The early Korean immigrants were largely uneducated young bachelors whose primary purpose for migration was to work temporarily on the Hawaiian plantations, rather than to settle here permanently. But who are the new Korean immigrants who constitute the overwhelming majority of the Koreans in America today? How do they adapt themselves to the new country? What are the major problems they face in the adaptation process? Why?

In this book, we have attempted to answer these questions by multidimensional and structural analyses of the new Korean immigrants' adaptation in terms of their historical background, demographic characteristics, and various patterns of adaptation in cultural, social, economic, and psychological dimensions.

In conclusion, we summarize our findings in two parts: (1) a descriptive summary of the immigrants' background, general adaptation patterns, and problems based on our Los Angeles data, and (2) the theoretical and practical implications of our study.

Descriptive Data on the New Immigrants

1. Socioeconomic Background

Generally, our respondents were in early middle adulthood, married, and come from an average size family of 3.5. About one-third of the respondents were homeowners, whereas half of them rented apartments. The majority of the respondents were college educated and held white-collar occupations prior to their emigration from Korea. One-third of the employed respondents were small-business owners and/or managers, one-fourth professionals and semiprofessionals, and another one-fourth semi-skilled and unskilled workers. The proportion of the employed female immigrants was higher than that of American women. The majority of our respondents came to the United States about six years ago and they were still in the process of settling in the new environment. During the last decade, the Korean community in the Los Angeles area grew in two aspects: the establishment of a discrete Koreatown in the inner city of Los Angeles as a reception area for many Korean newcomers and the rapid suburbanization within a sixty-mile radius of Greater Los Angeles. The immigrants' residential scattering to various suburban areas does not seem to have weakened their strong ethnic social ties.

2. Adaptation Patterns

The acculturation process has been very slow among the respondents. About half of them experienced language problems and were not exposed to the American-printed media at all. Nearly all of them did not speak English at home, although about 60 percent of our employed respondents used English at work. Being the first-generation immigrants, the respondents' ethnic attachment to Korean culture has persisted. Most of them indicated that family duty should be given priority over individual interest; nearly all of them thought it was necessary for their children to speak Korean language well; the majority of them prefered the Korean ethnic church over the American; and about half of them desired to return to Korean.

Their social participation and interpersonal relations were largely confined to their own ethnic group. For instance, most of the respondents actively participated in Korean voluntary associations, whereas only a very small portion of them were members of American voluntary organizations. This is particularly true for noncollege graduates whose individual adaptive capacity was relatively lower than those who graduated from Korean and/or American colleges. The respondents' primary group relations did not extend beyond their families, relatives, Korean friends, and neighbors. Two-thirds of our respondents were opposed to interracial marriage with Americans. Despite this seemingly "self-imposed" or voluntary segregation from American social networks, about half of the respondents desired close association with white Americans, approved of changing their Korean first names to American names, and many indicated that they prefered to live in predominantly American neighborhoods. The immigrants' psychological ambivalence can be observed in both cognitive and emotional dimensions.

For the respondents, occupational life, underemployment, job-information deprivation, and employment segregation were problematic. As mentioned earlier, almost all of the respondents were engaged in white-collar occupations in Korea; however, about half of them started their occupational career as low-skilled, blue-collar workers upon their arrival in the United States. Eventually, many of them managed to move up to a marginal level of white-collar occupations (generally in small businesses). On the whole, our respondents have been subjected to job-information deprivation, mainly as a result of limited social assimilation. Limited social assimilation and the structure of the American labor market have blocked or delayed the occupational mobility of the immigrants. Despite these hardships, the respondents reported that they were generally satisfied with their jobs, and the majority of them did not have feelings of relative deprivation, in spite of their objectively apparent status inconsistency. One may wonder how long this unrealistic perception of reality would last. Or would this phenomenon be unique to only the first-generation Korean immigrants? We address these questions later in our discussion on the theoretical implications of these findings.

Closely related to employment, another area of the immigrants' adjustment is the division of their household tasks. In the traditional Korean family, the wife is confined to home and bears the major responsibility of performing household tasks, whereas the husband is expected to be the breadwinner. As our data revealed, the traditional pattern of the marital roles persists. A high proportion (64%) of the wives in our sample were employed: however, irrespective of their employment, a substantial proportion of the wives still performed most of the household tasks—even more than they felt obliged to do. Moreover, the immigrant wives were no less traditional in their conception of marital roles than their husbands. Obviously, the traditional role expectation and role behavior are deeply rooted in the past socialization of the immigrants. Would there be any other factors contributing to the persistence of the traditional family role? We also defer this question until later.

In contrast to Chinese and Japanese immigrants, a great majority (70%) of our respondents were affiliated with Christian churches of various denominations. Of the church affiliates, the overwhelming majority (96.5%) belonged to Korean ethnic churches and the rest were members of American churches. About half of our respondents were already affiliated with churches prior to their emigration from Korea, but the proportion significantly increased after their arrival in the United States. Koreans also appear to be active Christians: the vast majority (84%) of our respondents attended church at least once a week and one-third of them held staff positions in the church. Religious participation thus appears to be one of the integral parts of the Korean immigrants' adaptation in the United States. Why is there such a heightened interest in church among the immigrants? Their expressed motives for attending church were primarily religious in nature, and the main advantages they gained from their church attendance were indicated as "peace of mind" and "meeting people." The implications of these findings are summarized later.

Our respondents generally expressed their life satisfaction in the United States for the following reasons: "In the United States honest and diligent work pays off," "good facilities for children's education and growth," and "free life, activities, and atmosphere" (Hurh and Kim, 1979b:80). On the whole, the majority of our respondents appeared to be satisfied with their immigrant life, despite half of them feeling lonely and powerless. It may be that loneliness and powerlessness are usually expected by minority immigrant in the new country. No wonder our immigrants generally evaluated their achievement in comparison primarily with their Korean fellow immigrants. Would this mean that our respondents limited or contained their own level of aspirations? Whether one may call this phenomenon "resignation" or realism, the majority of the respondents did not seem to have a strong sense of relative deprivation. The theoretical implications of this satisfaction associated with contained aspirations are summarized later.

3. Problem Areas

The most serious problem experienced by our respondents was that of language. Next to the problem of language were differences of the culture and social systems between Korea and the United States, and transportation problems. Other concerns were reflected in their suggestions to the government. They are, in order of frequency: reduction of prejudice and discrimination, facilitation of employment service, and effective law enforcement, especially in Koreatown and other business areas (Hurh and Kim, 1979b:85-89).

In sum, the Korean immigrants' adaptation is a dialectic process between the American social structure and the immigrants' performance of their adaptive capacities. We have, so far, described only the latter. A structural analysis of the mutual interaction between the two is now summarized.

Theoretical Implications

A study of immigrants is also a study of the host society. In other words, the degree of the Korean immigrants' adaptation depends not only on their adaptive capacities but also on the openness in the American social structure. Various patterns and problems of the immigrants' adaptation analyzed in this book reflect in many ways structural problems inherent both in the American society and in the immigrants' cultural and socioeconomic backgrounds. Adhesive adaptation, the general mode of adaptation among the first-generation Korean immigrants, is therefore basically a product of the confluence between ethnic segregation inherent in the American social structure and ethnic attachment embedded in the Korean immigrants' sociopsychological structure.

There is nothing particularly new in this theorizing. Any first-generation immigrants, whether Korean, Chinese, or even Irish, would generally have stronger ethnic attachments to their traditional culture and society and be less acculturated and assimilated to the new country than their posterity would. This tendency may be more pronounced for those immigrants whose racial and cultural backgrounds are radically different from that of the dominant group of the host society. The first-generation Korean immigrants are certainly not unique in this respect. As we discussed in Chapter 4, the Korean immigrants' perception of their social segregation from the mainstream of the American society and their own limited adaptive capacities (cultural unfamiliarity in general and language in particular) tend to even enhance their ethnic attachment as a defense. The bicultural and bilingual, but socially marginal, situation may thus be ubiquitous to all first-generation immigrants, although the extent and intensity of social marginality varies from one immigrant group to another.

What is new in our study, however, is that we have *empirically confirmed* the adhesive model in the major adaptation dimensions of the immigrants. In this respect, adhesive adaptation is not merely a conjecture, but it emerges as a viable theoretical model or paradigm that has survived empirical tests. As a theoretical model, adhesive adaptation offers a comprehensive analytical framework; thereby it helps us to understand the general pattern of the immigrant's adaptation in relation to structural sources (cultural, social, economic, and psychological). Furthermore, our theoretical model can also be used to predict the possible consequences of such a mode of adaptation by testing its derivative theories on various immigrant groups under similar circumstances. This would mean that the adhesive model of adaptation may have macrosociological implications beyond a case of Korean immigrants.

As we have empirically demonstrated throughout this book, the adhesive model applies to virtually all dimensions of the Korean immigrants' adaptation to the United States. The theoretical and practical implications of our entire study thus center around adhesive adaptation. The following summary highlights these implications.

1. Adhesive Adaptation as a General Theory

As we discussed in the introductory chapter, adhesive adaptation is one of the major types of ethnic adaptation in which certain aspects of the new culture and social relations with members of the host society are added on to the immigrants' traditional culture and social networks, without replacing or modifying any significant part of the old. In short, it is a nonzero-sum model of adaptation. For example, Korean immigrants' progressive Americanization and their strong ethnic attachment are not mutually exclusive. It is not to be equated, however, with the ideal pluralistic mode of adaptation since the scope and intensity of Americanization (especially social assimilation) is generally limited to a minimum. Two main factors are responsible for this "limited pluralism"—adhesive adaptation, ethnic segregation inherent in the American social structure (involuntary factor) and the immigrants' persistent ethnic attachment (voluntary factor). Each of these factors reinforces each other through intervening factors, such as the immigrants' inadequate adaptive capacities (e.g., language, economic resources), well-established ethnic enclaves, the dominant group's perception of threat, and the general economic and political climate of the host society at a particular point in time.

When ethnic confinement (imposed ethnic segregation) is inherent in the social structure of the host country, it is most likely that immigrants' assimilation into the dominant group's primary social structure is restricted in its scope and intensity, regardless of the immigrants' length of residence in the new country, socioeconomic status, degree of acculturation, and desire for assimilation. Under such circumstances, the immigrants' ethnic attachment tends to become stronger in order to satisfy their primary group needs, preserve their collective identity, and lower the levels of their frustration and dissatisfaction. In sum, the voluntary factor involved in adhesive adaptation is not strictly voluntary because of its structural roots; that is, the social segregation of racial and ethnic minorities in the United States.[1] As long as the structural roots are not eradicated, neither assimilation nor perfect pluralism is attainable but adhesive adaptation remains as a survival strategy for nonwhite immigrants, especially for the first-generation immigrants.

2. Adhesive Adaptation in Specific Dimensions

Having summarized the theoretical implications of adhesive adaptation on a paradigmatic level, we now cull their significance in relation to specific adaptive dimensions.

(a) Cultural Dimension. As shown in Chapter 4, the immigrants become acculturated as their length of stay in the United States extends, but their strong ethnic attachment is largely unaffected by these variables. Even among the "old-timers" (whose length of residence is eleven years or more), the vast majority of them indicate their strong sense of family priority, ethnic pride, exposure to Korean mass media, and the desire to teach Korean language to their children. Neither have the educational statuses any bearing on the degree of ethnic attachment. In short, progress in time, acculturation, and socioeconomic status do not accompany a regress in ethnic attachment. It is apparent, therefore, by adhesive adaptation that the immigrants do not resist acculturation but rather seek to adopt the new culture whenever possible without discarding or weakening the old.

(b) Social Dimension. Ethnic confinement is also pronounced in the intimate social relations of Korean immigrants as discussed in Chapter 5. As our data reveal, social assimilation is very limited for the immigrants; very few of the noncollege graduates have white friends and even among the American-college graduates, only half manage to have white friends. Only 8 percent of our Los Angeles sample participated in American voluntary associations, whereas three-fourths of them participated in Korean voluntary associations. In general, the immigrants' social interaction with white friends and participation in American voluntary associations vary with the length of residence and/or levels of education; however, the immigrants' strong attachment to their ethnic social ties is not largely affected by these variables. As a result, the immigrants' social assimilation is not accompanied by their dissociation from Korean friends or kin in the Los Angeles area, or from other Korean ties. As discussed in Chapter 3, the ethnic social ties of the Korean immigrants in the Los Angeles area have not been weakened even by their residential scattering to various suburban areas where whites predominantly reside. This means that the immigrants expand the dimension of their social networks without replacing the "old" social relations (adhesive social adaptation).

(c) Economic Dimension and Family Role Adjustment. The relevance of adhesive adaptation to the economic dimension of the immigrants' life is the effect of limited social assimilation and confinement of the immigrants on their occupational career. As discussed extensively in Chapter 6, the immigrant workers are generally deprived of adequate job information in part as a result of their lack of primary social contact with members of the dominant group in the new country. Our data reveal that personal contact is the most frequently used method of job information among the immigrants. However, most of the job informers for the immigrants are members of the same ethnic group (Koreans). Since whites are structurally better placed to introduce better jobs in the primary sector of the American market, the immigrants are deprived of better job information. This deprivation precipitates the immigrant workers to concentrate in the unfavorable labor market. It is thus not surprising that a high proportion of the Korean immigrant workers are segregated in the labor market. In short, limited social assimilation and minority confinement in the labor market (whether voluntary or involuntary) emerge as formidable barriers to the occupational assimilation of the immigrants.

Ironically, however, the majority of the Korean immigrant workers express that they are satisfied with their jobs despite occupational segregation. The major reasons accounting for this discrepancy are the immigrants' low levels of expectation on the job because of their perception of limited occupational opportunity, limited ability (language handicap), and their low comparison levels (ethnic attachment). As in the case of the immigrants' general life satisfaction, the discrepancy between the objectively precarious conditions and the subjectively perceived contentment can be explained by the immigrants' shrinking aspirations. Shrinking aspirations are a function of the confluence between limited Americanization and persisting ethnic attachment of the immigrants—adhesive adaptation.

As mentioned earlier, a higher proportion of the immigrants' wives are employed in the United States than they were in Korea; however, a great majority of the wives continue to carry the major burden of performing household tasks as they did in Korea, irrespective of their employment. Not only do the wives perform the traditional role but also *they feel they are expected* to perform the role. Undoubtedly, the main factor contributing to the persistence of the traditional Korean family role behavior and expectation is the past socialization of the immigrants in Korea. Another crucial factor, however, is the immigrants' adhesive mode of adaptation in the new country: their persisting and strong ethnic attachment functions not only to perpetuate but also to reinforce the traditional family ideology regardless of how long and how extensively they may have been exposed to the American culture and society.

(d) Religious Dimension. Religious participation in the form of church involvement has become an integral part of the Korean immigrants' adaptation in the United States as evidenced by our data. Now we ask the question we posed before: why is there such a heightened interest in church among the Korean immigrants? In other words, "What are the functions of the Korean ethnic church?"

As past theories on the ethnic roles of immigrant churches have generally emphasized, the Korean ethnic church provides a fellowship with communal bonds (ethnic fellowship). An ethnic fellowship could, however, also be provided by other ethnic voluntary associations. Why then does the church particularly provide this function? In addition to an ethnic fellowship, the ethnic church has become a focal point of the immigrants' "sociation" in their new country for three major reasons: (1) their intensified needs for a religious or spiritual fellowship because of the sociocultural marginality they face upon immigration; (2) the inclusive nature of the church as both a Gemeinschaft and a Gesellschaft; and (3) the idea and practice of religious pluralism inherent in the American society. Simply put, church involvement has become a modus vivendi for the Korean immigrants in America to pray, to seek peace of mind, to meet friends, to see new faces, to be recognized, or to be with a large crowd of Koreans, just like being in Korea. Thus, first-generation immigrants' gravitation to the ethnic churches reflects their adhesive mode of adaptation—persisting importance of an ethnic fellowship as well as a Christian fellowship. This would mean that the ethnic church will survive throughout the successive generations of the immigrants, if their adhesive adaptation persists in the form of a bilingual and bicultural church.

(e) Psychological Dimensions. As noted in Chapter 8, the social, religious, and psychological dimensions of adaptation are closely interrelated. In this book, the psychological adaptation of the immigrants has mainly been examined in terms of the immigrants' subjective perception of life satisfaction and related attitudes, such as cognitive ambivalence and alienation. After all, the immigrants' "successful" adaptation would ultimately be dependent upon their overall life satisfaction in the new country.

Feelings of satisfaction (or dissatisfaction) in life are highly personal and subjective; that is, the degree of one's life satisfaction is largely dependent on one's level of aspirations. The possibility of attaining one's aspirations is, however, determined not only by the individual's adaptive capacity but also by the *opportunity structure* of his or her environment. In this sense, four factors are deeply implication in the immigrants' life satisfaction: the American social structure, the immigrants' adaptive capacity, their socioeconomic status, and their aspiration levels. As shown in Chapter 9, the American social structure of ethnic confinement (social and employment segregation) limits the range of the immigrants' socioeconomic opportunities, and the immigrants' perception of such structural limitations (including their own) tends to lower the levels of their aspirations. As a consequence, they feel relatively satisfied with their immigrant life in spite of their objectively apparent status inconsistency in the new country. Thus, the lower aspiration levels serve as "shock absorbers" to cope with the marginal situation. To minimize their feelings of relative deprivation and discontentment, the Korean immigrants' comparative reference groups are predominantly Koreans either in the United States or in Korea. As examined in length in Chapter 9, Korean immigrants do not *shift* their comparative reference group from Koreans to white Americans. "Shifting" would mean to reject the old reference relationships with Koreans altogether and embrace new reference relationships with white Americans in their entirety. Those who shifted should have indicated decreasing ethnic attachment to the Korean immigrant community and increasing social participation in the white American society. As our data indicate, the immigrants' strong and pervasive ethnic attachment is unaffected by their choice of white reference groups and their length of residence. In short, white Americans are thus *added* to the immigrants' reference set as an ideal normative reference category (adhesive reference group). This pattern is very similar to the previously summarized adhesive mode of sociocultural adaptation.

Cognitive ambivalence of the immigrants is also closely related to adhesive adaptation since it is structurally rooted. Korean immigrants' ambivalence derives mainly from their marginal social position in which two different and often incompatible cultural values, normative expectations, and even racial visibilities are juxtaposed. To make the situation more complicated, the majority of recent Korean immigrants are employed in the segregated labor market as discussed in Chapter 6. In other words, the immigrants are also occupationally marginal and ambivalent.

By virtue of occupying such a social position embedded with ambivalence, Korean immigrants tend to develop a variety of ambivalent attitudes, as mentioned in our descriptive summary. As long as ethnic segregation and attachment persist, the immigrants' adhesive adaptation will continue and so will their ambivalence.

Practical Implications

In studying patterns and sources of adhesive adaptation, one can also foresee some of its possible consequences. As mentioned earlier, the adhesive mode of adaptation may serve to mitigate the immigrants' immediate feelings of daily frustrations, relative deprivation, and social isolation in the short run, but it also tends to perpetuate ethnic confinement of the Korean minority and their marginality acceptance in America in the long run, as was the case of the Chinese-Americans in Chinatowns. Moreover, the dominant group may even encourage such ethnic containment in the name of "ethnic pluralism" in order to perpetuate social segregation of nonwhite minorities. To the dominant group's rationalizations, American Indians are not contained but would be "contented" in reservations, Mexican-Americans would be "happy" in their *barrios*, black Americans would be "at home" in urban slums, and Chinese would prefer to stay in Chinatowns (Hurh, 1980). After all, the Japanese-Americans were "safe" at the relocation centers during World War II.

The ideal type of ethnic pluralism is, however, predicated on the democratic principle of freedom and equality; that is, a nation is ethnically plural when diverse ethnic groups can maintain or change their identities by their own free choice and no group is in a position of imposing acculturation or restricting social assimilation (Kallen, 1924; Bogardus, 1949; Newman, 1973:68–69). As long as involuntary elements (especially of restricting social assimilation) exist in the American social structure, ethnic confinement of Korean immigrants stays, and their adhesive adaptation will continue.

Again, one may argue that adhesive adaptation is typically a phenomenon of the first-generation nonwhite immigrants. True, the posterity of the first-generation Korean immigrants will be less ethnically attached and more Americanized than their predecessors. Unlike generations of European immigrants, however, Koreans' social assimilation to the WASP primary social structure is largely limited for reasons elaborated elsewhere in this book. Their race will be "hunted out" whenever it is convenient to the dominant group unless their racial visibility disappears through extensive intermarriage or unless a drastic change in the American value system makes "race" no longer a determining factor for social distance and thus causes the concept of race to lose its social meaning (Hurh, 1977a). The second-generation Japanese-Americans' (the Niseis') painful experience of social discrimination from whites during World War II is a heightened example (Hosokawa, 1969; Kitano, 1976).

Bogardus pointed out this second-generation (or the entire posterity of nonwhite immigrants for that matter) problem as early as 1930:

> The children of the Japanese and Mexicans have been undergoing assimilation in the schools and through many other contacts. They have been losing contact with the home-country culture, and have been particularly ostracized. But because of their conspicuous nature (color or cultural heritage), they have been only partially accepted in the land of their birth and citizenship. (1930:617)

Past empirical studies on social distance have also repeatedly demonstrated that the American people want to maintain distance in social relations with the Koreans (Bogardus, 1968; Hurh, 1977a). The effect of such ethnic confinement may thus be more profound and serious for the second- and third-generation Korean-Americans since they would have no recourse unless they gain their strong ethnic attachment (a renewed adhesive adaptation or Hansen's law of third-generation return?) or create a third identity for themselves (Hansen, 1937; Hurh, 1980). Reflecting upon the past experiences of Chinese- and Japanese-Americans, we conjecture that the former would most likely be the adaptation pattern for the generations of Korean immigrants (Lyman, 1974; Petersen, 1971).

The new immigrants from Asia may share similar demographic and socioeconomic characteristics, such as their young age, urban background, relatively high preimmigration socioeconomic status, and family immigration (often accompanied by elderly relatives). However, Koreans are especially noted for having the highest educational and professional background among all immigrant groups in the United States, wide geographic dispersion in settlement, pervasive involvement in religion, proliferation of ethnic organizations, heavy concentration in small business, high achievement motives, thrift, and hard work (cf. Bonacich, Light and Wong, 1980; Bok-Lim Kim, 1978c). Although it is too early to tell, the Korean immigrants' adaptation patterns generally resemble those of Japanese-Americans, or even closer, the Jewish-American patterns (Goldstein and Goldscheider, 1968).

To conclude, adhesive adaptation of Korean immigrants reflects multiple realities involved in the intergroup relations in the United States, such as acculturation, assimilation, separatism, and pluralism. More importantly, it also reveals the most salient aspect of an American dilemma: the idea of ethnic pluralism versus the reality of ethnic confinement.

Note

1. For the development of specific theories, see our Theoretical Propositions, pp. 171-73.

Theoretical Propositions

On Adhesive Adaptation in General

1. In general, the longer the immigrants' length of residence in the host society, the higher the degree of their acculturation becomes.
2. In general, the longer the immigrants' length of residence in the host society, the higher the levels of their socioeconomic status will be.
3. In general, the higher the levels of the immigrants' socioeconomic status, the higher the degree and the faster the rates of acculturation will be.
4. When ethnic confinement (involuntary ethnic segregation) is inherent in the social structure of the host country, it is most likely that:
    (a) the immigrants' assimilation into the dominant group's primary social structure is restricted in its scope and intensity regardless of the immigrants' length of residence, socioeconomic status, degree of acculturation, and desire for assimilation.
    (b) the first-generation immigrants tend to maintain or even enhance their strong ethnic attachment regardless of progressive acculturation and assimilation.
    (c) the immigrants' ethnic attachment tends to be enhanced by:
        (1) the dominant group's prejudice and discrimination.
        (2) the immigrants' perception of limited social assimilation.
        (3) the immigrants' perception of their limited adaptive capacities (e.g., language, economic resources).
        (4) relatively well-defined large ethnic communities.
    (d) the immigrant's strong ethnic attachment functions:
        (1) to satisfy primary group needs.
        (2) to preserve ethnic identity.

(3) to lower the levels of their frustration and dissatisfaction.
   (4) to evoke a false sense of success and satisfaction
   (5) to perpetuate ethnic confinement and marginality acceptance ("mobility trap").
   (6) to evoke in the dominant group a rationale that the immigrants "want to be with their own kind and resist assimilation."
  (e) the immigrants' strong ethnic attachment and their choice of the dominant group as an abstract reference are not mutually exclusive.
  (f) in general, the first-generation immigrants' mode of adaptation is adhesive; that is, certain aspects of the new culture and social relations with members of the host society are added on to the immigrants' traditional culture and social networks, without replacing or modifying any significant part of the old.
  (g) the first-generation immigrants expect social (structural) assimilation least, and perceive its limited possibility most.
  (h) the second-generation immigrants expect social assimilation most and perceive its limited possibility least.
  (i) the third-generation immigrants expect social assimilation most and perceive its limited possibility most.
5. The degree of pluralistic adaptation depends on:
  (a) the extent of openness in the socioeconomic structure and value systems of the host society for absorbing immigrants into its mainstream.
  (b) the extent of the immigrants' educational, occupational, and linguistic capacities including their cultural heritage for competing effectively with the dominant group.
  (c) demographic, socioeconomic, and ecological conditions of the immigrant community in relation to those of the dominant group and other minorities at a particular time.
  (d) the extent of immigrants' perception of the host society's structural conditions, their own adaptive capacities, social acceptance by the dominant group, and their willingness to participate in the mainstream of the host culture and society.

On Life Satisfaction

1. The immigrants' levels of aspirations tend to decline:
  (a) when they perceive limited opportunity because of ethnic

confinement inherent in the social structure of the host society.
    (b) when they perceive limitations in their own capacity to adapt to the new culture and society.
    (c) when they perceive they cannot change either of these situations.
2. The immigrants' low levels of expectations tend:
    (a) to lower the levels of their frustration, disappointment, and dissatisfaction.
    (b) to build tolerance for discrimination and deprivation.
    (c) to evoke in the immigrants a false sense of "success" and satisfaction.
    (d) to perpetuate ethnic confinement and marginality acceptance.
3. When ethnic confinement is pervasively inherent in the social structure of the new country, it is most likely that:
    (a) the immigrant minority accepts ethnic segregation from the dominant group as a matter of fact, especially the first-generation immigrants.
    (b) the immigrant minority expects social assimilation the least.
    (c) the immigrants voluntarily confine themselves within their own ethnic enclaves for primary group needs and self-protection.
    (d) the dominant group attempts to maintain the status quo with a rationale that the immigrants want ethnic attachment and solidarity.
    (e) even a slight degree of social acceptance of the immigrants by the dominant group may evoke in the immigrants a sense of accomplishment and well-being.
    (f) the immigrant's comparative reference groups are predominantly their fellow immigrants.
4. Objective conditions of life (job, income, housing, family, etc.) have a bearing on the degree of life satisfaction *only* through the immigrant's subjective perception (evaluation) of the conditions.
5. Subjective variables (perceptions or attitudes) are pervasively related to both structural (socioeconomic) variables and the degree of life satisfaction of immigrants.

Appendix A
Qualitative Analysis of Interviewers' Comments

Interviewers' Comments as Qualitative Data

Adaptation patterns of immigrants can be studied in various ways, such as questionnaire surveys, document analyses, interviews, and participant or detached observations. In our study on Korean immigrants in the Los Angeles area, we used primarily the interview method. After each interview, our interviewers were encouraged to write down freely on the last page of the interview schedule any comments they wished to make regarding their interviewing and/or the research project itself. All of our interviewers were native-born Koreans (14 females, 4 males).

Most of our interviewers wrote at least a paragraph or two, and some even made extensive comments ranging from one to three pages in length for each case. The number of cases on which comments were made totaled 290 (155 female cases and 135 male cases). Usually these comments were considered peripheral to the main research data; however, in our study they seemed to provide the investigator with rich qualitative data not only for methodological refinement but also for theoretical serendipity.

The content of our interviewers' comments can be divided into two general categories: (1) the methodological and (2) the substantive. The first includes structural and logistic problems involved in interviewing, such as incorrect addresses of respondents, high refusal rates, unreliable appointments, interactional difficulties (inhibitors and distorters of communication between the interviewer and interviewee), and transportation problems. (Cf. Gorden, 1975; Hurh and Kim, 1979a.)

The second category includes our interviewers' serendipitous findings or spontaneous observations on the respondents' day-today life conditions and their subjective experiences that were not usually revealed by the interviewees' responses to the structured questionnare items in the interview schedule. In this appendix, we analyze the second category, i.e., qualitative or symbolic data obtained through the spontaneous observations of respondents during the entire process of interviewing (preinterview, during the interview, and postinterview situations).

Serendipitous are such findings in the sense that neither the investigator nor the interviewer anticipated from the "interviewers' comments" any theoretically relevant information except some possible methodological footnotes. Such a surprise may come from the fact that we are relatively ignorant of the latent functions of interviewing as a social act. Once our interviewers were involved in the process of interviewing, most of them acted not only as "inquiries" but also soon found themselves acting as participant observers, and later some of them even became personal friends and counselors of the respondents.

For instance, the informal postinterview situation (a chat or dinner) functioned not only to establish a good rapport between the interviewer and interviewee but also to provide the interviewer with a chance to participate in certain activities of the respondent's everyday life. It was not uncommon that our interviewers were invited by their respondents to a dinner either at the respondents' homes or at restaurants after the interview. When this situation occurred, the interviewer became an impromptu participant observer of the respondent as well as of his or her social networks (family members, relatives, and friends). As soon as the formal interview was over, both the interviewer and interviewee usually redefined their interacting situation as just fellow Koreans who had something to share—a common plight of immigrants. Interviewing of fellow immigrants, therefore, often opened a channel of emotional catharsis for both the interviewer and interviewee. The following excerpts from the comments by one of our female interviewers illustrates these observations:[1]

> When I phoned Mrs. A for an appointment, she responded kindly. She wanted to know first about my background. After listening to what I had to say about myself (a UCLA student), she said she too went to UCLA and would be glad to be interviewed. Since her husband had to go to work that evening, she wanted to invite me to supper at a local Korean restaurant and wished to be interviewed there.... After the interview and

supper, we had a good chance to exchange our views and feelings on many things. She was a very sympathetic person. She gave me a great deal of encouragement. I have interviewed many fellow immigrants but I have never met such a wonderful person as Mrs. A. I felt like I met my own sister.

Mr. B. wanted to be interviewed at his home located in a suburb of Los Angeles. Since I don't have a car, one of my relatives gave me a ride. We were rather surprised to see Mr. B's plush home. Mr. B looked much older than his age. After the interview, we were invited to stay for dinner or at least for a drink. We stayed a couple of hours mainly to listen to his talk. He said he was a high-ranking government official in Korea, but in the United States he felt lonelier and lonelier every day in spite of his family and material affluency. After a couple of drinks, he started to shed tears. I wondered if he were more alienated than some of the poor Koreans in the inner city. Through interviewing I am learning a lot.

As one can imagine from these examples, the extent and intensity of the interviewer's involvement in the postinterview situation varied depending on various factors, such as the personalities of the interviewer and interviewee, their socioeconomic characteristics, and the interview setting (time and place). Also diverse are the interviewers' interpretations of the respondents' conditions as expressed in the interviewers' comments. In fact, the contents of the interviewers' comments ranged from objective description and personal impressions to subjective value judgments and suggestions. Problems of reliability, validity, and generalization become serious if the symbolic data from our interviewers' comments are to be used to test hypotheses; however, they can be used to construct ideal types for analytical purposes (cf. Festinger and Katz, 1966:438, 448). Moreover, when such qualitative data are examined in conjunction with quantitative data, avenues for new hypotheses and inquiries can be opened. In short, the interviewers' comments in this appendix are not to prove but to generate new hypotheses that may eventually enlarge the existing theoretical framework (cf. Merton, 1964:105).

In his extensive study on the absorption of immigrants in Israel, Eisenstadt identifies six main types of immigrant groups that "portray some of the basic problems of absorption and institutionalization of immigrant behavior" (1954b:143). The six types are (1) the isolated, apathetic family, (2) the isolated, stable family, (3) the isolated, active family, (4) the cohesive, traditional group, (5) the self-transforming, cohesive group, and (6) the instrumentally cohesive group. For the construction of these ideal types, Eisenstadt used two general criteria: (1) participation within the social system, and (2) identification with its values and symbols (1954b:142).

In our study, various types of Korean immigrants were constructed according to the dimension and degree of the immigrant's adaptation in the United States. Included in the dimension are (1) the economic, (2) the social, and (3) the personal or psychological. The degree of adaptation is also divided into three categories: (1) successful or highly satisfying, (2) intermediate, and (3) failing or extremely dissatisfying. A cross-tabulation of the three dimensions thus yields nine categories, and measuring each category in three degrees of adaptation, we can identify (or construct) twenty-seven types of Korean immigrants as shown in Figure 11.

			Economic Dimension		
		Personal Dimension	S	I	F
Social Dimension	S	S	1	2	3
		I	4	5	6
		F	7	8	9
	I	S	10	11	12
		I	13	14	15
		F	16	17	18
	F	S	19	20	21
		I	22	23	24
		F	25	26	27

"S" indicates: economically successful; socially participating; personally (or psychologically) satisfied.

"I" indicates: economically struggling or working hard, limited social participation; personally (or psychologically) ambivalent.

"F" indicates: economically failing; socially isolated (or alienated); psychologically dissatisfied.

Figure 11. Types of Korean Immigrants Based on Adaptation Dimensions and Degrees

Each type indicated in Figure 11 is an analytical construct as an ideal type. None of them, therefore, corresponds to the concrete reality perfectly. All of them, however, are accentuated from the real-life conditions of immigrants to an abstraction for comparative analysis. For instance, the variations among twenty-seven types—from the highly satisfactory adaptation pattern (Type 1) to the lowest adaptation pattern (Type 27)—are relative and diffuse rather than absolute and definitive. Moreover, it is not our intention merely to classify particular individuals into various categories in order to justify our typology, but rather, it is our attempt to understand the individual immigrants as social collectivities under various ideal typically defined situations. In this sense, the individual patterns of adaptation observed by our interviewers are not only psychologically significant but also sociologically (structurally) relevant.

It may not be totally impossible to examine all twenty-seven types through various empirical methods against real concrete situations; however, as an exploratory study, we limit our illustration to a few selected types in order of saliency.

(1) Economically Failing Category

I felt so sad coming home from an interview this afternoon. It was the poorest family I have ever visited. When I first met Mr. C, I was shocked to see his thin and undernourished face. He said he was sick but had to work in a sewing factory as a janitor to support his family. He has a wife and four young children to support but his income is $400 per month. Since last year, they have been on welfare. They live in a deteriorated black neighborhood, and, of course, they don't have a car. They are not only economically poor but psychologically depressed. I wish I could help them in some way.
When I visited Mrs. D, I was really heartbroken. She lives in a one-bedroom apartment in a rundown black neighborhood. She is a divorcee with two children. They are on social welfare, and Mrs. D does not speak English. A daughter of her former husband invited her to come to the United States, but she (her step-daughter) lives in another state with whom Mrs. D seldom has contact. Mrs. D is originally from a remote rural village in South Korea, illiterate, and has no skill. The atmosphere in their home was utterly depressing. I could never believe such a living condition was possible in the United States. When I finished the interview, she thanked me politely for coming for an interview. Mrs. E was widowed in Korea, 1945. She immigrated to the United States with her seven children. Now they are all grown

and live in the Los Angeles Area. Mrs. E, however, lives alone in destitution. No one comes to visit her except a Korean church minister who often brings food to her. Without the minister, she would starve. She does not speak English nor drive. Her only joy is occasional telephone calls from her youngest son in Texas. I have never seen such an alienated mother. She wanted to thank the U.S. government for welfare money on which she survives. She said the American government is much, much better than her seven children.

(2) **Economically Intermediate Category**

Mrs. F works with her husband in a coffee shop 16 hours a day. They own the shop. She looked tired, and yet she told me she was satisfied with her life in the U.S. She especially enjoys going to church. She goes to the church 5 to 6 times every week. Before she came to the United States, she worked as a nurse in Germany for several years. Two things keep her going: business and church.

Among the 53 respondents I have contacted so far, Mr. G was the most friendly person. Mr. and Mrs. G live in an old apartment but the inside was freshly painted and everything was neatly arranged. Mr. G looked 10 years younger than his age (67). In spite of his age, Mr. G works as an upholsterer, and has been supporting his youngest son who just entered Medical School at the University of Southern California. His older son is already a lawyer practicing in New York. More than anyone else, he looked happy with a sense of accomplishment and satisfaction. He said his immigration to the United States has been very meaningful and fulfilling. I think he meant it.

Mrs. H was a physician in Korea. After her immigration to the United States, she could not pass the required tests for obtaining a license to practice medicine mainly due to her lack of English proficiency. She gave up her hope of practicing medicine and went into private business, a grocery store. The store was, however, robbed 4 times within a year. Finally, she sold her store and now is back again with her English study in the hope of passing the test some day. Her husband is a Protestant minister. She regrets that she immigrated to the United States.

Mr. I came to the United States 15 years ago, obtained a Ph.D. in engineering, once was employed by one of the largest engineering firms in America, and now is employed by a local government agency. Throughout his professional career, Mr. I felt he has been discriminated against on the job (pay, promotion, etc.) because of his race. He said the higher he climbed the occupational ladder, the severer became racial discrimination on the job. Once he brought a legal suit against an establishment for their discriminatory practices, but it was of no avail. Mr. I thinks most of the American establishments, private or public, are entrenched with institutional racism. He is disillusioned and plans to return to Korea.

(3) Economically Successful Category

Mr. J came to the United States in 1972 after he failed in his business in Korea. He did not have an immigrant visa but eventually obtained one and joined the U.S. Army. He was sent to Korea, finished his duty there, married and returned to the United States with his wife. He purchased a grocery market from a Jewish-American, and his business has been successful. While he was expanding his business, he witnessed many of his friends receiving academic degrees, and he felt inferior. In the midst of his dilemma, whether to continue his business or to begin his study, I visited him for an interview. We had a long talk after the interview.

Mrs. K lives in a huge, luxurious home located in an exclusive neighborhood. She and her husband jointly own a few import-export business firms in the United States and in Europe. They seem to be, however, one of those who are economically very successful but socially and personally dissatisfied. Mrs. K complained that her husband was having affairs with other women. She feels lonely, depressed and homesick for Korea. She is such an attractive lady and yet her life is unfulfilling. I felt sorry for her and wondered about the meaning of wealth.

Mr. L was a son of a wealthy family in Korea to begin with. Since his immigration, everything has been successful except his marriage. He obtained a Ph.D., started a wig business, accumulated considerable wealth, but his marriage of 10 years has failed. Presently, he lives with his brother's family. Mr. L feels his past life was too self-centered. He wants to start life anew doing something good for others. He was very cooperative with our project.

Methodological and Theoretical Implications

In this appendix, we have analyzed our interviewers' comments as qualitative data that seem to involve three elements of the serendipity patterns in Merton's terms. According to Merton: "The serendipity pattern refers to the fairly common experience of observing *an unanticipated, anomalous and stragetic datum* which becomes the occasion for developing a new theory or for extending an existing theory" (1964:104). Our findings are unanticipated, surprising, and appear to be theoretically relevant.

First, we did not expect any substantive information from the interviewers' comments except some suggestions for methodological improvement. Our interviewers' extensive (290 cases) and intensive (sometimes two to three pages for each case) comments on the respondents' life conditions were also unanticipated. Furthermore, it was not a part of our research project to construct a typology of Korean immigrants' adaptation through the content anlaysis of the interviewers' comments.

Second, we were surprised to discover that most of our respondents were willing to share their personal feelings with our interviewers after the formal interview was over. Not only the old and poor but also the young and well-to-do spontaneously utilized the postinterview situation for their emotional catharsis. Our interviewers became, in fact, impromptu participant observers and often their friendships with interviewees continued to later days. Such latent functions (emotional catharsis and friendship) of interviewing have not generally been mentioned in the sociological research manual. Is the postinterview situation among our Korean immigrant interviewees and interviewers anomalous? Borrowing Merton's words, how do we "make sense of the datum" in this case (1964:104)?

More significantly, through the content analysis of the interviewers' comments, we were able to construct twenty-seven ideal types of adaptation patterns of Korean immigrants. Instead of using elaborated sociopsychological indices, we used very simple and yet seemingly most important criteria for Korean immigrants —money, friends, and happiness. When these three dimensions (the economic, social, and psychological) were crisscrossed with the degree of adaptation, we were able to portray a comprehensive picture of the immigrant life of Koreans in America. It was anomalous that the interviewers' comments could contain such a rich qualitative data to illustrate many salient aspects of the adaptation patterns. Also anomalous is the fact that very few of our respondents confided to our interviewers that they were personally satisfied regardless of their economic status. A careful review of our quantitative data on their life-satisfaction patterns indicates to the contrary. As discussed in Chapter 9, the general level of life satisfaction of our respondents is above the midpoint as indicated by a mean score of 13.9 in a twenty-point scale. Which one is the real "human coefficient" of Korean immigrants (Znaniecki, 1934:37)?

And third, our findings may have strategic implications, if we consider the following points. Methodologically, our data may be strategic in the sense that: (1) the interviewer can also function as a participant observer, and (2) the interviewer's comments may contain theoretically as well as methodologically relevant information. Theoretically, (1) a typology of immigrants' adaptation can be constructed through the content analysis of the interviewers' comments, (2) for a comprehensive typology of adaptation, dimensions and degrees of adaptation need to be specified, (3) the higher the socioeconomic status the lower the consistencies become among the adaptation dimensions, (4) satisfactory social adaptation has a greater bearing than satisfactory economic adaptation on personal satisfaction, and (5) life satisfaction measured by quantitative data need to be checked against qualitative data, such as interviewers' comments.

Note

1. All illustrations are contextually translated from Korean and are structurally rearranged in order to protect the anonymity of the respondents and to save space. The respondents in our illustrations are identified alphabetically from A to L. The initials have no relation to our respondents' actual names.

Appendix B
Methodological Problems in the Study of Korean Immigrants

Even within the same culture, we often hear people say to one another: "I hear you but what do you mean?" It has also been a classic joke for instructors in an undergraduate methodology class to mention the respondent's nonchalant answer to the interviewer: "My age? Thirty-nine. And my marital status? Just fine. So far, we have no problems" (Goode and Hatt, 1952:133).

Such miscommunication becomes more problematic when one attempts to conduct a study on non-Western subjects using the Western research methodology. For instance, a large number of our Korean respondents in our previous study in the Chicago area reported combined income for their families, despite the fact that our interviewers were instructed to elicit the individual respondent's annual income (Hurh, Kim, and Kim, 1978). Although both interviewers and investigators were raised in Korea, we overlooked the Korean social unit of orientation—the group rather than the individual. Koreans seldom refer to "my home" or "my family" but "our home" or "our family." It was indeed natural for them to report their family incomes when they were simply asked by our interviewers: "What is your income?"

The semantic problem is just one of many difficulties in cross-cultural research. The difficulties include not only the language barrier and conceptual differences but also situational equivalence of sampling, interviewer training, and interviewing (not to mention interpretation of findings). In other words, the entire process of the research act—from conceptualization to interpretation—must be transculturally equivalent (cf. Sears, 1961;

A condensed version of this appendix appeared in *California Sociologist*, vol. 4, no. 1 (1981). Reprinted by permission of *California Sociologist*.

Warwick and Osherson, 1973; Warwick and Lininger, 1975). Another crucial problem related to the study of non-Western subjects is the so-called protection of human subjects. How do we obtain "informed consent" (either written or oral) from non-Western subjects? By means of signature or thumbprint? The following was mentioned in the recent *Anthropology Newsletter* (American Anthropological Association 1978:11): "Western models are felt to be difficult to apply to non-Western research. Particularly in nonliterate societies, the difficulty of translating consent into native terms is formidable, especially when one is, in the next breath, going to try to explain and guarantee anonymity while at the same time requesting a signature (or thumbprint)." Korean immigrants in the United States are not, of course, nonliterates; on the contrary, 78 percent of our Chicago sample had received four years of college education or more. Nevertheless, we learned that the solicitation of a written consent from the Koreans makes any type of interview virtually impossible, mainly because of the so-called signature phobia of Korean immigrants (cf. Elena Yu, 1979).

These problems are, by no means, new. Since Emile Durkheim and Franz Boas, anthropologists have always stressed that "the use of *a priori* definitions and conceptual models" needs to be avoided in the study of culture (cf. Romney and D'Andrade, 1964; Noroll, 1970). Especially, ethnoscience, a branch of cognitive anthropology, has recently dealt with the problem in terms of "etics" versus "emics" dichotomy. Etic is the outsider's view of a culture based on his or her cognitive categories and assumptions; emics, on the other hand, concerns the inside or native view of a culture (Hunter and Whitten, 1976:142, 152; Sturtevant, 1964: Pike, 1954). "To understand the behavior of subjects, then," as Stone emphasizes, "it is crucial that the field research identify the cognitive properties of these emic categories, otherwise interpretations of behavior cannot claim to reflect units of behavior which are meaningful to the people studied" (Stone, 1976).

Since Weber, Mead, and Thomas, the actor's subjective meaning or definition of the situation has also been a crucial methodological concern for many sociologists, such as, Blumer's symbolic interactionism, Goffman's frame analysis, Schütz's phenomenology of social world, and Garfinkel's ethnomethodology. And yet, the research methods employed by American sociologists for studying ethnic minorities have largely been based on Western cognitive categories and assumptions (etics). Whether the researcher is a Korean, a black American, or a white Anglo-Saxon, his or her epistemological orientation and frame of analysis are predominantly Western as long as the Western sociological methodology is used (cf. Vermeulen and de Ruijter, 1975; Hsu, 1973).

What then is non-Western methodology? Is there such a thing as "Eastern methodology"? Perhaps not. We hope that both non-Western and Western methodologies are misnomers. What we are actually looking for may be a transcultural methodology that takes into account both outsider's and insider's views (cf. Merton, 1972). The questions posed are fundamentally in the domain of the sociology of knowledge, which is far beyond the subject of this appendix (cf. Frazier, 1947). The main purpose of this appendix is to discuss some key methodological problems involved in the study of Korean immigrants based on our field experiences from our recent studies.

Throughout our past research, we discovered some methodological problems unique to Korean subjects and others similar to Western subjects but with higher intensity. The problems are discussed in three categories: (1) problems of linguistic and conceptual equivalence; (2) interactional difficulties between the interviewer and respondent; and (3) sampling problems unique to the Korean immigrant community.

Linguistic and Conceptual Problems

In most non-Western research, the first obstacle to overcome is the language barrier. Since some of our interviewers and the majority of our respondents had difficulty in the use of both spoken and written English, our interview schedules had to be translated into Korean. The questionnaire items were thus translated by the investigators themselves (all are native-born Koreans and bilingual), and the translated versions were administered usually to thirty or forty immigrants for pretesting. On the basis of suggestions and comments given by the respondents, a number of questions were reworded, added, or eliminated. Pretest interviewers and our consultants participated also in the preparation of the final version of the interview schedule. Difficulties involved in translation are well known, especially between Western and non-Western languages. Many words are just not translatable, even literally, such as "full-time or part-time," "random sampling," or even "community." As in the case of other Oriental languages, one must also pay a great deal of care to honorifics when translating from English to Korean.

The most difficult problem was, however, conceptual ambiguity. For example, in our Chicago study, social invitations were used as an index of social assimilation. Our respondents were asked: "How often have you been invited by Americans to their homes in the past year (excluding business-related ones)?" We also asked, "How often have you invited Americans to your home in the past year?" Invitation was translated into Korean as "cho dae." Whereas "invitation" in English can be used to request the presence of a person at a variety of occasions, "cho dae" means to request the presence of a person at a formal dinner or occasion, usually for well-prepared entertainment. "Cho dae" has thus a more restricted meaning than "invitation" in English. In our Los Angeles study, we changed the term "cho dae" to "nolo kanda" (literally "to go to play" but meaning "to visit" or "to drop in"). For most of the respondents, no semantic problem occured. Some respondents indicated, however, that they visited American homes almost everyday! They were generally apartment dwellers who usually dropped in on their American neighbors for a chat everyday. Certainly the problem of conceptual equivalence becomes paramount.

The following are some more examples. In our Chicago study, we investigated marital roles in Korean immigrant families. We used the instrument which Blood and Wolfe (1960) had developed for their study of American families in the Detroit area. The Korean translation of some terms resulted in negative connotations which could stiffen the Korean male's resistence to the sharing of marital roles (e.g., "grocery shopping" or "dishwashing"). In another study in the Chicago area, we wanted to know if our respondents would like to return to Korea after their retirement. Only about 18 percent indicated they would remain in the United States. The translated Korean version of the question did not specifically refer to retirement. The literal translation of the question from Korean to English was: "When you get old, would you like to return to Korea and wish to spend the rest of your life there?" Originally, we did not use the Korean term "twae jik" (retirement) because the connotation of the word is much narrower than the English equivalent. Normally, "twae jik" means disengagement from an official or public position accompanied by pension or retirement benefit. Disengagement from one's self-employment, for instance, is not "twae jik." The conceptual equivalence of "retirement," we thought, would be a composite of events to the effect: "when you get old, you don't have to work and can take things easy for the rest of your life." No wonder the overwhelming majority of our respondents wanted to go back to their native country and take things easy for the rest of their life! It turned out that we asked about their dreams, rather than their plans.

Another question asked in the Chicago study was whether our respondents felt that most Americans accepted them as their equal. Half of our respondents (52 percent) answered this question, "definitely yes" or "probably yes." In light of Bogardus's repeated findings on social distance in which Koreans rank socially almost at the bottom, our observation was rather surprising (Bogardus, 1968; Hurh, 1977a). By virtue of their unfamiliarity with the American way of social life, many of our respondents might have thought of equality as used in a formal or legal sense, rather than in an informal or social sense.

Similarly, when Korean immigrants were asked in our Chicago study: "Do you think your present occupation is commensurate with the educational level you achieved?" their responses were equally divided into two groups—either yes or no. This seems to reflect their different perception of postimmigration social life, or it may be related to their particular social status—the first-generation immigrant. As the first-generation immigrants, our respondents have two sets of socioeconomic statuses, preimmigration and postimmigration. Some of our respondents might have answered the question in terms of the educational level they had achieved in Korea, whereas others answered it in terms of the educational level they had achieved in the United States. What this domonstrates is that the immigrant status itself also creates conceptual ambiguity.

Some of our ethnic identity questionnaire items for the Korean church study were too general and, more importantly, they put our respondents on the defensive. Not very many people could really disagree with such statements as: "Once one is born a Korean, he/she is always Korean"; "Korean culture should be preserved in American life"; "There is no need to feel unfortunate about having been born a Korean." Since our respondents were interviewed by their fellow Korean interviewers, disagreement with any of these items would produce a strain for the respondent and the interviewer (a threat to self-esteem and offense against Koreans as a whole). Ego threat has been found to be one of the most significant inhibitors or distorters of communication in our studies on Korean immigrants (cf. Gorden, 1975:104–20). More about this ego threat is discussed later.

The linguistic and conceptual problems are thus compounded by inhibitors and distorters of communication, derived from the particular sociocultural context of the interview setting unique to non-Western subjects.

Interactional Difficulties in the Interview

Interactional difficulties in the interview involve not only verbal and nonverbal miscommunication between the interviewer and the respondent but also the time and place of the interview, the nature of the questions asked, the sponsoring organization, the credentials of the investigators, the provisions for anonymity and confidentiality, the length of the interview, and even the personalities of the interviewer and the interviewee. In other words, the interview is a *process* taking place in the larger social and cultural context. It is a dynamic Gestalt or microcosm as Gorden aptly put it: "Interviewing is a microcosm of many forces operating within the human personality, within the interaction situation we call interview, and within the whole community, society, or culture" (Gorden, 1975:104). In this sense, much of the interview situation is determined even before the interaction between the interviewer and respondent takes place, such as the interview schedule, purpose of the study, and the sponsoring organization (cf. Gorden, 1975:85–101). We, therefore, discuss the problems involved in *the entire process* of interviewing (preinterview, during the interview, and postinterview situations). Each situation is discussed as it happened and analyzed in terms of difficulties and some possible solutions.

1. Preinterview Situation

Usually about two weeks prior to the actual interview, we informed Korean residents (e.g., general purpose, procedure, investigators, sponsoring organization, funding agency) through the local Korean daily newspaper. A week later, letters were sent out to the selected interviewees, explaining the nature of our prospective research and asking for their cooperation. In the letter, we emphasized that the individual's participation in the interviewing would be strictly voluntary and also that all information obtained through interviewing would be kept completely confidential. Approximately one week to ten days were allowed to ensure that the prospective respondents would receive the letters. The interviewers then visited their homes and either interviewed them there, if allowed, or made appointments to meet with them at later dates. Our interviewers normally contacted the prospective respondents by telephone to make appointments. Oral informed consent was a prerequisite for our interviewers' visitation to the respondents' homes. We dropped the idea of soliciting a written consent because of its impracticality, if not impossibility, as mentioned earlier. Such situations contain problems as well as advantages.

a. Problems

(1) Reaction of Korean Immigrants. In order to enhance the immigrants' motive to cooperate with our studies, we stressed in the newspaper announcement and subsequent letters that we would report the findings to the U.S. government and welfare agencies so that these agencies could use our data for the welfare of Korean immigrants. This was a technique to appeal to the altruism of the respondents. This appeal aroused a considerable interest among Koreans in our first Chicago study (1975–76). By the time we started our third Chicago study (1978), this technique was found to be, however, no longer effective. Two factors seem to contribute to this development. First, most of our respondents were looking for immediate solutions to their pressing problems, such as the financial, marital, and juvenile. Yet, they saw that no significant action had been taken to alleviate their problems. In other words, they questioned the "practical relevance and efficacy" of our studies (or for that matter, any sociological studies), however scholarly meritorious such studies may be. Second, since our first study, several other Korean scholars, ministers, and students had also studied Korean immigrants through interviews or mailed questionnaire surveys. Under this condition, Koreans in the Chicago area seemed to be annoyed by these research activities, which most of them considered irrelevant and time demanding.

Some of our respondents in Los Angeles, however, clearly cooperated with our research activity from altruistic motivations. They were reported to be deeply concerned with the general welfare of Korean immigrants, problems of Korean youth, racial discrimination, job opportunity for Korean immigrants, and so on. Because of their interest in these public issues, our Los Angeles respondents wanted to help our research project.

(2) Incorrect Address. In our first Chicago study, 22 percent of our sample population were found to have wrong addresses with no forwarding addresses to follow up. The immigrants' mobility was found to be unusually high. Not only were incorrect addresses problematic but telephone numbers were also incorrect. In the Los Angeles area, about 60 percent of our prospective respondents' telephone numbers were outdated.

(3) High Refusal Rates. In the Chicago study about 26 percent of the remaining sample ($N = 284$) either could not be reached despite repeated attempts or refused to be interviewed for one reason or another: "too busy," "not interested," "why me?" "leave me alone," and the like. In the Los Angeles study, slightly more than one-fourth of prospective respondents refused to be interviewed. The highest refusal rates were among young males, and the lowest were among older females. Gorden (1975:311) argues that the attempt to make an appointment in advance by mail or telephone only increases the refusal problem because it is easier to refuse when the interviewer is not face-to-face with the respondent. Gorden cites Brunner and Carroll's (1967-68) experiments: "Those contacted by telephone had a refusal rate of 63 percent in contrast to only 33 percent for the face-to-face contacts" (Gorden, 1975:311).

Apparently, Gorden suggests the personal and surprise call. There are, however, a number of problems in making an unannounced personal call on Korean immigrants. First, the oral informed consent cannot be obtained in advance, it must be done on the spot. Second, most of the Korean immigrants work both day and night, and even on Sundays and holidays for extra income as shown in our Los Angeles study. It has been found through our experience that even with a definite appointment, our interviewers could not reach the respondent easily. Often, they deliberately did not keep appointments, or because of unexpected events, such as sickness of children and sudden visits from friends and relatives, they refused the interviewer. Third, in large metropolitan areas, such as Chicago and Los Angeles, the distance and time involved in paying personal purprise calls for the interviewer is simply too great. Gorden (1975:313-314) suggests that if the respondent is too busy, the interviewer should make a favorable impression on the respondent and motivate him or her to give an interview some other time. If no one is home, Gorden suggests further, "the interviewer can ask neighbors the best time to return." In the inner city of Chicago, such a procedure would be extremely futile. A high proportion of our respondents in Chicago and Los Angeles broke their appointment with the interviewers, whether the appointment was made through telephone or personal contact. Breaking an appointment was, in fact, a convenient means to express one's refusal to be interviewed.

b. Suggestions

The announcement of the prospective research in the ethnic community can be expedited beyond local ethnic newspapers. For instance, announcements through television radio, church bulletins, and newsletters of voluntary associations would also be effective. The vast majority of the Korean immigrants attend their ethnic churches and are affiliated with many ethnic social organizations as revealed in our Los Angeles study.

Because of the prevalent mobility of Korean immigrants, the problem of incorrect addresses is hard to mitigate; however, telephone directories were found to be the most reliable sources. The next best reliable source would be church membership lists. This point is discussed in more detail later in conjunction with sampling problems.

The refusal rates may be reduced by persuasive and persistent telephone calls by trained interviewers. The interviewer's knowledge about the social network of the prospective respondent would expedite such persuasive calls. To know the social circle of the respondent is important not only for gaining access to the respondent but also for interviewing itself. Our interviewers also carried a copy of the article that appeared in the local Korean newspaper about our research and showed it to their prospective respondents. This potentially reduced the refusal rate (cf. Gorden, 1975:312).

2. Interview Situation

The interview situation refers to the setting of the actual interview, such as time, place, and interaction between the interviewer and respondent. Problems are generally what Gorden calls "inhibitors" of communication during the interview. Gorden identifies eight inhibitors: competing time demands, ego threat, etiquette, trauma, forgetting, chronological confusion, inferential confusion, and unconscious behavior (Gorden, 1975:104-120). Among these, we found "ego threat," "time demands," and "etiquette" to be highly relevant.

a. Problems

(1) Time of Interviewing. Just like for any other population, evenings and weekends are generally the best time to interview Korean immigrants. As mentioned earlier, however, many Koreans have no definite time for leisure. Since there is no pattern of leisure time, one must "catch" them whenever possible.

In our studies, several respondents were interviewed during their lunch hours or coffee breaks. In such cases, the main problem was time pressure as the interview had to be completed in a short period of time. Some respondents were interviewed right after their work. Some were relaxed and responded to the interview willingly without any immediate time pressure; others had to hurry home or to their next work place.

(2) Place of Interview. There are several places where Koreans can be interviewed such as their home, work place, and church. Hence, the problems in setting a place for the interview are diverse. Homes can provide privacy for the interview, and the interview, as a sort of self-report, needs such privacy for a self-diagnosis of one's attitudes and experiences (Sellitz et al., 1961: 237). Privacy can also reduce mistakes in responses that result from simple forgetting or confusion. But the home also contains distractions, such as children, visitors, telephone calls, and other family happenings. Moreover, some of our respondents did not want to be bothered by an interview simply because they wanted to relax at home after a hard day of work.

Some respondents in our Los Angeles study were reluctant to be interviewed at their homes. For instance, one respondent was so reluctant to show his home to our interviewer that they finally met at a McDonald's hamburger shop. In another case, when one female respondent was interviewed at her home, she repeatedly apologized for the poor condition of her apartment. This illustrates Gorden's observation that: "In other cases, lower status respondents may feel defensive about their economic conditions as reflected by the home. This is particularly true of minority groups who are forced to live in slum housing..." (1975:251).

Our interviews often took place at the respondent's work place. Although the work place was more easily located than a home address, the interview in the workplace was inhibited by the time limit (e.g., lunch hour). Moreover, the respondents who were interviewed at their work place appeared to respond less candidly to the job-related questions than those who were interviewed at home. In fact, some of our respondents were afraid that their supervisors might know about the interview.

Church was another convenient place for interviewing. The Korean church on Sunday was, however, a busy place where our respondents had to see their friends and relatives. Thus, one can easily locate the prospective respondents at the Korean church, but it is just not a suitable place for an interview.

In a few cases, the interview was conducted over the telephone. The telephone interview usually took longer time to complete than the face-to-face interview, and it required a considerable patience on the part of the interviewer and respondent. In addition, the telephone interview missed some crucial aspects of nonverbal communication (e.g., proxemics and kinesics). This deficiency made the interviewer less capable of controlling the interview situation.

(3) Ego Threat. As Gorden elaborates, the effect of an ego threat can range from mild hesitancy to complete repression (Gorden, 1975:108). Through our experiences, we learned that complete repression was rare. Our respondents, however, tended to exaggerate or understate information in order to defend their self-esteem or to save "face" (cf. Hu, 1944). For example, they usually exaggerated their familiarity with the American culture, especially sports, music, and their consumer purchases, such as cars, televisions, and clothing. Especially to their fellow Korean interviewers, they were reluctant to reveal their weaknesses. As one of our interviewers put it, "I have never known that Koreans have such high self-pride or need to have high self-esteem. Everyone would like to say that they are university graduates and engage in white-collar jobs, although they never went to college and currently work in factories as manual laborers." This also means that the respondents understated their plight, whether economic or social. For instance, in our Chicago study, we asked our respondents: "What is the most important problem or

difficulty you are experiencing in the course of your immigrant life?" The language problem was found to be the most important, as mentioned earlier, but racial discrimination and inadequate income were the least important problems, in spite of the immigrants' apparent underemployment or even unemployment.

(4) Length of Interview. Our interviews in the Los Angeles area usually took one and one-half hours, although some extreme cases ranged from under an hour to over three hours. When the interview was exceptionally long, it was the result of one of the following reasons: the interviewer's explaining the interview questions to the respondents who did not understand them, or listening to the respondent's talk on his or her personal experiences beyond the formal interview. As mentioned in Appendix A, our interviewers were often invited by their respondents to a dinner either at the respondents' homes or at restaurants after the interview.

The optimal length of an interview seems to be less than one hour. Some respondents even suggested to the interviewer to leave the interview schedule so that they could fill the questionnaire out by themselves and mail it to the interviewer. According to our experience, this is not a desirable practice. The majority of such respondents never returned the interview schedule. A few respondents lost and interview schedule and some report that the interview schedule was torn by their children or uncooperative spouses (usually husbands). When the respondents returned the interview schedule, several crucial questions were often left blank. In a few cases, we suspected that a family member filled out the interview schedule for our respondents.

(5) Age and Sex of the Interviewer. The social life of Korean immigrants is dominated by two cultures: Korean and American. Such a bicultural situation generates a great deal of uncertainty and friction in their interpersonal relations. This problem inevitably affects the interaction between the interviewer and respondent. The problem is further accelerated by several ethnic factors such as the divisiveness of the Korean immigrant community, the general distrust among Koreans (e.g., suspicion of covert activity of Korean Central Intelligence Agency), and the social distance between the interviewer and respondent because of the difference between their social class background (ethclass).

Under these circumstances, female interviewers were found to be more successful in accomplishing their tasks than male interviewers. This has consistently been the case throughout our studies. Compared with male interviewers, females were less suspected by their respondents and were perceived as being less threatening. In addition, female interviewers were somehow more determined to complete their interviews than were the males. However, female interviewers also had some problems. They had to consider their physical safety before contacting their respondents, especially in the inner city. And some of our female interviewers did not have a car, which restricted their geographic mobility.

In traditional Korean culture, elderly persons are highly revered. This suggests that an elderly interviewer might command more respect and trust from the respondent than a younger interviewer. However, elderly male interviewers were found to be less reliable, less productive, and less responsible than younger interviewers.

b. Suggestions

The interviewer should pay very close attention to minimizing ego threat in the respondents. In this sense, female students seem to be the best interviewers. On the average, the optimal time and place for the interview appears to be in the evening for the male respondents and in the afternoon for the female respondents at their respective homes if possible. A humble and cordial approach was found to be the most efficient way to yield the maximum result. Information on income, English proficiency, occupational status, and educational attainment needs to be double-checked by some objective measures other than the respondent's statements. The interview schedule should be concise and preferably printed (often the respondent wanted to read it by him or herself). Some sort of compensation (extrinsic reward) would facilitate the interview situation favorably. Money may be given in exchange for the respondent's time as Gorden suggests (1975:133). As mentioned, our respondents in Los Angeles were compensated for their time ($10). Some of the respondents were apparently attracted by the compensation. It was reported that upon receiving monetary compensation, some respondents could hardly restrain an expression of their gladness. At the same time, some respondents declined to accept our monetary compensation, suggesting that this money could be used for some other research expense.

3. Postinterview Situation

Whenever we completed interviews, we had a meeting with our interviewers for an exchange of problems they had experienced and possible solutions for the future study. The findings of our research were also made available to the Korean community, normally through newspapers. Each interviewer received a copy of the final report of our study. Furthermore, some social policy implications of our study were made public, so that our respondents would know the practical relevance of the research to their everyday life.

Sampling Problems

The sampling problems unique to the study of Korean immigrants largely derive from the particular demographic characteristics and ecological setting of the Korean community in the United States. Among others, two major factors seem to most significantly contribute to the sampling problem: the rapid growth of the Korean population in the United States and their broad geographic dispersion. As a result, the Korean immigrants are constantly on the move.

As mentioned in Chapter 2, the Korean population is also more dispersed than other Asian counterparts, in regional as well as in urban-rural distribution. These ecological patterns certainly present problems of defining a population universe. For example, how would one operationally define the universe of the Korean population in such large metropolitan areas as Chicago, Los Angeles, and New York, especially when they are widely dispersed into outlying suburban communities?

Together with these two factors (population growth and dispersion), age and education variables seem to make Koreans one of the most highly mobile ethnic groups in the United States. Altough no comprehensive data are available on the mobility rate of Koreans, the average Korean family moves every other year according to our study of Korean church affiliates in Chicago (Kim, Hurh and Kim, 1978). If this rate is typical, the Korean family is twice as mobile as the average American family (cf. Packard, 1972; Toffler, 1970:78). No wonder addresses of Koreans are becoming rapidly obsolete. A number of directors are published each year, such as the Korean community association directories, Korean church directories, telephone directories, and directories from alumni associations, professional associations, business and trade associations, and even *Go* and fishing clubs. However, none of these including the immigration office, can keep track of the Korean immigrants accurately. Even if the U.S. Immigration and Naturalization Service had a relatively accurate list, it would not give out the information anyway. We approached the Immigration and Naturalization Service in Chicago in 1975 but without any result. A Korean language daily in Chicago was also approached for its subscription list, but the efforts proved to be fruitless. The task of securing the names and current addresses of the target population was one of the most frustrating and time-consuming problems we experienced.

Ironically, the most accessible, least costly, and up-to-date source turned out to be local telephone directories. One major problem with telephone directories, however, is in identifying Korean names. Although Kim is the most popular Korean name, the next popular names, such as Lee and Park, are not uniquely Korean. Recently, Eui-Young Yu has introduced a new sampling technique for the study of Koreans—the "Kim sample technique":

> Kim sample technique: Kims listed in the public telephone directories in the United States provide a unique and the most updated sampling frame for the Korean population. Key assumption behind this method is that Kims constitute a good representative sample of the total Korean population. Two arguments can be brought about to support this assumption. One is the fact that Kims constitute a significant proportion of the Korean population. The 1975 Korean Census revealed that persons with the surname Kim comprised 22 percent of the total Korean household heads. As examination of Kims in the 1977 Korean Directory of Southern California reveals that the proportions of the Kim listings in each of the four largest zipcode areas of Korean concentration does not deviate significantly from 22 percent: 90004, 23.4%; 90005, 22.1%; 90006, 22.9%; 90019, 21.7%. Whether the Kims constitute the cross-section of socioeconomic strata of the Korean population is hard to prove, although there is no known evidence that Kims represent any one particular class. We contend that a group comprising such a high proportion of the total population must represent the general population fairly well. Another argument is that Kim is a typical Korean surname and no other nationalities are known to have such a name in any significant number. Furthermore, all Koreans with the surname Kim spell their names KIM in the United States with rare exception. (Yu, 1980:95).

Although Yu's contention is quite convincing, we did not use the Kim sample technique mainly because of possible class biases associated with a particular surname group. As soon as Yu's conjecture that the Kims constitute a cross section of socioeconomic strata of the Korean population is empirically proved, the Kim sample technique may be utilized.

How do we compile, then, a reasonably accurate list of Korean immigrants? We collected as many directories and membership lists as possible, which were published by various Korean voluntary organizations, such as the Korean Association of Chicago, Korean ethnic churches, alumni associations, occupational or professional associations, and social clubs. Some of these directories were more accurate than others; for instance, the directory of the Korean Association of Chicago and the customer lists compiled by Korean businesmen. In the Los Angeles area, *The Korean Directory of Southern California* is the most updated and comprehensive source.[1] It is published annually by Keys Advertising and Printing Company. In any case, all addresses needed to be checked against local telephone directories. Even such double-checked and updated lists still pose another crucial problem in sampling: the list compiled from community directories and telephone directories usually contain only the names of the heads of the families. Kish's method (1965:396–401) has been found very useful.

Obtaining lists of some specified groups of Koreans (e.g., church affiliates, blue-collar workers), raises different problems. In our Korean ethnic church study, we found that almost half of the members listed in church directories were no longer regular members of their respective churches. For our study on occupational assimilation, we selected eight factories that hired many Korean immigrants. The employment and work conditions were found to fit the characteristics of the secondary labor market; that is, no active union, low wages, low skilled jobs, little chance for promotion, job instability, and little respect of due process in the consideration of labor grievances (cf. Doeringer and Piore, 1971). Under such circumstances, we did not expect that the management would cooperate with us in obtaining a list of the prospective respondents. At the same time, it was extremely difficult to obtain any information on the employees in each factory on the basis of the personal knowledge of friendly Korean employees.

Conclusion

Our main purpose in this appendix was to share with the reader our Western methodological experiences (etics) in studying Korean immigrant's everyday life (emics). We discussed primarily problematic issues in the study of non-Western subjects; that is, the outsider's mistakes in an attempt to study the insider's subjective categories using his or her own assumptions, categories, and instruments. Simply put, we elaborated on what went wrong, rather than on what went right. Certainly not everything went wrong—something must have gone right, too. We agree with Weber that "one need not be Caesar in order to understand Caesar" (Weber, 1913; cf. Merton, 1972:31). At the same time, however, one does not have to be Genghis Khan to understand Caesar either. The truth seems to lie somewhere in the middle. Merton has already given us excellent advice in this regard: "Insiders and Outsiders in the domain of knowledge, unite. You have nothing to lose but your claims. You have a world of understanding to win" (1972:44).

Since the basic problem is transcultural equivalence of verbal materials, measuring instruments, interview situations, and the large sociocultural context of research settings, both Western and non-Western methodologies are misnomers. What we are striving for seems to us to be "transcultural" methodology and we do not have it yet. Until then, our methodologies, whether they be Western, Eastern, Southern, or Northern, are vulnerable, refutable, and subjected to critical tests. To borrow Karl Popper's words: "They may survive these tests; but they can never be positively justified; they can neither be established as certainly true or even as 'probable'" (Popper, 1965:vii). We believe that a testable methodology is still better than an untestable dogmatic methodology.

Note

1. Limitations of using this directory were discussed in the methodology section of this book.

Appendix C
Interview Schedule

Korean Immigrants in America

A STUDY OF KOREAN IMMIGRANTS IN THE LOS ANGELES AREA

Interview Schedule

Investigators:

Won Moo Hurh
Kwang Chung Kim

Funded by NIMH, U.S. Department of Health, Education, and Welfare, Grant Number 1 RO 1 MH 30475-01 (1979)

TO: The Respondent:

The data obtained through this interview questionnaire will be statistically analyzed in order to assess the assimilation patterns of Korean immigrants <u>as a group</u>, and therefore, all information about the individual respondent will be kept in strict confidence. For the protection of confidentiality of data and anonymity of respondents, only persons directly engaged in the study will handle this interview schedule. Your candid response to each questionnaire item will be deeply appreciated. The U.S. Department of Health, Education, and Welfare requires all investigators to safeguard the rights and welfare of human subjects. The entire interview will take approximately an hour and a half, and you will be compensated for the time as announced ($10).

Questionnaire Items

1. When (in what year) did you come to the United States?

   Year _____

2. When (in what year) did you come to the Los Angeles area?

   Year _____

3. Do you read any American newspaper(s)?

   ___ A. Yes, I subscribe to American newspaper(s) and read regularly.
   The name(s) of the newspaper(s):
   _____
   _____
   _____

   ___ B. No, I don't subsribe, but I buy it (them) at newsstands and read occasionally.
   The name(s) of the newspaper(s):
   _____
   _____

1

___ C. No. I don't read it at all.

If you read American newspaper(s), what section do you mainly read? (Please check all that apply)

political _____   business _____   culture _____
editorial _____   family _____   sport _____
comic _____   advertisement _____   other (specify) _____

Do you read any American magazine(s)? (except professional journals)

___ A. Yes, I subscribe to American magazine(s) and read regularly. The name(s) of the magazine(s):
_____
_____

___ B. No, I don't subscribe, but I buy it (them) at newsstands and read occasionally. The name(s) of the magazine(s):
_____
_____

___ C. No, I don't read it at all.

. Do you read Korean newspaper(s)?

   ___ A. Yes, I subscribe to Korean newspaper(s) and read regularly.
   ___ B. No, I don't subscribe but buy it (them) at newsstands and read occasionally.
   ___ C. No, I don't read it at all.

If you read (either regularly or occasionally), how many different kinds of newspapers? _____ (indicate number).

2

---

7. If you read Korean newspaper(s), what section do you mainly read?

   ___ A. I am more interested in news on Korea than on America (including Koreans in America).
   ___ B. I am more interested in news on America (including Koreans in America).
   ___ C. I am interested in both.

8. When you were in Korea, did you study English?

   ___ A. Yes.
   ___ B. No.
   C. If yes, how did you study English? (method, duration, etc.)
   Reading _____
   Writing _____
   Conversation _____

9. Since you arrived in the U.S., how have you been doing with your English? (e.g., formal schooling, informal learning, no particular learning, etc.)
   Reading _____
   Writing _____
   Conversation _____

10. Reflecting on your experience in America, how well do you think you can express yourself in English? (Please check which applies)

Not at all	Almost not at all	About a half	Moderately well	Fluently

11. How well can you read American newspapers and magazines?

Not at all	Almost not at all	About a half	Moderately well	Fluently

3

12. How well can you write letters in English?

Not at all	Almost not at all	About a half	Moderately well	Fluently

13. Do you speak English at home?

	Always	Often	Once in a while	Never	Does not apply
A. With spouse?					
B. With children?					
C. With siblings?					
D. With parents?					

14. Do you speak English at work?

___ A. Always
___ B. Often
___ C. Once in a while
___ D. Never

15. How do you feel about Koreans changing their names to American names?

___ A. Strongly approve
___ B. Approve
___ C. Don't know
___ D. Disapprove
___ E. Strongly disapprove

Why do you think the way you indicated above?
_____
_____

16. Do you agree that some Korean customs which are disadvantageous to your life in America should be discarded?

___ A. Strongly agree
___ B. Agree
___ C. Don't know
___ D. Disagree
___ E. Strongly disagree

17. How should a wife react to her husband who comes home late at night after drinking with his colleagues or friends?

___ A. She should be understanding always.
___ B. She should be understanding in most of times.
___ C. Don't know.
___ D. Generally, she should not allow it.
___ E. Absolutely, she should not allow it.

18. What would you do when your guests stay late at night, even though you are very tired?

___ A. I would not express my fatigue at all.
___ B. If possible, I would not express my fatigue.
___ C. Don't know.
___ D. I would express my fatigue somewhat.
___ E. I would express my fatigue and ask them to meet again some other time.

19. In your life in America do you feel some aspects of Korean culture need to be modified? If so, what are they?
_____
_____
_____
_____

20. Are you a member of any voluntary social and/or cultural organizations in the Los Angeles area, such as a social club, church, or alumni association?
If yes, list the name(s) of organization(s) and your activity (activities) in it (them). In case of the organization(s) to which you belong is (are) multi-racial in composition, please indicate as such under "American Organization(s)" below:

Name of Korean Organization	Frequency of Attendance	Official Position, Committee Assignment, & Other Activity

Name of American Organization	Frequency of Attendance	Official Position, Committee Assignment, & Other Activity

21. During the last year have you been invited to the home(s) of any American(s)?

Yes ___   No ___
If yes, how often? _____

22. During the last year have you invited any American(s) to your home?

Yes ___   No ___
If yes, how often? _____

23. Do you think it is generally difficult to make friends with Americans?

___ A. Definitely yes.
___ B. More or less yes.
___ C. Don't know.
___ D. More or less no.
___ E. Definitely no.

24. Do you have any close friends (Korean, American or both) in the Los Angeles area?

Yes ___   No ___
If yes, how many? _____

Please complete the following information blank (list the middle name(s) of your Korean friend(s) and the first name(s) of your friend(s) who are other than Korean):

A. Close Korean Friend:

Middle Name	How did you meet	How long have you been known each other	Approx. age	Educational Status		Present Occupation
				Korean	U.S.	

B. Close American Friend:

First Name	Race	How did you meet	How long have you been known each other	Approx. age	Educational Status	Present Occupation

25. Would you feel more comfortable to live in predominantly American neighborhood than Korean?

___ A. Definitely yes.
___ B. More or less yes.
___ C. Don't know.
___ D. More or less no.
___ E. Definitely no.

Why do you think so?

_____
_____
_____

26. If circumstances allowed, whom would you like your children to play with?

___ A. Exclusively with American children.
___ B. More with American children than with Korean children.
___ C. Equally with American and Korean children.
___ D. More with Korean children than with American children.
___ E. Exclusively with Korean children.

27. Do you approve Korean-American (white) marriage?

___ A. Strongly approve
___ B. Approve
___ C. Don't know
___ D. Disapprove
___ E. Strongly disapprove

28. Do you have relatives in the Los Angels area?

Yes ___   No ___
If yes, how many (adults only)? ___
Relations: _____
_____

How often do you visit each other? _____
_____

29. Do you have someone in your neighborhood who is (are) close to you?

Yes ___   No ___
If yes, how many (adults only)? ___
  Koreans? _____
  Americans? _____
  Other? (specify) _____

How often do you contact (or visit) each other?
_____

30. How strongly do you agree or disagree with the following statements?

A. When I am with Americans, I often feel "left out" or isolated.
___ (a) Strongly agree
___ (b) Agree
___ (c) Don't know
___ (d) Disagree
___ (e) Strongly disagree

B. Most of Americans who I personally know do not seem to understand how I feel about things.
___ (a) Strongly agree
___ (b) Agree
___ (c) Don't know
___ (d) Disagree
___ (e) Strongly disagree

31. When you have difficult personal problems, with whom do you mainly discuss? (check as many as apply)

___ (a) Spouse
___ (b) Parent(s)
___ (c) Children
___ (d) Other relatives (specify) _____
___ (e) Korean friend(s)
___ (f) American friend(s)
___ (g) Colleague(s) at work
___ (h) Minister, priest, or other clergy people
___ (i) Other (specify) _____
___ (j) No one

32. How strongly do you agree or disagree with the following statements?

A. As long as Koreans have immigrated to the U.S., they must learn actively the American way of life and associate mainly with Americans, rather than with Koreans.
___ (a) Strongly agree
___ (b) Agree
___ (c) Don't know
___ (d) Disagree
___ (e) Strongly disagree

B. When my personal interest is in conflict with my family need, family duty should be given priority.
___ (a) Strongly agree
___ (b) Agree
___ (c) Don't know
___ (d) Disagree
___ (e) Strongly disagree

C. I am ashamed of being born a Korean.
___ (a) Always, yes
___ (b) Frequently, yes
___ (c) Once in a while, yes
___ (d) Definitely, no

D. After Korean immigrants are accustomed to American life, it's better for them in many respects to attend American churches than Korean churches.
___ (a) Strongly agree
___ (b) Agree
___ (c) Don't know
___ (d) Disagree
___ (e) Strongly disagree

E. Although Korean immigrants need to adjust themselves to the American society occupationally, they must associate mainly with Koreans in other areas of life.
___ (a) Strongly agree
___ (b) Agree
___ (c) Don't know
___ (d) Disagree
___ (e) Strongly disagree

F. It is necessary for children of Korean immigrants to speak Korean language well.
___ (a) Strongly agree
___ (b) Agree
___ (c) Don't know
___ (d) Disagree
___ (e) Strongly disagree

33. How do you feel about returning to Korea eventually and spending the rest of your life there?

_____
_____

Appendix C

34. Among your family members (e.g., wife, husband, and other*) how do you divide your household tasks? Please indicate in terms of <u>actual</u> task performance.

Household Tasks	Family Members Who <u>Actually</u> Perform the Tasks (those who do the most, first and the least, last)		
	1	2	3
A. Grocery			
B. House-keeping			
C. Laundry			
D. Dish Wash			
E. Garbage			
F. Finance			

*Specify "other" family members _____

35. In your opinion, how should the above household tasks be divided in principle? Please indicate below who <u>should</u> do what in terms of percentages.

Household Tasks	Family Members Who <u>Should</u> Perform the Tasks (in percentage)		
	Husband(%)	Wife(%)	Other(%)*
A. Grocery			
B. House-keeping			
C. Laundry			
D. Dish Wash			
E. Garbage			
F. Finance			

*Specify "other" family members _____

36. Please list all of the full-time or part-time jobs that you (have) ever held for more than a month since you came to the U.S., and answer the following questions:

	Nature of Work Organization (e.g., wig business, electronic plant)	Period of Employment	Required Educational Level for the Job
Present Job			
1st Job			
2nd Job			
3rd Job			
4th Job			
5th Job			

	Job Title and Description	Main Source of Job Information: How did you obtain job information which led you to the following job(s) below?
Present Job		
1st Job		
2nd Job		
3rd Job		
4th Job		
5th Job		

37. If you obtained job information from someone (contact person) you knew, please answer the following:

	Your Relationship with Contact Person at the Time of Job Information Transmission (e.g., friend, colleague)	Did your contact person belong to your church?	Contact Person's Ethnicity	How did your contact person know about the job?
Present Job				
1st Job				
2nd Job				
3rd Job				
4th Job				
5th Job				

38. (The following questions deal with those who are unemployed)

A. How long have you been unemployed? _____

B. Have you been looking for a job?

Yes ____ No ____ Other ____ (specify)

If yes, please describe in detail what kind of effort have you been making for getting a job (within the past 4 weeks).

_____
_____
_____
_____

(Questions 39-42 apply to those who are presently employed)

39. On the Present Job:

A. How long did it take you to learn the skill or ability required for your present job?

__(a) None at all
__(b) Less than a month
__(c) Less than 3 months (1 - 3 months)
__(d) Less than 6 months (3 - 6 months)
__(e) Less than a year (6 months - 1 year)
__(f) Less than 2 years (1 - 2 years)
__(g) Less than 4 years (2 - 4 years)
__(h) Approximately 4 years
__(i) More than 4 years but less than 6 years
__(j) More than 6 years
__(k) Don't know

B. Among your work colleagues which one of the following categories is the numerical majority? (Please rank them)

__(a) Whites
__(b) Blacks
__(c) Mexicans
__(d) Koreans
__(e) Asians (other than Korean)
__(f) Other _____(specify)

(The following question is for those who deal with customers in their work)

C. Among your customers which one of the following categories is the numerical majority? (Please rank them)

__(a) Whites
__(b) Blacks
__(c) Mexicans
__(d) Koreans
__(e) Asians (other than Korean)
__(f) Other _____(specify)

D. On the average how many hours per day do you work at your current job?

Hours?_____ What time of the day? _____

(c) Do you work on Saturdays?

    Yes_____   No_____

    If yes, always?_____

           often? _____

           once in a while? _____

    How many hours do you work on Saturdays on the average?
    _____

(d) Do you work on Sundays?

    Yes_____   No_____

    If yes, always? _____

           often? _____

           once in a while?_____

    How many hours do you work on Sundays on the average?
    _____

E. What was your _personal_ annual income last year?

    ___ $0   ___ $13,000 - 14,999
    ___ 3,000 and below   ___ 15,000 - 16,999
    ___ 3,000 - 4,999   ___ 17,000 - 18,999
    ___ 5,000 - 6,999   ___ 19,000 - 20,999
    ___ 7,000 - 8,999   ___ 21,000 - 22,999
    ___ 9,000 - 10,999   ___ 23,000 - 24,999
    ___ 11,000 - 12,999   ___ 25,000 and above

F. What was your _family_ annual income last year?

    ___ $3,000 and below   ___ $13,000 - 14,999
    ___ 3,000 - 4,999   ___ 15,000 - 16,999
    ___ 5,000 - 6,999   ___ 17,000 - 18,999
    ___ 7,000 - 8,999   ___ 19,000 - 20,999
    ___ 9,000 -10,999   ___ 21,000 - 22,999
    ___ 11,000 -12,999   ___ 23,000 - 24,999
                                  ___ 25,000 and above

G. Do you find your present job boring or tiresome?
_____
_____

H. What are your personal relationships with your colleagues, boss, and/or customers?
_____
_____
_____

I. What are the future prospect of your present job and chances of promotion?
_____
_____
_____

J. Is your income from the present job sufficient to support your family?
_____
_____

What are the chances of getting a raise in the future?
_____
_____

K. Is the knowledge and skill obtained through your past education and experience sufficiently utilized at your present job?
_____
_____

L. As a whole, how well are you satisfied with your present job?

    ___ (a) Very much satisfied
    ___ (b) Somewhat satisfied
    ___ (c) Don't know
    ___ (d) Somewhat dissatisfied
    ___ (e) Very much dissatisfied

M. If you quit your present job, what kind of job would you most likely get?
_____

1. In your opinion, is your occupation commensurate with your education (attained in Korean and/or in the U.S.)?

    ___ (a) Definitely yes
    ___ (b) More or less, yes
    ___ (c) Don't know
    ___ (d) More or less, no
    ___ (e) Definitely no

.. In your opinion, is your present income commensurate with your education (attained in Korea and/or in the U.S.)?

    ___ (a) Definitely yes
    ___ (b) More or less, yes
    ___ (c) Don't know
    ___ (d) More or less, no
    ___ (e) Definitely no

. In your opinion, is your present income commensurate with income of American workers who are doing similar jobs with yours?

    ___ (a) Definitely yes
    ___ (b) More or less, yes
    ___ (c) Don't know
    ___ (d) More or less, no
    ___ (e) Definitely no

Why do you think the way you indicated above (questions 40-42)?
_____
_____
_____
_____

43. Do you attend church?

    No_____ (If no, skip questions 43-49)

    Yes_____

    If yes, what church (indicate denomination, e.g., Catholic, Methodist, Presbyterian, etc.)?
    _____

44. Do you take part in any of the activities of your church other than attending services (e.g., choir, committee, etc.)?

    Yes_____   No_____

    If yes, what activity (activities)? _____

    Any offices or position? _____

45. About how often have you attended regular church services (or Mass) in the past year?

    ___ (a) Two or more times a week
    ___ (b) Once a week
    ___ (c) Twice a month
    ___ (d) Once a month
    ___ (e) A few times a year

46. Which of the reasons listed below is the main reason for you to attend church? If more than one, please rank the reasons.

    ___ (a) Because it has been a habit to attend.
    ___ (b) For the sake of peace and security of mind.
    ___ (c) To see friends and relatives.
    ___ (d) Because ministers (or priests) have been so kind to me.
    ___ (e) Because it's one of believer's obligations.
    ___ (f) To worship God.
    ___ (g) To hear sermon.
    ___ (h) To seek salvation.
    ___ (i) Other _____(specify)

47. How long have you been attending your present church?
_____

48. Did you attend church in Korea?

    Yes_____   No_____

    If yes, what denomination? _____

49. What would be the advantages and disadvantages of attending church?

    Advantages: _____
    _____
    _____

    Disadvantages: _____
    _____
    _____

50. (The following questions apply only to Buddhists)

    A. How often do you visit the Buddhist temple in the Los Angeles area?
       _____

    B. Please describe your activities (other than worship) in the temple.
       _____
       _____

    C. What are your major reasons for visiting the Buddhist temple?
       _____
       _____

51. Do you think Koreans in the U.S. can be more successful in certain areas but less in other areas regardless of their efforts?

    Yes_____   No_____

    If yes, please specify the areas below: (next page)

    Successful areas: _____
    _____

    Less successful areas: _____
    _____

52. In accessing your achievement in the U.S., for what group of persons do you get your standard for comparison?

    ___(a) Koreans in Korea
    ___(b) Koreans in America
    ___(c) White Americans
    ___(d) Black Americans
    ___(e) Mexican Americans
    ___(f) Asian Americans (other than Korean)
    ___(g) Don't know
    ___(h) None
    ___(i) Other _____ (specify)

53. In terms of your children's future achievement, what group of persons would you compare?

    ___(a) Koreans in Korea
    ___(b) Koreans in America
    ___(c) White Americans
    ___(d) Black Americans
    ___(e) Mexican Americans
    ___(f) Asian Americans (other than Korean)
    ___(g) Don't know
    ___(h) None
    ___(i) Other _____ (specify)

54. In what aspect of your immigrant life do you find the sense of fulfillment?
    _____
    _____

55. Do you regret that you came to the U.S.?

    ___(a) Always, yes
    ___(b) Often, yes
    ___(c) Don't know
    ___(d) Nearly, no
    ___(e) Absolutely, no

56. How strongly do you agree or disagree with the following statement?

    "Since the world is run by a few powerful people, Korean immigrants' influence on the American society is negligible."

    ___(a) Strongly agree
    ___(b) Agree
    ___(c) Don't know
    ___(d) Disagree
    ___(e) Strongly disagree

57. Since your immigration, do you think everything has progressed as you planned?

    ___(a) Almost, yes
    ___(b) Somewhat, yes
    ___(c) Don't know
    ___(d) Somewhat, no
    ___(e) Not at all

58. How well are you generally satisfied with your immigrant life?

    ___(a) Very satisfied
    ___(b) More or less, satisfied
    ___(c) Don't know
    ___(d) More or less, dissatisfied
    ___(e) Very dissatisfied

59. How strongly do you feel about the following statement?

    A. Since immigration I feel more lonely than ever.

    ___(a) Strongly agree
    ___(b) Agree
    ___(c) Don't know
    ___(d) Disagree
    ___(e) Strongly disagree

    B. One thing I have learned through immigrant life for sure is that one should employ whatever the means in order to survive.

    ___(a) Strongly agree
    ___(b) Agree
    ___(c) Don't know
    ___(d) Disagree
    ___(e) Strongly disagree

60. Because you are a Korean or a member of minority group:

    A. Have you had difficulties in getting a job?

       Yes_____   No_____

       If yes, please describe your experience: _____
       _____
       _____

    B. Have you lost your job?

       Yes_____   No_____

       If yes, please describe your experience: _____
       _____
       _____

    C. Have you had difficulties in promotion at work?

       Yes_____   No_____

       If yes, please describe your experience: _____
       _____
       _____

    D. Have you ever experienced that you did not get raises regularly as compared to others?

       Yes_____   No_____

       If yes, please describe your experience: _____
       _____
       _____

61. A. Generally, what have been the major difficult problems in your immigrant life in the U.S.? Please list the most essential ones.

    _____
    _____
    _____

    B. Generally, what have been the major satisfying and worth-while experiences in your life in the Los Angeles area?

    _____
    _____
    _____

62. Personal Items:

    A. Sex: Male _____ Female _____

    B. Age: _____

    C. Age at Immigration _____

    D. Marital Status: Single ___ Married ___ Divorced ___
                      Widowed ___ Other ___

    E. Family Members (in the same household)

Relations	Age	Birth Place	Present Occupation (position, activity)

    F. Type of Residence:

    Own____ Renting_____ Apartment_____
    Other _____(specify)

    G. How often have you moved since you arrived in the Los Angeles area?

    _____(number of moving)

    H. How long have you been living at the current address?

    _____

    I. Your Education Completed in Korea:

    _____

    J. Your Education Completed in the U.S.:

    _____

    K. Your Final Occupation Held in Korea (specify the nature of work and position):

    _____

Thank you for your time. Using this opportunity, would you like to suggest anything to the U.S. government for promoting life conditions of Korean immigrants in the United States?

_____
_____
_____

(continue in the next page)

_____
_____
_____
_____
_____
_____
_____
_____
_____
_____
_____
_____
_____
_____
_____
_____
_____

Interviewer's Name: _____
Date _____ Time _____ Place of Interview:_____
Interviewer's Comment (if any): _____
_____
_____

Appendix D
Tables

Table 0.1. Adhesive Adaptation in Comparison to Other Modes of Ethnic Adaptation

Modes of Adaptation	Ethnic Attachment (Koreanism)		Americanization (Anglo-Conformity)	
	Korean Culture	Korean Society	American Culture	American Society
Assimilation	−	−	+	+
Separatism	+	+	−	−
"Ideal" Pluralism	+	+	+	+
Adhesion	+	+	±	±

+ means acceptance
− means detachment
± means limited acceptance

Table 1.1. Korean Immigration to the United States, 1903-1978

Year	Number of Immigrants* Admitted	Category
1903-1905	7,226	Labor Immigration to Hawaii
1910-1924	1,100	Picture Brides
* * * * * * * * * * * * * * * *		
1951-1964	14,027	Post-Korean War Immigration: mostly wives of American servicemen (6,423) and war orphans (5,348). Others are professional migrants.
* * * * * * * * * * * * * * * *		
1965	2,139	New Wave of Family Immigration: Effect of the Immigration Act of 1965 (P.L. 89-236) is gradually evident.
1966	2,492	
1967	3,956	
1968	3,811	
1969	6,045	
1970	9,314	
1971	14,297	
1972	18,876	
1973	22,930	
1974	28,028	
1975	28,362	
1976	30,803	
1977	30,917	
1978	29,288	

*Number of bona fide immigrants who entered the United States with immigrant visas. Non-immigrants, such as students and political refugees, are not included, although many of them changed their statuses to immigrant status.

Source: Warren Kim (1971)
U.S. Commissioner of Immigration and Naturalization (1952-1978)
Bok-Lim Kim (1977:99)
Ministry of Health and Social Affairs (1967)
Yu (1977)

Table 2.1 East Asian Immigrants by Country of Birth, 1965-1977

	Korea	Phillippines	Japan	China, Taiwan & Hong Kong	Total
1965	2,165	3,130	3,180	4,769	13,244
1966	2,492	6,093	3,394	17,608	29,587
1967	3,956	10,865	3,946	25,096	43,863
1968	3,811	16,731	3,613	16,434	40,589
1969	6,045	20,744	3,957	20,893	51,639
1970	9,314	31,203	4,485	17,956	62,958
1971	14,297	28,471	4,457	17,622	64,847
1972	18,876	29,376	4,757	21,730	74,739
1973	22,930	30,799	5,461	21,656	80,846
1974	28,028	32,857	4,860	22,685	88,430
1975	28,362	37,751	4,274	23,427	87,814
1976	30,803	37,281	4,258	24,589	96,931
1977	30,917	39,111	4,178	25,396	99,602

Source: U.S. Commissioner of Immigration and Naturalization, 1966-1977

Table 2.2 Socioeconomic Characteristics of Asian Americans, 1970

Population Distribution	U.S. Total	Japanese	Chinese	Filipinos	Koreans
Number:	203.2 mill.	588,324	431,583	336,731	70,598
Male	98.9 mill.	271,453	226,733	183,175	28,491
Female	104.3 mill.	316,871	204,850	153,556	42,107
Foreign-born (%)	5	21	47	53	54
Age Distribution:					
% under 18	34	29	32	36	35
% 65 & over	10	8	6	6	3
Education:					
High School Graduates (%)	55	69	60	57	71
College Graduates (%)	11	15	21	21	36
Labor Force:					
% in labor force					
Male	77	79	73	79	76
Female	41	49	50	55	42
Income:					
Persons with Incomes under $4,000 (%)					
Male	34	30	41	40	36
Female	69	58	65	56	64
$10,000 and over (%)					
Male	25	33	24	12	28
Female	3	5	5	5	5
Median Income (Family)	$9,590	$12,515	$10,610	$9,318	NA
Urban-Rural Distribution:					
Urban (%)	74	89	97	86	67
Rural (%)	26	11	3	14	33

Source: U.S. Department of H. E. & W., 1974:17, 25, 70, 83, 105, 134.
U.S. Department of Commerce (Bureau of Census), 1977a.
U.S. Department of Commerce, 1977:27.
Ryu, 1977:209, 213.

Table 2.3 Respondents' Ages by Sex

Age	Male		Female		Total	
	N	%	N	%	N	%
20	3	1.1	5	1.5	8	1.3
21-30	43	15.3	101	30.2	144	23.4
31-40	104	37.0	118	35.3	222	36.1
41-50	74	26.3	52	15.6	126	20.5
51-60	23	8.2	25	7.5	48	7.8
61-70	23	8.2	19	5.7	42	6.8
71 and over	11	.9	14	4.2	25	4.1
Totals			334	100.0	615	100.0
Mean			38.75		40.33	
SD			13.78		13.63	

T̲ ̲ ̲ence in the U.S.

Length of R̲ (Number of Y̲			Female		Combined	
			N	%	N	%
2 or less		15.0	45	13.5	87	14.1
3-4	o6	23.5	84	25.2	150	24.4
5-6	70	24.9	78	23.4	148	24.1
7-8	48	17.1	58	17.4	106	17.2
9-10	24	8.5	26	7.8	50	8.1
11 or more	31	11.0	43	12.7	74	12.1
Total	281	100.0	334	100.0	615	100.0
Mean	6.34		6.61		6.49	
SD	5.20		6.60		6.00	

Table 3.1 Rank Order of Korean-Concentrated Neighborhoods by Zip Code

Rank	Zip	1972 Household	(%)	Zip	1975 Household	(%)	Zip	1979 Household	(%)
1	90006	496	(14.9)	90006	660	(13.2)	90006	1,226	(9.6)
2	90005	257	(7.7)	90005	421	(8.4)	90005	842	(6.6)
3	90019	235	(7.0)	90019	301	(6.0)	90004	740	(5.8)
4	90007	144	(4.3)	90004	257	(5.2)	90019	575	(4.5)
5	90004	125	(3.7)	90026	127	(2.5)	90020	384	(3.0)
6	90016	79	(2.4)	90007	124	(2.5)	90029	298	(2.3)
7	90029	75	(2.2)	90029	113	(2.3)	90038	244	(1.9)
8	90027	70	(2.1)	90038	99	(2.0)	90250	229	(1.8)
9	90057	66	(2.0)	90027	98	(2.0)	90027	195	(1.5)
10	90033	65	(1.9)	90034	85	(1.7)	91754	170	(1.3)
11	90018	64	(1.9)	90020	82	(1.6)	90701	162	(1.3)
12	90026	59	(1.8)	90018	80	(1.6)	90026	158	(1.2)
13	90247	59	(1.8)	90057	71	(1.4)	90247	156	(1.2)
14	90008	47	(1.4)	90250	69	(1.4)	90057	148	(1.0)
15	90038	47	(1.4)	90247	68	(1.4)	91745	129	(1.0)
Total Percentage			(57.7)			(54.6)			(45.2)
Total Households in Southern California		3,430	(100.0)		5,036	(100.0)		12,722	(100.0)

Source: Korean Directory of Southern California 1972, 1975, 1979

Table 3.2 Distribution of Korean Households in Southern California

	1972 Household	%	1975 Household	%	1979 Household	%
City of Los Angeles	2,404	70.1	3,399	67.5	6,374	50.1
Los Angeles County	3,248	94.7	4,833	96.0	11,256	88.5
Santa Ana	55	1.6	67	1.3	868	6.8
Anaheim	11	0.3	7	0.1	167	1.3
St. Bernardino	18	0.5	32	0.6	94	0.7
Riverside	12	0.3	13	0.3	53	0.4
Palm Springs	3	0.1	1	0.0	12	0.1
San Diego	15	0.4	10	0.2	185	1.5
Total	3,362	98.0	4,963	98.6	12,635	99.4
Total Listing*	3,430	100.0	5,036	100.0	12,722	100.0

*Total Listing represents the total number of households listed in the Korean Directory of Southern California that includes some households in northern California.

Source: Korean Directory of Southern California 1972, 1975, 1979

Appendix D

Table 4.1 Proficiency in English

	Self-Evaluation of English Proficiency	Speaking		Reading		Writing	
		N	%	N	%	N	%
Male	Fluent	10	3.6	22	7.9	35	12.6
	Moderately Well	42	15.0	46	16.4	41	14.6
	About Half	97	34.6	80	28.6	76	27.1
	Almost Not At All	111	39.7	101	36.0	101	36.1
	Not At All	20	7.1	31	11.1	27	9.6
	Total	280	100.0	280	100.0	280	100.0
Female	Fluent	18	5.5	49	14.8	61	18.4
	Moderately Well	64	19.3	58	17.5	71	21.4
	About Half	132	39.9	114	34.3	95	28.6
	Almost Not At All	109	32.9	95	28.6	88	26.5
	Not At All	8	2.4	16	4.8	17	5.1
	Total	331	100.0	332	100.0	332	100.0

Table 4.2 Length of Residence in the U.S., Current Age, Age at Immigration and Current Occupation of Respondents Classified by the Levels of Education

Types of Respondents		Length of Residence		Current Age		Age at Immigration		Current Occupation							
		Mean	SD	Mean	SD	Mean	SD	1		2		3		4	
								N	%	N	%	N	%	N	%
Male	Non-College Graduates (76)	4.68	2.64	47.32	15.65	43.03	15.46	5	8.3	16	26.7			39	65.0
	Korean-College Graduates (118)	5.47	3.11	42.87	10.53	37.74	10.36	27	25.0	46	42.6	13	12.0	22	20.4
	American-College Graduates (54)	11.13	8.89	40.24	11.89	28.50	10.28	24	49.0	13	26.5	9	18.4	3	6.1
	Students (30)	5.50	2.30	29.67	8.42	24.10	8.36								
	Statistical Test	F=23.76*** df=3,274		F=15.59*** df=3,274		F=27.31*** df=3,274		Chi-Square Value=68.84*** Degree of Freedom=6							
Female	Non-College Graduates (116)	6.66	6.80	45.80	15.90	39.29	15.63	4	6.0	18	26.9	7	10.4	38	56.7
	Korean-College Graduates (149)	5.56	3.00	35.23	7.27	29.99	7.10	31	27.2	39	34.2	20	17.5	24	21.1
	American-College Graduates (25)	10.24	5.45	33.40	10.23	23.32	9.85	5	31.3	4	25.0	4	25.0	3	18.8
	Students (33)	5.00	3.59	26.03	7.31	21.06	6.51								
	Statistical Test	F=7.31*** df=3,319		F=34.77*** df=3,319		F=34.15*** df=3,319		Chi-Square Value=30.96*** Degree of Freedom=6							

1: Professionals and Semi-professionals
2: Proprietors and Managers
3: Other White Collar Workers
4: Blue Collar Workers
***: Significant at the .001 Level

Table 4.3 English Proficiency by the Length of Residence in the United States and Level of Education

		Male			Female		
		N	Mean*	SD	N	Mean*	SD
Number of Years in the United States	2 or Less	42	7.86	2.93	45	7.91	2.78
	3 - 4	66	8.61	2.71	83	8.33	2.63
	5 - 6	70	9.37	2.96	78	8.21	2.92
	7 - 8	48	10.65	2.61	57	9.12	2.79
	9 - 10	24	11.42	2.59	26	9.46	3.28
	11 or More	31	12.49	2.54	43	10.63	3.31
	F Test	F=15.24***,		df=5,275	F=5.80***,		df=2,327
Level of Education Received	1	76	6.87	2.67	115	6.73	2.85
	2	118	9.86	2.50	149	9.51	2.00
	3	54	12.44	1.74	24	12.08	2.12
	F Test	F=86.68***,		df=2,245	F=71.84***,		df=2,285

1: Non-College Graduates
2: Korean College Graduates
3: American College Graduates
*: Mean of English proficiency scores which are the total points assigned to responses to three statements on English proficiency. When all three responses are "fluent" the score will be a maximum of 15 points, but if all three are "not at all" the score will be a minimum of 3.
***: Significant at the .001 Level

Table 4.4 Cultural Assimilation and Length of Residence in the U.S.

			Number of Years in the United States												Chi-Square Test
			2 or Less		3 - 4		5 - 6		7 - 8		9 - 10		11 or More		
			N	%	N	%	N	%	N	%	N	%	N	%	
M	American Newspaper	1	4	9.5	8	12.3	14	20.2	9	18.8	9	37.5	20	64.5	52.20***
		2	12	28.6	26	40.0	24	34.3	25	52.1	8	33.3	5	16.1	df=10
		3	26	61.9	31	47.7	32	45.7	14	29.2	7	29.2	6	19.4	
		Total	42	100	65	100	70	100	48	100	24	100	31	100	
	American Magazine	1	5	11.9	11	16.9	19	27.5	14	29.2	9	37.5	20	64.5	46.92***
		2	7	16.7	16	24.6	11	16.0	18	37.5	8	33.3	5	16.1	df=10
		3	30	71.4	38	58.5	39	56.5	16	33.3	7	29.2	6	19.4	
		Total	42	100	65	100	69	100	48	100	24	100	31	100	
	Name Change	For	10	27.8	27	45.8	36	55.4	27	58.7	16	72.7	22	75.9	20.69***
		Against	26	72.2	32	54.2	29	44.6	19	41.3	6	27.3	7	24.1	df=5
		Total	36	100	59	100	65	100	46	100	22	100	29	100	
F	American Newspaper	1	4	8.9	10	11.9	14	17.9	15	25.9	7	26.9	20	46.5	34.08***
		2	13	28.9	27	32.1	26	33.4	21	36.2	12	46.2	8	18.6	df=10
		3	28	62.2	47	56.0	38	48.7	22	37.9	7	26.9	15	34.9	
		Total	45	100	84	100	78	100	58	100	26	100	43	100	
	American Magazine	1	2	4.4	19	22.9	10	13.0	17	29.8	11	44.0	20	46.5	34.13***
		2	12	26.7	19	22.9	21	27.3	12	21.1	6	24.0	7	16.3	df=10
		3	31	68.9	45	54.2	46	59.7	28	49.1	8	32.0	16	37.2	
		Total	45	100	83	100	77	100	57	100	25	100	43	100	
	Name Change	For	19	48.7	37	49.3	38	54.3	34	63.0	20	83.3	29	76.3	16.18**
		Against	20	51.3	38	50.7	32	45.7	20	37.0	4	16.7	9	23.7	df=5
		Total	39	100	75	100	70	100	54	100	24	100	38	100	

1: Regular Subscription; 2: Occasional Purchase at Newsstand; 3: Do Not Read At All
M: Male Respondents; F: Female Respondents
**: Significant at the .01 Level
***: Significant at the .001 Level
Otherwise Not Significant

Appendix D

Table 4.5 Ethnic Attachment and Length of Residence in U.S.

			Number of Years in the United States											Chi-Square Test
			2 or Less		3 - 4		5 - 6		7 - 8		9 - 10		11 or More		
			N	%	N	%	N	%	N	%	N	%	N	%	
M	Korean Newspaper	1	32	76.2	56	86.1	54	77.1	39	81.3	17	70.8	24	77.4	6.81
		2	8	19.0	7	10.8	13	18.6	6	12.5	4	16.7	4	12.9	df=10
		3	2	4.8	2	3.1	3	4.3	3	6.3	3	12.5	3	9.7	NS
		Total	42	100	65	100	70	100	48	100	24	100	31	100	
	Association With Koreans	A	22	55.0	36	57.1	36	52.9	32	68.1	12	57.1	16	51.6	3.25
		B	18	45.0	27	42.9	32	47.1	15	31.9	9	42.9	15	48.4	df=5
		Total	40	100	63	100	68	100	47	100	21	100	31	100	NS
	Preferred American Church	A	11	28.9	11	22.0	9	15.3	6	13.0	6	33.3	5	21.7	6.14
		B	27	71.1	39	78.0	50	84.7	40	87.0	12	66.7	18	78.3	df=5
		Total	38	100	50	100	59	100	46	100	18	100	23	100	NS
F	Korean Newspaper	1	37	84.1	62	73.8	57	73.1	49	84.5	19	76.0	29	67.4	11.25
		2	3	6.8	16	19.0	10	12.8	5	8.6	3	12.0	6	14.0	df=10
		3	4	9.1	6	7.2	11	14.1	4	6.9	3	12.0	8	18.6	NS
		Total	44	100	84	100	78	100	58	100	25	100	43	100	
	Association With Koreans	A	24	57.1	46	56.8	52	70.3	32	55.2	14	53.8	24	57.1	4.80
		B	18	42.9	35	43.2	22	29.7	26	44.8	12	46.2	18	42.9	df=5
		Total	42	100	81	100	74	100	58	100	26	100	42	100	NS
	Prefer Korean Church	B	4	11.4	20	29.0	7	10.6	12	22.6	4	18.2	6	16.7	9.44
		A	31	88.6	49	71.0	59	89.4	41	77.4	18	81.8	30	83.3	df=4
		Total	35	100	69	100	66	100	53	100	22	100	36	100	NS

1: Regular Subscription; 2: Occasional Purchase at Newsstand; 3: Do Not Read At All
A: Agree; B: Disagree
M: Male Respondents; F: Female Respondents

Table 4.6 Response to Statements on Ethnic Attachment by the Length of Residence in U.S. and Levels of Education*

		Male						Female					
		A		B		C		A		B		C	
		N	%	N	%	N	%	N	%	N	%	N	%
Number of Years in U.S.A.	2 or Less	39	92.9	39	100.0	38	92.7	42	93.3	43	97.7	40	97.6
	3 - 4	59	90.8	61	95.3	61	95.3	71	86.6	73	100.0	81	96.4
	5 - 6	63	92.6	62	100.0	68	98.6	72	94.7	71	97.3	74	94.9
	7 - 8	44	91.7	43	97.7	46	85.8	52	94.5	54	100.0	54	94.7
	9 - 10	20	90.9	21	100.0	24	100.0	21	87.5	24	100.0	25	96.2
	11 or More	29	96.7	26	92.9	29	93.5	38	95.0	39	97.5	41	95.3
Level of Education Received	Non-college Grad.	68	91.6	68	97.1	73	97.3	101	91.8	106	98.1	109	94.8
	Korean-college Grad.	109	94.8	107	98.2	113	96.6	137	93.2	136	99.3	145	98.0
	American-college Grad.	50	94.3	47	97.9	49	92.5	22	100.0	21	95.5	22	91.7

*Responses to five statements on ethnic attachment are grouped in two categories: one for "strongly agree" and "agree"; the other for "strongly disagree" and "disagree". The "don't know" category was eliminated due to its smallness.

A: The Respondents who think that family duty should be given priority.
B: The Respondents who do not feel ashamed of being born a Korean.
C: The Respondents who think that their children should speak Korean well.

Table 4.7 Cultural Assimilation and Ethnic Attachment by Level of Education

		Non-College Graduates		Korean-College Graduates		American-College Graduates		Chi-Square Test
		N	%	N	%	N	%	
American Newspaper	1	15	7.8	60	22.6	38	48.1	107.90*** df = 4
	2	40	20.8	102	38.3	33	41.8	
	3	137	71.4	104	39.1	8	10.1	
	Total	192	100.0	266	100.0	79	100.0	
American Magazine	1	15	7.9	76	28.7	40	51.3	98.10*** df = 4
	2	26	13.7	71	26.8	22	28.2	
	3	149	78.4	118	44.5	16	20.5	
	Total	190	100.0	265	100.0	78	100.0	
Name Change	For	70	41.9	146	59.3	56	73.7	24.4*** df = 2
	Against	97	58.1	100	40.7	20	26.3	
	Total	167	100.0	246	100.0	76	100.0	
Korean Newspaper	1	144	75.4	225	84.6	56	71.8	9.26* df = 4
	2	32	16.8	26	9.8	15	19.2	
	3	15	7.8	15	5.6	7	9.0	
	Total	191	100.0	266	100.0	78	100.0	
Association With Koreans	A	129	69.0	140	54.5	31	40.8	19.68*** df = 2
	B	58	31.0	117	45.5	45	59.2	
	Total	187	100.0	257	100.0	76	100.0	
Preference of Korean Church	A	131	79.9	180	80.7	49	79.0	.40 df = 2
	B	33	20.1	43	19.3	13	21.0	
	Total	164	100.0	223	100.0	62	100.0	

1: Regular Subscription
2: Occasional Purchase at Newsstand
3: Do Not Read At All
A: Agree
B: Disagree
*: Significant at the .05 Level
**: Significant at the .01 Level
***: Significant at the .001 Level
    Otherwise Not Significant

Appendix D

Table 4.8 Relationship Between Cultural Assimilation and Ethnic Attachment (I)

			Male N	Male %	Female N	Female %
Reading of American Newspaper	A	1	57	90.5	64	94.1
		2	90	92.8	94	93.1
		3	106	93.0	138	90.2
	B	1	59	98.3	63	100
		2	88	98.9	98	100
		3	104	96.3	143	97.3
	C	1	60	95.2	68	97.1
		2	95	96.0	99	95.2
		3	110	96.5	148	95.5
Reading of American Magazine	A	1	71	94.7	69	89.6
		2	58	92.1	66	93.0
		3	123	91.1	157	92.4
	B	1	67	98.5	70	98.6
		2	59	100	74	100
		3	124	96.1	156	98.1
	C	1	72	94.7	75	94.9
		2	63	98.4	75	98.7
		3	129	95.6	161	94.7
Favoring of Name Change	A		127	93.4	154	90.1
	B		120	97.6	162	98.3
	C		131	96.3	166	94.7

1: Regular Subscription
2: Occasional Purchase at Newsstand
3: Do Not Read At All
A: Those who think that family duty should be given priority.
B: Those who do not feel ashamed of being born a Korean.
C: Those who think their children should speak Korean well.

Table 4.9 Relationship Between Cultural Assimilation and Ethnic Attachment (II)

		Korean Newspaper 1 N	1 %	2 N	2 %	3 N	3 %	Total N	Total %	Association with Koreans Agree N	Agree %	Disagree N	Disagree %	Total N	Total %	Preferred Church Agree N	Agree %	Disagree N	Disagree %	Total N	Total %
American Newspaper	1	108	81.2	11	8.3	14	10.5	133	100	62	47.7	68	52.3	130	100	18	16.8	89	83.2	107	100
	2	162	78.6	34	16.5	10	4.9	206	100	112	56.3	87	43.7	199	100	36	20.6	139	79.4	175	100
	3	204	75.0	40	14.7	28	10.3	272	100	172	65.4	91	34.6	263	100	47	20.3	185	79.7	232	100
		Chi-Square Value = 9.54*, df = 4								Chi-Square Value = 11.81**, df = 2						Chi-Square Value = .69, df = 2					
American Magazine	1	123	78.3	18	11.5	16	10.2	157	100	80	53.0	71	47.0	151	100	29	22.7	99	77.3	128	100
	2	106	75.2	27	19.1	8	5.7	141	100	78	56.1	61	43.9	139	100	21	17.9	96	82.1	117	100
	3	244	79.0	39	12.6	26	8.4	309	100	184	62.0	113	38.0	297	100	50	18.8	216	81.2	266	100
		Chi-Square Value = 5.89, df = 4								Chi-Square Value = 3.66, df = 2						Chi-Square Value = 1.08, df = 2					
Name Change	For	250	79.9	37	11.8	26	8.3	313	100	173	56.7	132	43.3	305	100	53	20.5	206	79.5	259	100
	Against	183	75.9	36	14.9	22	9.2	241	100	145	62.0	89	38.0	234	100	42	20.1	167	79.9	209	100
		Chi-Square Value = 1.38, df = 2								Chi-Square Value = 1.30, df = 1						Chi-Square Value = 0, df = 1					

1: Regular Subscription
2: Occasional Purchase at Newsstand
3: Do Not Read At All
*: Significant at the .05 Level
**: Significant at the .01 Level; Otherwise Not Significant

Table 4.10 English Proficiency by Three Items of Ethnic Attachment

		Male			Female		
		N	Mean	SD	N	Mean	SD
Korean Newspaper	Regular Subscription	251	8.86	2.78	251	8.86	2.78
	Occasional Purchase	42	9.02	3.43	43	8.53	3.55
	Do Not Read	16	11.00	3.20	36	8.56	3.70
	Statistical Test	F=2.44, df=2,306			F=.33, df=2,327		
Association With Koreans	Agree	154	9.21	3.36	190	8.40	3.02
	Disagree	116	10.26	2.66	131	9.39	2.77
	Statistical Test	F=7.61**, df=1,268			F=8.81**, df=1,319		
Preferred Church	Agree	48	9.48	3.49	53	8.75	2.73
	Disagree	186	9.84	2.93	226	8.63	3.00
	Statistical Test	F=.53, df=1,232			F=.07, df=1,277		

** Significant at the .01 Level; Otherwise Not Significant

Table 5.1 Korean Friends

How Did You Meet Your Friends?	Male		Female		Total	
	N	%	N	%	N	%
Kin	152	18.8	233	24.4	385	21.8
(Old) Friends	118	14.6	101	10.6	219	12.5
Alumni	133	16.4	130	13.6	263	14.9
Church	142	17.6	172	18.0	314	17.8
Workplace	90	11.1	95	10.0	185	10.5
School	52	6.4	58	6.1	110	6.2
Neighborhood	42	5.2	62	6.5	104	5.9
Other	80	9.9	103	10.8	183	10.4
Total	809	100	954	100	1,763	100

Appendix D

Table 5.2 Non-Korean Friends

How Did You Meet Your Friends?	Male						Female					
	White Friends		Asian Friends		Black or Mexican Friends		White Friends		Asian Friends		Black or Mexican Friends	
	N	%	N	%	N	%	N	%	N	%	N	%
School	22	13.4	10	35.7	3	12.5	37	19.4	11	20.8	7	25.9
Workplace	82	50.0	11	39.3	14	58.4	72	37.9	24	45.3	14	51.9
Church	6	3.7			2	8.3	19	10.0	1	1.9		
Neighborhood	11	6.7	1	3.6	2	8.3	33	17.4	7	13.1	4	14.8
Kin	4	2.4	1	3.6			2	1.1	1	1.9	1	3.7
Others	39	23.8	5	17.8	3	12.5	27	14.2	9	17.0	1	3.7
Total	164	100	28	100	24	100	190	100	53	100	27	100

Table 5.3 Association with White Friends and Participation in American Voluntary Association Among Three Groups of Respondents

			White Friends			American Voluntary Association		
			Yes	No	Total	Yes	No	Total
Male	Non-College Graduates	N %	14 18.4	62 81.6	76 100	3 3.9	73 96.5	76 100
	Korean-College Graduates	N %	39 33.1	79 66.9	118 100	3 2.5	115 97.5	118 100
	American-College Graduates	N %	31 57.4	23 42.6	54 100	10 18.5	44 81.5	54 100
	Chi-Square Value Degree of Freedom		21.49*** 2			16.81*** 2		
Female	Non-College Graduates	N %	19 16.4	97 83.6	116 100	2 1.7	114 98.3	116 100
	Korean-College Graduates	N %	57 38.3	92 61.7	149 100	12 8.1	137 91.9	149 100
	American-College Graduates	N %	12 48	13 52	25 100	7 28	18 72	25 100
	Chi-Square Value Degree of Freedom		18.80*** 2			21.44*** 2		

***: Significant at the .001 Level

Table 5.4 Length of Residence in the U.S. and Association with White Friends and Participation in American Voluntary Associations

Length of Residence		White Friend			American Voluntary Association		
		Yes	No	Total	Yes	No	Total
2 Years or Less	N	21	66	87	3	84	87
	%	24.1	75.9	100	3.4	96.6	100
3-4 Years	N	45	105	150	6	144	150
	%	30.0	70.0	100	4.0	96.0	100
5-6 Years	N	39	109	148	9	139	148
	%	26.4	73.6	100	6.1	93.9	100
7-8 Years	N	38	68	106	8	98	106
	%	35.8	64.2	100	12.0	92.5	100
9-10 Years	N	24	26	50	6	44	50
	%	48.0	52.0	100	12.0	88.0	100
11 Years or More	N	34	40	74	18	56	74
	%	45.9	54.1	100	24.3	75.7	100
Chi-Square Value		17.81**			33.84***		
Degree of Freedom		5			5		

**Significant at the .01 level.
***Significant at the .001 level.

Appendix D

Table 5.5 Length of Residence in the U.S. and Social Assimilation Among Three Groups of Respondents

			2 Years or Less N	%	3 - 4 Years N	%	5 - 6 Years N	%	7 - 8 Years N	%	9 - 10 Years N	%	11 Years or More N	%	Chi-Square
1	AVA	Yes	1	3.2	0		1	1.9	2	6.5	1	3.6			3.39
		No	30	96.8	50	100	51	98.1	29	93.5	27	96.4			df=4
		Total	31	100	50	100	52	100	31	100	28	100			
	AF	Yes	6	19.4	7	14.0	8	15.4	6	19.4	6	21.4			1.03
		No	25	80.6	43	86.0	44	84.6	25	80.6	22	78.6			df=4
		Total	31	100	50	100	52	100	31	100	28	100			
2	AVA	Yes	1	2.3	1	1.4	2	3.1	3	6.5	8	19.5			19.10***
		No	42	97.7	72	98.6	63	96.9	43	93.5	33	80.5			df=4
		Total	43	100	73	100	65	100	46	100	41	100			
		Yes	10	23.3	24	33.3	17	26.2	23	50.5	22	53.7			15.46**
		No	33	76.7	48	66.7	48	73.8	23	50.5	19	46.3			df=4
		Total	43	100	72	100	65	100	46	100	41	100			
3		Yes					5	25.0	2	11.8	3	25.0	7	23.3	1.25
		No					15	75.0	15	88.2	9	75.0	23	76.7	df=3
		Total					17	100	17	100	12	100	30	100	
	AF	Yes					12	60.0	7	41.2	9	75.0	15	50.0	3.74
		No					8	40.0	10	58.8	3	25.0	15	50.0	df=3
		Total					20	100	17	100	12	100	30	100	

1: Non-college graduates; 2: Korean-college graduates; 3: American-college graduates
AVA: Joining American voluntary associations; AF: Association with American friends
***Significant at .001 level; **Significant at .01 level

Table 5.6 Association with Korean Friends, Kin, and Participation in Korean Voluntary Associations Among Three Groups of Respondents

			Korean Friends			Kin			Korean Voluntary Association		
			Yes	No	Total	Yes	No	Total	Yes	No	Total
Male	Non-College Graduates	N	68	8	76	58	18	76	59	17	76
		%	89.5	10.5	100	76.3	23.7	100	77.6	22.4	100
	Korean-College Graduates	N	114	4	118	90	28	118	90	28	118
		%	96.6	3.4	100	76.3	23.7	100	76.3	23.7	100
	American-College Graduates	N	51	3	54	40	14	54	39	15	54
		%	94.4	5.6	100	74.1	25.9	100	72.2	27.8	100
	Chi-Square Value Degree of Freedom		4.17 2			1.30 2			.53 2		
Female	Non-College Graduates	N	105	11	116	89	27	116	89	27	116
		%	90.5	9.5	100	76.7	23.3	100	76.7	23.3	100
	Korean-College Graduates	N	137	12	149	104	45	149	110	39	149
		%	91.9	8.1	100	69.8	30.2	100	73.8	26.2	100
	American-College Graduates	N	21	4	25	19	6	25	20	5	25
		%	84	16	100	76	24	100	80.0	20.0	100
	Chi-Sqaure Value N Degree of Freedom %		1.61 2			1.71 2			.60 2		

All of the Chi-square tests are not significant

Table 5.7 Length of Residence in the U.S. and Association With Korean Intimate Groups Among Male Respondents

Number of Years		Korean Friends			Kin			Korean VA		
		Yes	No	Total	Yes	No	Total	Yes	No	Total
2 or less	N	42	0	42	35	7	42	30	12	42
	%	100		100	83.3	16.7	100	71.4	28.6	100
3 - 4	N	61	5	66	51	15	66	51	15	66
	%	92.4	7.6	100	77.3	22.7	100	77.3	22.7	100
5 - 6	N	66	4	70	52	18	70	51	19	70
	%	94.3	5.7	100	74.3	25.7	100	72.9	27.1	100
7 - 8	N	45	3	48	29	19	48	42	6	48
	%	93.8	6.2	100	60.4	39.6	100	87.5	12.5	100
9 - 10	N	21	3	24	19	5	24	16	8	24
	%	87.5	12.5	100	79.2	20.8	100	66.7	73.3	100
11 or more	N	28	3	31	24	7	31	23	8	31
	%	90.3	9.7	100	77.4	22.6	100	74.2	25.8	100
Chi-Sqaure Value			5.12			7.46			5.56	
Df			5			5			5	

VA: Voluntary Association
All of the Chi-Square tests are not significant

Table 5.8 Length of Residence in the U.S. and Association With Korean Intimate Groups Among Female Respondents

Number of Years		Korean Friends			Kin			Korean VA		
		Yes	No	Total	Yes	No	Total	Yes	No	Total
2 or less	N	43	2	45	35	10	45	34	11	45
	%	95.6	4.4	100	77.8	22.2	100	75.6	24.4	100
3 - 4	N	73	11	84	65	19	84	58	26	84
	%	86.9	13.1	100	77.4	22.6	100	69.0	31.0	100
5 - 6	N	72	6	78	57	21	78	61	17	78
	%	92.3	7.7	100	73.1	26.9	100	78.2	21.8	100
7 - 8	N	54	4	58	41	17	58	46	12	58
	%	93.1	6.9	100	70.7	29.3	100	79.3	20.7	100
9 - 10	N	23	3	26	19	7	26	22	4	26
	%	88.5	11.5	100	73.1	26.9	100	84.6	15.4	100
11 or more	N	35	8	43	35	8	43	34	9	43
	%	81.4	18.6	100	81.4	18.6	100	79.1	20.9	100
Chi-Square Value		7.00			2.15			3.86		
Df		5			5			5		

VA: Voluntary Association
All of the Chi-square tests are not significant

Appendix D

Table 5.9 Presence of Kin in the Los Angeles Area, Association with Korean Friends, and Participation in Korean Voluntary Association

				Korean Friends			Korean Voluntary Association		
				Yes	No	Total	Yes	No	Total
Presence of Kin in the Los Angeles Area	Male	Yes	N	198	12	210	157	53	210
			%	94.3	5.7	100	74.8	25.2	100
		No	N	65	6	71	56	15	71
			%	91.5	8.5	100	78.9	21.1	100
	Female	Yes	N	228	24	252	187	65	252
			%	90.5	9.5	100	74.2	25.8	100
		No	N	72	10	82	68	14	82
			%	87.8	12.2	100	82.9	17.1	100
	Chi-Square Value			Male	Female		Male	Female	
				.66	.48		.29	2.14	
	Df			1	1		1	1	

All of Chi-square tests are not significant

Table 5.10 Social Assimilation in Relation to Association with Korean Friends, Kin, and Participation in Korean Voluntary Association

				Korean Friends			Kin			Korean Association		
				Yes	No	Total	Yes	No	Total	Yes	No	Total
To Have White Friends	Male	Yes	N	88	7	95	74	21	95	68	27	95
			%	92.6	7.4	100	77.9	22.1	100	71.6	28.4	100
		No	N	175	11	186	136	50	186	145	41	186
			%	94.1	5.9	100	73.1	26.9	100	78.0	22.0	100
	Female	Yes	N	101	5	106	79	27	106	88	18	106
			%	95.3	4.7	100	74.5	25.5	100	83.0	17.0	100
		No	N	199	29	228	173	55	228	167	61	228
			%	87.3	12.7	100	75.9	24.1	100	73.2	26.8	100
	Chi-Square Value			Male	Female		Male	Female		Male	Female	
				.22	4.23*		.76	.07		1.09	3.31	
	Df			1	1		1	1		1	1	

*Significant at .05 level; otherwise not significant

Table 5.11 Distribution of the Persons With Whom Respondents Discuss Their Personal Problems

Types of Persons	Number of Respondents					
	Male (N=272)		Female (N=324)		Total (N=596)	
	N	%	N	%	N	%
Spouse	203	74.6	206	63.6	409	68.5
Parent(s)	59	21.7	77	23.8	136	22.8
Child(ren)	44	16.2	59	18.2	103	17.3
Other kin	66	24.3	71	21.9	137	22.9
Korean Friend(s)	126	46.3	125	38.9	257	42.1
American Friend(s)	34	12.5	25	7.7	259	9.9
Colleague(s) at Work	29	16.7	14	4.3	43	7.2
Minister or Priest	55	20.2	64	19.8	119	20.1
Others	9	3.3	11	3.4	20	3.4

Table 5.12 Types of Voluntary Association Participated*

Types of Voluntary Association Participated In	Korean Association						American Association					
	Male		Female		Combined		Male		Female		Combined	
	N	%	N	%	N	%	N	%	N	%	N	%
Social Club	22	8.5	9	3.1	31	5.6	17	60.0	5	16.1	22	37.9
Student Club	6	2.3	2	.7	8	1.5						
Church	189	73.0	241	83.7	430	78.6	3	11.1	15	48.4	18	31.0
Religious Group	6	2.3	13	4.5	19	3.5	6	22.2	5	16.1	11	19.2
Senior Citizen's Group	12	4.6	4	1.4	16	2.9			1	3.2	1	1.7
Alumni Group	20	7.7	18	6.3	38	6.9	1	3.7	1	3.2	2	3.4
Social Service Group	1	.4			1	.2			2	6.5	2	3.4
Academic or Artistic Group	1	.4	1	.3	2	.4			2	6.5	2	3.4
Others	2	.8			2	.4						
Total	259	100.0	288	100.0	547	100.0	27	100.0	31	100.0	58	100.0

*N of this table is based on all of the voluntary associations participated by the respondents.

Table 6.1 Current Occupations of Respondents

Occupational Categories	Male		Female		Combined	
	N	%	N	%	N	%
Professionals and Semi-Professionals	62	25.7	44	20.7	106	23.4
Proprietors and Managers	82	34.0	62	28.9	144	31.6
Other White-Collar Workers	26	10.8	37	17.2	63	13.8
Skilled Workers	23	9.6	6	2.8	29	6.4
Semi-Skilled or Unskilled Workers	48	19.9	65	30.4	113	24.8
Total	241	100.0	214	100.0	455	100.0

Table 6.2 Methods of Job Information Transmission in Relation to Quality of Job Introduced

Indices of Quality of Job		Methods of Job Information Transmission				Chi-Square Test
		Personal Contact		Other Methods		
		N	%	N	%	
A	Good	52	33.1	71	49	Chi-Square Value=7.19** df=1
	Bad	105	66.9	74	51	
	Total	157	100.0	145	100.0	
B	Sufficient	58	38.7	86	58.9	Chi-Square Value=11.33*** df=1
	Insufficient	92	61.3	60	41.1	
	Total	150	100.0	146	100.0	
C	$10,999 or less	81	51.9	50	31.8	Chi-Square Value=21.04*** df=3
	$11,000-$16,999	47	30.1	44	28.0	
	$17,000-$24,999	16	10.3	33	21.0	
	$25,000 or More	12	7.7	30	19.2	
	Total	156	100.0	157	100.0	

A: Promotion Chance or Future Prospect at the Current Job
B: Opportunity to Use One's Ability at the Current Job
C: Individual Annual Income
**: Significant at the .01 Level
***: Significant at the .001 Level

Table 6.3 Distribution of Respondents by Occupation and Ethnicity of Major Work Colleagues or Customers

		Ethnicity of Major Work Colleagues or Customers							
		Whites		Whites & Minorities		Minorities		Total	
		N	%	N	%	N	%	N	%
Male	Professionals & Semi-Professionals	27	49.1	6	10.9	22	40.0	55	100
	Proprietors & Managers	26	33.8	16	20.8	35	45.4	77	100
	Other White-Collar Workers	3	12.5	5	20.8	16	66.7	24	100
	Blue-Collar Workers	25	37.9	3	4.5	38	57.6	66	100
Female	Professionals & Semi-Professionals	26	63.4	6	14.6	9	22.0	41	100
	Proprietors & Managers	26	43.3	11	18.3	23	38.4	60	100
	Other White-Collar Workers	12	37.5	4	12.5	16	50.0	32	100
	Blue-Collar Workers	12	20.3	9	15.3	38	64.4	59	100

Table 6.4 Distribution of Respondents by Occupation and Proportion of Those Who Work on Saturday or for More than 8 Hours a Day

		Work on Saturday								Work for More Than 8 Hours A Day	
		Every Saturday		Certain Saturdays		Not at All		Total			
		N	%	N	%	N	%	N	%	N	%
Male	Professionals & Semi-Professionals	16	29.6	13	24.1	25	46.3	54	100	19	35.8
	Proprietors & Managers	57	71.3	16	20.0	7	8.8	80	100	54	72.0
	Other White-Collar Workers	4	17.4	12	52.2	7	30.4	23	100	6	26.1
	Blue-Collar Workers	25	37.3	22	32.8	20	29.9	67	100	22	33.3
Female	Professionals & Semi-Professionals	6	14.6	21	51.2	14	34.2	41	100	3	7.3
	Proprietors & Managers	44	73.4	8	13.3	8	13.3	60	100	39	65.0
	Other White-Collar Workers	5	14.7	11	32.4	18	52.9	34	100	2	6.3
	Blue-Collar Workers	11	19.0	20	34.5	27	46.5	58	100	15	25.9

Table 6.5 Distribution of Respondents by Their Annual Individual and Family Incomes

		Annual Income									
		$10,999 or Less		$11,000–$16,999		$17,000–$24,999		$25,000 or More		Total	
		N	%	N	%	N	%	N	%	N	%
Male	I	68	30.4	64	28.6	41	18.3	51	22.7	224	100
	F	27	12.1	44	19.6	63	28.1	90	40.2	224	100
Female	I	83	47.4	42	24.0	24	13.7	26	14.9	175	100
	F	33	17.9	37	20.1	39	21.2	75	40.8	184	100

I: Annual Individual Income
F: Annual Family Income

Table 6.6 Distribution of Respondents by Occupation and Annual Individual Income

		\$10,999 or Less N	\$10,999 or Less %	\$11,000-\$16,999 N	\$11,000-\$16,999 %	\$17,000-\$24,999 N	\$17,000-\$24,999 %	\$25,000 or More N	\$25,000 or More %	Total N	Total %
Male	Professionals & Semi-Professionals	13	23.6	15	27.3	12	21.8	15	27.3	55	100
Male	Proprietors & Managers	20	25.3	19	24.1	12	15.2	28	35.4	79	100
Male	Other White-Collar Workers	10	41.6	6	25.0	4	16.7	4	16.7	24	100
Male	Blue-Collar Workers	24	38.7	23	37.1	11	17.7	4	6.5	62	100
Male	Chi-Square Test	Chi-Square Value=20.4*, df=9									
Female	Professionals & Semi-Professionals	12	33.4	16	44.4	7	19.4	1	2.8	36	100
Female	Proprietors & Managers	10	17.5	11	19.3	14	24.6	22	38.6	57	100
Female	Other White-Collar Workers	21	75.0	5	17.9	0		2	7.1	28	100
Female	Blue-Collar Workers	40	78.4	9	17.6	2	4.0			51	100
Female	Chi-Square Test	Chi-Square Value=82.7***, df=9									

*: Significant at the .05 Level
***: Significant at the .001 Level

Table 6.7 Multiple Classification Analysis of Annual Individual Income by Education, Ethnicity, Occupation and Length of Residence in U.S. (Employed Non-Small Business Males)

Variables		N	A	B	C
Occupation	1	48	1.32	.70	.37
Occupation	2	21	-.27	.06	.49
Occupation	3	55	-1.05	-.64	-.51
Occupation	(Eta & beta)		.32	.18	.13
Ethnicity	Whites	49	1.46	1.06	1.05
Ethnicity	Minority Members	75	-.96	-.76	-.69
Ethnicity	(Eta & beta)		.35	.28	.25
Education	Non-College	36	-1.13	-.47	.08
Education	Korean-College	57	-.51	-.55	-.14
Education	American-College	31	2.26	1.56	.17
Education	(Eta & beta)		.39	.26	.04

Multiple R .502 .636
Multiple R Squared .252 .404
Grand Mean = 8.74

A: unadjusted; B: adjusted for independent variables;
C: adjusted for independent variables and covariate;
1: professionals or semi-professionals
2: other white-collar workers
3: blue-collar workers

Appendix D

Table 6.8 Multiple Classification Analysis of Annual
Individual Income by Ethnicity, Education
and Length of Residence in U.S.
(Small Businessmen)

	Variables	N	\multicolumn{3}{c}{Deviation from Grand Mean}
			A	B	C
Ethnicity	Whites	23	.74	.72	.66
	Minority Members	46	-.37	-.36	-.32
	(Eta & beta)		.14	.14	.12
Education	Non-College	14	-3.23	-3.18	-2.61
	Korean-College	43	.43	.39	.54
	American-College	12	2.21	2.30	1.11
	(Eta & beta)		.47	.47	.36
Multiple R				.448	.571
Multiple R Squared				.238	.326
Grand Mean = 9.87					

A: unadjusted; B: adjusted for independent variables;
C: adjusted for independent variables and covariate

Table 6.9 Multiple Classification Analysis of Annual
Individual Income by Occupation and Ethnicity
(Employed Females)

		Variables	N	\multicolumn{2}{c}{Deviation from Grand Mean}
				A	B
I	Ethnicity	Whites	68	1.04	.56
		Minority Members	101	-.70	-.38
		(Eta & beta)		.23	.13
	Occupation	1	35	.16	-.03
		2	57	2.96	2.91
		3	26	-1.78	-1.80
		4	51	-2.51	-2.32
		(Eta & beta)		.63	.61
	Multiple R				.645
	Multiple R Squared				.416
	Grand Mean = 7.67				
II	Ethnicity	Whites	42	.98	.32
		Minority Members	70	-.59	-.19
		(Eta & beta)		.28	.09
	Occupation	1	35	1.67	1.46
		3	26	-.28	-.37
		4	51	-1.00	-.81
		(Eta & beta)		.43	.37
	Multiple R				.494
	Multiple R Squared				.244
	Grand Mean = 6.16				

(continued)

I: all employed females
II: females employed in occupations other than small business
A: unadjusted; B: adjusted for independent variable
1: professionals and semi-professionals
2: small businesswomen
3: other white-collar workers
4: blue-collar workers

Table 6.10 Subjective Work Experiences of Respondents

	Male		Female		Combined	
	N	%	N	%	N	%
(1)	157	70.1	117	62.9	274	66.8
(2)	97	45.5	74	38.9	171	42.4
(3)	132	57.9	84	44.4	216	51.8
(4)	137	59.1	109	57.7	246	58.4
(5)	114	52.8	110	62.9	224	57.3
(6)	122	57.5	102	61.1	224	59.1
(7)	138	70.8	117	79.6	255	74.6
(8)	168	62.9	210	67.3	378	65.3

Table 6.11 Occupation of Respondents and Their Subjective Work Experiences

Items	Occupation							
	Professionals and Semi-Professionals		Proprietors and Managers		Other White-Collar Workers		Blue-Collar Workers	
	N	%	N	%	N	%	N	%
1	70	72.9	94	70.7	36	66.7	68	56.7
2	38	43.2	82	63.6	21	38.2	26	20.8
3	44	45.8	109	78.0	17	29.8	41	34.5
4	81	82.7	78	56.5	36	64.3	46	37.4
5	77	81.9	63	52.5	35	62.5	46	39.3
6	58	65.2	87	71.9	27	50.0	50	45.0
7	70	77.8	84	75.4	30	73.2	68	70.8
8	75	72.9	89	64.0	40	65.6	70	51.5

Table 6.12 Subjective Work Experiences Among Three Groups of Respondents(1)

Items	Male							Female						
	A		B		C		Chi-Square Value	A		B		C		Chi-Square Value
	N	%	N	%	N	%		N	%	N	%	N	%	
2	13	24.5	48	49.5	26	60.5	13.91***							
4	23	39.7	61	58.1	39	83.0	20.10***	24	44.4	65	6.13	11	73.3	5.92*
5	28	52.8	44	44.9	32	74.4	10.49**							
6	41	56.9	65	58.6	42	80.8	9.11**	71	65.1	89	62.7	21	91.3	7.30*

(1) Present only the work experience items which show significant differences among the three groups of respondents; A: Non-College Graduates; B: Korean-College Graduates; C: American-College Graduates; ***: Significant at the .001 Level; **: Significant at the .01 Level; *: Significant at the .05 Level

Table 7.1 Distribution of Married Respondents' Families by Six Categories of Task Performance

Category of Performer	Task Items											
	Grocery Shopping				Housekeeping				Laundry			
	RB		RE		RB		RE		RB		RE	
	N	%	N	%	N	%	N	%	N	%	N	%
A	266	55.0	263	54.5	278	57.4	225	46.6	286	59.2	250	51.8
B	57	11.8	143	29.6	23	4.8	129	26.6	17	3.5	99	20.4
C	61	12.6	17	3.5	24	5.1	10	2.1	36	7.5	19	3.9
D	9	1.9	29	66.0	22	4.6	69	14.3	38	7.9	51	10.6
E	52	10.8	5	1.0	84	17.4	27	5.6	58	12.0	40	8.3
F	38	7.9	26	5.4	52	10.7	23	4.8	48	9.9	24	5.0
Total	483	100.0	483	100.0	483	100.0	483	100.0	483	100.0	483	100.0

Category of Performer	Dishwashing				Disposal of Garbage				Family Budget			
	RB		RE		RB		RE		RB		RE	
	N	%	N	%	N	%	N	%	N	%	N	%
A	287	59.4	275	56.9	129	26.7	81	16.8	191	39.5	146	30.2
B	12	2.5	75	15.5	12	2.5	87	18.0	42	8.7	214	44.3
C	28	5.8	10	2.1	182	37.6	108	38.9	208	43.1	91	18.8
D	46	9.5	44	9.1	66	13.7	36	7.5	7	1.4	6	1.2
E	64	13.3	53	11.0	53	11.0	63	13.0	10	2.1	4	.8
F	46	9.5	26	5.4	41	8.5	28	5.8	25	5.2	22	4.7
Total	483	100.0	483	100.0	483	100.0	483	100.0	483	100.0	483	100.0

RB: Role Behavior
RE: Role Expectation
A: Wife alone performs; wife performs more than husband
B: Husband and wife performs equally
C: Husband alone performs; husband performs more than wife
D: Children perform less than **parent(s)**
E: Children alone perform; children perform more than parent(s)
F: Other family members perform

Table 7.2 Discrepancy Between Role Behavior and Role Expectation Among Family Members (Percentage)

Task Items	Families With No Children*		Families With Children					
			A		B		C	
	(1)	(2)	(3)	(4)	(5)	(6)	(7)	(8)
Grocery Shopping	9.5	13.1	10.3	-2.8	5.0	8.3	1.5	12.4
Housekeeping	13.3	17.2	26.5	3.8	21.7	22.3	1.4	12.4
Laundry	16.4	13.7	21.1	.9	13.4	11.1	-1.5	10.6
Dishwashing	21.0	7.0	16.2	-2.9	13.4	9.2	-3.0	10.5
Garbage Disposal	20.0	6.7	22.1	13.4	18.3	10.2	2.9	12.3
Family Budget	18.7	13.2	13.1	16.2	10.0	9.3	- .01	3.8

A: Percent of wives who perform tasks more than they feel obliged.
B: Percent of husbands who perform tasks less than they feel obliged.
C: Percent of children or other family members who perform more than wives think that they are obliged.
(1) Families in which husband alone is employed.
(2) Families in which both husband and wife are employed.
(3) Non-employed wives.
(4) Employed wives.
(5) Husbands of non-employed wives.
(6) Husbands of employed wives.
(7) Children or other family members of non-employed wives.
(8) Children or other family members of employed wives.
*A and B are combined.

Table 7.3 Distribution of Respondents' Families With Children By Three Categories of Actual Performance (Role Behavior)

		Wives				Chi-Square Test	Husbands				Chi-Square Test
		A		B			C		D		
		N	%	N	%		N	%	N	%	
Grocery Shopping	(1)	47	69.1	55	52.4	5.91* DF=2	40	66.7	48	44.4	8.30* DF=2
	(2)	14	20.6	26	24.7		12	20.0	29	26.9	
	(3)	7	10.3	24	22.9		8	13.3	31	28.7	
	Total	68	100.0	105	100.0		60	100.0	108	100.0	
Housekeeping	(1)	55	80.9	44	41.9	26.00*** DF=2	42	70.0	46	42.6	11.74** DF=2
	(2)	1	1.5	10	9.5		3	5.0	13	12.0	
	(3)	12	17.6	51	48.6		15	25.0	49	45.4	
	Total	68	100.0	105	100.0		60	100.0	108	100.0	
Laundry	(1)	55	80.9	50	47.6	19.80*** DF=2	42	70.0	51	47.2	8.56* DF=2
	(2)	4	5.9	10	9.5		5	8.3	11	10.2	
	(3)	9	13.2	45	42.9		13	21.7	46	42.6	
	Total	68	100.0	105	100.0		60	100.0	108	100.0	
Dishwashing	(1)	58	85.3	48	45.7	27.27*** DF=2	41	68.3	48	44.4	10.24** DF=2
	(2)	1	1.5	7	6.7		5	8.3	8	7.4	
	(3)	9	13.2	50	47.6		14	23.4	52	48.2	
	Total	68	100.0	105	100.0		60	100.0	108	100.0	
Garbage	(1)	28	41.2	28	26.7	14.48** DF=2	20	33.3	14	13.0	10.44** DF=2
	(2)	27	39.7	27	25.7		22	36.7	45	41.6	
	(3)	13	19.1	50	47.6		18	30.0	49	45.4	
	Total	68	100.0	105	100.0		60	100.0	108	100.0	
Family Budget	(1)	32	47.1	46	43.8	.36 DF=2	22	36.7	34	31.5	3.16 DF=2
	(2)	32	47.1	54	51.4		36	60.0	62	57.4	
	(3)	4	5.8	5	4.8		2	3.3	12	11.1	
	Total	68	100.0	105	100.0		60	100.0	108	100.0	

A: Non-employed wives
B: Employed wives
C: Husbands of non-employed wives
D: Husbands of employed wives
(1) Wife performs predominantly
(2) Husband performs substantially
(3) Children of other family members are involved.
* Significant at the .05 level
** Significant at the .01 level
*** Significant at the .001 level

Appendix D

Table 7.4 Distribution of Respondents' Families With Children By Three Categories of Expected Performance (Role Expectation)

		Wives					Husbands				
		A		B		Chi-Square Test	C		D		Chi-Square Test
		N	%	N	%		N	%	N	%	
Grocery Shopping	(1)	40	58.8	58	55.2	.25 DF=2	42	70.0	51	47.2	9.55** DF=2
	(2)	22	32.4	36	34.3		15	25.0	38	35.2	
	(3)	6	8.8	11	10.5		3	5.0	19	17.6	
	Total	58	100.0	105	100.0		60	100.0	108	100.0	
House-keeping	(1)	37	54.4	40	38.1	8.51** DF=2	32	53.3	36	33.3	6.64* DF=2
	(2)	20	29.4	27	25.7		16	26.7	37	34.3	
	(3)	11	16.2	38	36.2		12	20.0	35	32.4	
	Total	68	100.0	105	100.0		60	100.0	108	100.0	
Laundry	(1)	40	58.8	49	46.7	6.80* DF=2	38	63.3	46	42.6	9.34** DF=2
	(2)	18	26.5	22	21.0		13	21.7	23	21.3	
	(3)	10	14.7	34	32.3		9	15.0	39	36.1	
	Total	68	100.0	105	100.0		60	100.0	108	100.0	
Dish-washing	(1)	47	69.1	51	48.6	9.36** DF=2	37	61.7	49	45.4	8.29** DF=2
	(2)	10	14.7	15	14.3		13	21.7	18	16.6	
	(3)	11	16.2	39	37.1		10	16.6	41	38.0	
	Total	68	100.0	105	100.0		60	100.0	108	100.0	
Garbage	(1)	13	19.1	14	13.3	7.57* DF=2	12	20.0	10	9.3	5.66* DF=2
	(2)	44	64.7	54	51.4		33	55.0	56	51.8	
	(3)	11	16.2	37	35.3		15	25.0	42	38.9	
	Total	58	100.0	105	100.0		50	100.0	108	100.0	
Family Budget	(1)	23	33.8	29	27.6	4.76 DF=2	14	23.3	28	25.9	.20 DF=2
	(2)	41	60.3	75	71.4		42	70.0	78	66.7	
	(3)	4	5.9	1	1.0		4	6.7	8	7.4	
	Total	68	100.0	105	100.0		60	100.0	108	100.0	

A: Non-employed wives
B: Employed wives
C: Husbands of non-employed wives
D: Husbands of employed wives
(1) Wife should perform predominantly
(2) Husband should perform substantially
(3) Children or other family members should be involved
 * Significant at the .05 level
** Significant at the .01 level

Table 8.1 Foremost Reasons for Attending Church

Reasons	N	%
Because it's been a habit to attend	20	4.7
For the sake of peace and security of mind	100	23.6
To see friends and relatives	15	3.5
Because minister (or priest) have been so kind to me	9	2.1
Because it's a believers' obligation	23	5.4
To worship God	95	22.4
To hear sermon	60	14.2
To seek salvation	81	19.1
Other	21	5.0
Total	424	100.0

Table 8.2 Ranked Reasons for Attending Church by Sex

	Reasons	Religious*	Psychological**	Social***	Other	Total
Male	First	118 (61.8%)	40 (20.9%)	17 (8.9%)	16 (8.4%)	191 (100%)
	Second	84 (64.6%)	19 (14.6%)	18 (13.8%)	9 (6.9%)	132 (100%)
	Third	65 (73.0%)	9 (10.1%)	12 (13.5%)	3 (3.4%)	89 (100%)
	Fourth	33 (63.5%)	9 (17.3%)	7 (13.5%)	3 (5.7%)	61 (100%)
Female	First	141 (60.5%)	60 (25.8%)	7 (3.0%)	25 (10.8%)	233 (100%)
	Second	145 (83.8%)	13 (7.5%)	10 (5.8%)	5 (2.9%)	173 (100%)
	Third	99 (72.8%)	25 (18.4%)	9 (6.6%)	3 (2.2%)	136 (100%)
	Fourth	48 (60.8%)	15 (19.0%)	7 (8.9%)	9 (11.4%)	79 (100%)

*Religious Reasons: "To seek salvation," "to worship God," "to hear sermon," and "because it's believers' obligation."
**Psychological Reason: "For the sake of peace and security of mind."
***Social Reasons: "To see friends and relatives," and "because ministers (or priests) have been so kind to me."

Table 8.3 Advantages and Disadvantages in Attending Church*

Advantages	(N=354)	Disadvantages	(N=119)
Peace of mind	173 (48.8%)	Gossiping	30 (25.2%)
Meeting people	109 (30.8%)	Seeking self interest	26 (21.8%)
Listening to sermons	59 (16.7%)	Wasting time	25 (21.0%)
Self improvement	41 (11.6%)	Schism and conflict	23 (19.3%)
Strengthening faith	24 (6.8%)	Solicitation of money	12 (10.1%)
Other**	83 (40.8%)	Other***	11 (9.2%)

*Frequency in this table is based on the addition of all expressed experiences of advantages and disadvantages reported by the respondents.
**Includes "receiving help when needed,", "learning," etc.
***Includes "hypocrisy," "exploitation of church members," "lack of harmony in the church," etc.

Table 8.4 Foremost Reason for and Foremost Advantage in Attending Church — A Cross-Tabulation

Foremost Advantage in Attending Church		Foremost Reason for Attending Church			
		Religious Motive	Peace of Mind	Meeting People	Total
Religious Aspect*	N	45	10	5	60
	%	75.0	16.7	8.3	100.0
Peace of Mind	N	75	51	3	129
	%	58.2	39.5	2.3	100.0
Meeting People	N	36	13	10	59
	%	61.0	22.0	17.0	100.0

*Included in "religious aspect"; "strengthening faith"; "listening to sermon"; "receiving grace".

Appendix D

Table 9.1 Economic Adaptation and Choice of Comparative Reference Group in Relation to Length of Residence in U.S.

Length of Residence	N	Economic Adaptation			Comparative Reference Group
		A (%)	B (%)	C (%)	D (%)
2 or less	87	37.9	11.5	5.7	20.2
3 - 4	150	44.0	14.8	18.7	22.3
5 - 6	148	46.6	40.5	24.5	20.4
7 - 8	106	65.1	52.4	56.6	30.8
9 - 10	50	64.1	53.1	75.0	34.7
11 or more	74	59.0	74.3	64.2	47.2

A: Proportion of respondents in white-collar occupations
B: Proportion of respondents who own their own homes
C: Proportion of high income earners ($17,000 or more annually)
D: Proportion of respondents who indicate white Americans as their comparative reference group

Table 9.2 Factor Analysis of Six Life-Experience Items by Varimax Rotation

Items	Factor 1	Factor 2
Regret	.77	-.06
Progress	.70	.11
Life Satisfaction	.81	.00
Loneliness	.66	.10
Powerlessness	-.02	.75
Normlessness	.10	.72

Table 9.3 Degree of Job Satisfaction and Score of Life Satisfaction

Degree of Job Satisfaction	Life Satisfaction Scores		
	N	Mean	SD
Very Much Dissatisfied	17	10.00	3.82
Somewhat Dissatisfied	91	12.25	3.46
Don't Know	18	11.56	3.50
Somewhat Satisfied	225	13.74	2.99
Very Much Satisfied	74	15.92	3.59

$F = 69.69$, Significant at the .001 Level

Table 9.4 Life Satisfaction Scores of Respondents in Relation to Length of Residence

Length of Residence (Years)	Male Respondents (N=281)			Female Respondents (N=334)		
	N	Mean	SD	N	Mean	SD
2 or Less	42	12.29	3.70	45	12.87	3.84
3 - 4	66	13.64	3.52	84	12.61	3.14
5 - 6	70	14.07	3.22	78	14.09	2.99
7 - 8	48	14.52	3.29	58	14.59	3.60
9 - 10	24	14.79	3.65	26	14.88	3.55
11 or More	31	14.61	3.98	43	15.53	2.88
	$F=2.76$ df=5,275 Sig. at .05			$F=6.61$ df=5,328 Sig. at .001		

Table 9.5 Life Satisfaction Scores of Male Professionals and Semi-Professionals in Relation to Length of Residence

Length of Sojourn (Years)	Life Satisfaction of Male Professionals and Semi-Professonals		
	N=62	Mean	SD
2 or Less	7	13.86	4.10
3 - 4	10	13.90	4.81
5 - 6	8	16.00	3.21
7 - 8	15	16.13	1.96
9 -10	9	15.56	3.57
11 or More	13	15.08	3.23

$F=.83$
df=5.56
N.S.

Appendix D

Table 9.6 Differential Effects of Dominant Group as a Reference Group on Minority's Life Satisfaction

Degree of Ethnic Attachment	Dominant Group as New Reference Group	Relation to Old Reference Group	Life Satisfaction
Strong	Abstract Aspiration Group	Adding	High
Weak	Concrete Comparative Group	Shifting	Low

Table 9.7 Variables Related to Relatively High Degree of Life Satisfaction of Respondents

Variables	Relationship	
	Male	Female
Length of Residence in U.S.	Longer	Longer
Age	Older	Older
Marital Status	Single	n.s.
Type of Residence	Homeowner	Homeowner
Education	American College	American College
Occupation	Professional or Semi-Professional	n.s.
Income	Higher	n.s.
Employment Status	n.s.	Non-Employment
Degree of Job Satisfaction	Satisfied	Satisfied
Acculturation	English Proficiency	n.s.
	American Newspapers	n.s.
	Name Change	n.s.
Perceived Social Acceptance	Perceived Acceptance	Perceived Acceptance
Ethnic Attachment	Korean Voluntary Assoc.	n.s.
	Ethnic Church Affiliation	n.s.
	Ethnic Church Attendance	n.s.

n.s.: Not Significant

References

Abrams, Franklin
1980 Immigration law and its enforcement: reflections of American immigration policy. Pp. 27–35 in Roy Simon Bryce-Laporte, ed., *Sourcebook on the New Immigration*. New Brunswick, N. J.: Transaction Books.

Adams, Bert N.
1970 Isolation, function, and beyond: American kinship in the 1960's. *Journal of Marriage and the Family* 32:575–97.

Adams, J. S.
1963a Toward an understanding on inequality. *Journal of Abnormal and Social Psychology* 67:422–36.
1963b Wage inequities, productivity and work quality. *Industrial Relations* 3:9–16.
1965 Just injustice in social exchange. Pp. 267–99 in L. Berkowitz, ed., *Advances in Experimental Social Psychology*.

Adams, Romanzo
(1937) *Interracial Marriage in Hawaii*. Montclair, N. J.
1967 Patterson Smith.

Aldous, Joan
1969 Occupational characteristics and males' role performance in the family. *Journal of Marriage and the Family* 31:707–12.

American Anthropological Association (Executive Board Committee on External Relations)
1978 Report on survey on HEW regulations on human subjects. *Anthropology Newsletter* 19:9–12.

Andrews, F., and Withey, S.
1976 Developing measures of perceived life quality: Results from several national surveys *Social Indicators Research* 1:1–26.

Araji, Sharon K.
1977 Husbands' and wives' attitude-behavior congruence on family roles. *Journal of Marriage and the Family* 39:309–20.

The Asian Student
1968 Kim, most popular Korean family name. March 10.

Axelson, Leland J.
1963 The marital adjustment and marital role definitions of husbands of working and nonworking wives. *Marriage and Family Living* 25:189–95.

Babchuk, Nicholas
1965   Primary friends and kin: A study of the associations of middle class couples. *Social Forces* 43:483–93.

Babchuk, Nicholas, and Edwards, John N.
1965   Voluntary associations and the integration hypothesis. *Social Inquiry* 35:149–62.

Babchuk, Nicholas, and Thompson, Ralph V.
1962   The voluntary associations of friends. *American Sociological Review* 27:647–55.

Barnett, Milton L.
1960   Kinship as a factor affecting Cantonese economic adaptation in the United States. *Human Organization* 19:40–46.

Becker, Henry Jay
1978   Racial segregation among places of employment. Paper presented at the Annual Meeting of the American Sociological Association, San Francisco, September 1–4.

Becker, Tamar
1968   Patterns of attitudinal changes among foreign students. *American Journal of Sociology* 73:431–42.

Berry, Brewton, and Tischler, Henry L.
1978   *Race and Ethnic Relations.* Boston: Houghton Mifflin.

Blau, Francine
1978   The data on women workers. Pp. 29–62 in A. H. Stromberg and S. Harkess, eds., *Women Working: Theories and Facts in Perspective.* Palo Alto, Calif.: Mayfield.

Blau, Francine, and Jusenius, Carol L.
1976   Economists' approaches to sex segregation in the labor market: An appraisal. Pp. 181–99 in M. Blaxall and B. Reagan, eds., *Women and the Workplace.* Chicago: University of Chicago Press.

Blau, Peter M., and Duncan, Otis D.
1967   *The American Occupational Structure.* New York: Wiley.

Blood, R. O., and Wolfe, W.
1960   *Husbands and Wives: The Dynamics of Married Living.* New York: The Free Press.

Bogardus, Emory S.
1930   A race-relations cycle. *American Journal of Sociology* 35:612–17.
1949   Cultural pluralism and acculturation. *Sociology and Social Research* 34:125–29.
1968   Comparing racial distance in Ethiopia, South Africa, and the United States. *Sociology and Social Research* 52:149–56.

Bonacich, Edna
1972   A theory of ethnic antagonism: the split labor market. *American Sociological Review* 37:547–59.
1978   U.S. capitalism and Korean immigrant small business: A study in the relationship between class and ethnicity. Paper

presented at the 9th World Congress of Sociology in Uppsala, Sweden, August 14–19.
1979 New immigrant small business as a form of cheap labor. Paper presented at the 145th National Meeting of the American Association for the Advancement of Science, Houston, Texas, January 3–8.

Bonacich, Edna, and Jung, Tae Hwan
1979 A portrait of Korean small business in Los Angeles, 1977. Paper presented at the meeting of Korean Community in Los Angeles: Problems and Issues in Settlement. Koryo Research Institute, Los Angeles, March 10.

Bonacich, Edna; Light, Ivan; and Wong, Charles Choy
1980 Korean immigrant small business in Los Angeles. Pp. 167–84 in Roy Simon Bryce-Laporte ed., *Sourcebook on the New Immigration*, New Brunswick, N. J.: Transaction Books.

Bott, Elizabeth
1971 *Family and Social Network*. New York: The Free Press.

Bowman, Mary Jean
1966 The human investment: Revolution in economic thought. *Sociology of Education* 39:111–37.

Brown, David G.
1965 *The Market for College Teachers*, Chapel Hill: University of North Carolina Press.

Bruce, J. M.
1970 Intragenerational occupational mobility and visiting with kin and friend. *Social Forces* 49:117–27.

Brunner, G. A., and Carroll, S. J.
1967– Effect of prior telephone appointments on completion rates
1968 and response content. *Public Opinion Quarterly* 31:652–54.

Bryce-Laporte, Roy S.
1980 *Sourcebook on the New Immigration*. New Brunswick, N. J.: Transaction Books.

Burgess, Ernest; Park, Robert E.; and McKenzie, Roderick D.
1925 *The City*. Chicago: University of Chicago Press.

Burr, Wesley R.
1972 Role transitions: A reformulation of theory, *Journal of Marriage and the Family* 34:407–16.

Campbell, A.; Converse, P. E.; and Rodgers, W. L.
1976 *The Quality of American Life: Perceptions, Evaluations, and Satisfaction*. New York: Russell Sage Foundation.

Cha, Marn J.
1975 Ethnic political orientation as function of assimilation: With reference to Koreans in Los Angeles. *Journal of Korean Affairs* 5:14–25.

Chakerian, Charles G.
1968 *From Rescue to Child Welfare*, New York: Church World Service.

Choy, Bong-youn
1979   *Koreans in America*. Chicago: Nelson Hall.

Cohen, Yehidi A., ed.
1974   *Human Adaptation*, 2d ed. Chicago: Aldine.

Converse, Jean M., and Schuman, Howard
1974   *Conversations at Random: Survey Research as Interviewers See It*. New York: Wiley.

Crain, Robert L.
1970   School integration and occupational achievement of Negroes. *American Journal of Sociology* 75:593–606.

Curtis, Russell L., Jr., and Zurcher, Louis A., Jr.
1971   Voluntary associations and the social integration of the poor. *Social Problems* 18:339–57.

Cutler, Stephen J.
1973   Voluntary association membership and the theory of mass society. Pp. 133–59 in Edward O. Laumann, *Bonds of Pluralism: The Form and Substance of Urban Social Network*, New York: Wiley.

Doeringer, Peter, and Piore, Michael J.
1971   *Internal Labor Markets and Manpower Analysis*. Lexington, Mass.: Heath Lexington Books.

Dohrenwend, Bruce P., and Smith, Robert J.
1962   Toward a theory of acculturation. *Southwestern Journal of Anthropology* 18:30–39.

The Dong-A Ilbo
1978   Mikunae hanin kyohoe sabaek ishipkae. (The number of Korean churches in the U.S. is 420), January 10.

Douvan, Elizabeth
1963   Employment and the adolescent. Pp. 142–64 in Ivan Nye and Lois Hoffman, ed., *The Employed Mother in America*. Chicago: Rand McNally.

Durkheim, E.
1951   *Suicide: A Study in Sociology*. New York: The Free Press.

Eisenstadt, S. N.
1951   Research on the cultural and social adaptation of immigrants. *International Social Science Bulletin* 3:258–62.
1952   The process of absorption of new immigrants in Israel. *Human Relations* 5:223–46.
1954a   Reference group behavior and social integration: An exploratory study. *American Sociological Review* 19:175–85.
1954b   *The Absorption of Immigrants*. London: Routledge and Kegan Paul.

Ericksen, Julia A.; Yancey, William L.; and Ericksen, Eugene P.
1979   The division of family roles. *Journal of Marriage and the Family* 41:301–13.

Everitt, John C.
1976   Community and propinquity in a city. *Annals of the*

Association of American Geographers 66:104.

Festinger, L., and Katz, D., eds.
1966   *Research Methods in Behavioral Sciences.* New York: Holt, Rinehart and Winston.

Form, William H., and Geschwender, James A.
1962   Social reference basis of job satisfaction: The case of manual workers. *American Sociological Review* 27:228-37.

Francis, E. K.
1945   The nature of the ethnic group. *American Journal of Sociology* 52:393-400.
1948   The Russian Mennonites: From religion to ethnic group. *American Journal of Sociology* 54:101-7.

Frazier, E. Franklin
1947   Sociological theory and race relations. *American Sociological Review* 12:265-71.

Freedman, Jonathan L.
1978   *Happy People: What Happiness Is, Who Has It and Why.* New York: Harcourt Brace Jovanovich.

Freedman, Marcia
1969   *The Process of Work Establishment.* New York: Columbia University Press.
1976   *Labor Markets: Segments and Shelters.* Montclair, N. J.: Allanheld, Osmun.

Frijda, N., and Jahoda, G.
1966   On the scope and methods of cross-cultural research. *International Journal of Psychology* 1:110-27.

Gallup, George H.
1980   *The Gallup Poll: Public Opinion 1979.* Wilmington, Del.: Scholarly Research.

Gardner, Arthur L.
1970   *The Koreans in Hawaii: An Annotated Bibliography.* Honolulu, Hawaii: Social Science Research Insitute, University of Hawaii.

Gillin, John, and Raimy, Victor
1940   Acculturation and personality. *American Sociological Review* 5:371-80.

Ginsburgs, George, and Ginsburgs, Herta
1977   A statistical profile of the Korean community in the Soviet Union. *Asian Survey* 17:952-66.

Glazer, Nathan
1954   Ethnic groups in America: from national culture to ideology. Pp. 158-73 in M. Berger, et al., eds., *Freedom and Control in Modern Society*, New York: Octagon Books.

Glazer, Nathan, and Moyhnihan, Daniel P.
1963   *Beyond the Melting Pot.* Cambridge, Mass: MIT Press.

Goldstein, Sidney, and Goldscheider, Calvin
1968   *Jewish Americans.* Englewood Cliffs, N. J.: Prentice-Hall.

Goode, William J., and Hatt, Paul K.
1952   *Methods in Social Research.* New York: McGraw-Hill.

Gorden, Raymond L.
1975   *Interviewing: Strategy, Techniques and Tactics.* Homewood, Ill.: Dorsey Press.

Gordon, Milton M.
1964   *Assimilation in American Life.* New York: Oxford University Press.

Granovetter, Mark S.
1974   *Getting a Job.* Cambridge, Mass.: Harvard University Press.

Greeley, Andrew M.
1971   *Why Can't They Be Like Us?: American White Ethnic Group.* New York: E. P. Dutton.
1972   *The Denominational Society: A Sociological Approach to Religion in America.* Glenview, Ill.: Scott, Foresman.

Greenstone, J. David
1975   Ethnicity, class and discontent: The case of Polish peasant immigrants. *Ethnicity* 2:1–9.

Gross, Neal; Mason, Ward S.; and McEachern, Alexander W.
1958   *Explorations in Role Analysis.* New York: Wiley.

Hankuk Ilbo
1979   Kyohwoesu 14 nyonkan 20 baero jungka. (The number of Korean churches has increased 20 times in 14 years) May 18.

Hansen, Marcus L.
1937   *The Problem of the Third Generation Immigrant.* Rock Island, Ill.: The Augustana Historical Society.
1940   *The Immigrant in American History.* New York: Harper Torch Books.

Harris, Keith D.
1971   Ethnic variations in Los Angeles business patterns. *Annals of the Association of American Geographers* 61:743.

Hays, William C., and Mindel, Charles H.
1973   Extended kinship relations in black and white families. *Journal of Marriage and the Family* 35:39–49.

Hendrix, Lewelly
1976   Kinship, social networks and family integration among Ozark residents and out-migrants. *Journal of Marriage and the Family* 38:97–104.

Herberg, Will
1955   *Protestant, Catholic, Jew.* Garden City, N. Y.: Doubleday.

Homans, George C.
1950   *The Human Group.* New York: Harcourt, Brace and World.
1961   *Social Behavior: Its Elementary Forms.* New York: Harcourt, Brace and World.

Honigmann, John J.
1964   Adaptation. Pp. 8–9 in J. Gould and W. L. Kolb, eds., *A*

Dictionary of the Social Sciences. New York: The Free Press.

Hosokawa, Bill
1969   *Nisei: The Quiet Americans.* New York: William Morrow.

Hsu, Francis L. K.
1973   Prejudice and its intellectual effect in American anthropology: An ethnographic report. *American Anthropologist* 5:1–19.

Hu, Hsien Chin
1944   "The Chinese concepts of 'face.'" *American Anthropologist* 46:45–65.

Hunter, David E., and Whitten, Philip
1976   *Encyclopedia of Anthropology.* New York: Harper & Row.

Hurh, Won Moo
1972   Marginal children of war: An exploratory study of American-Korean children. *International Journal of Sociology of the Family* 2:10–20.
1977a   *Comparative Study of Korean Immigrants in the United States: A Typological Approach.* San Francisco: R and E Research Associates, Inc.
1977b   *Assimilation of the Korean Minority in the United States.* Elkins Park, Penn.: Philip Jaisohn Foundation.
1978   *Hangkuk Imin ui Miguk Chongchak kwa Donghwa Kwajong* (Korean Translation of the above). Translated by Heedok Bang. Elkins Park, Penn.: Philip Jaisohn Foundation.
1980   Towards a Korean-American ethnicity: Some theoretical models. *Ethnic and Racial Studies* 3:444–63.

Hurh, Won Moo; Kim, Hei Chu; and Kim, Kwang Chung
1978   *Assimilation Patterns of Immigrants in the United States: A Case Study of Korean Immigrants in the Chicago Area.* Washington, D. C.: University Press of America.
1980   Cultural and social adjustment patterns of Korean immigrants in the Chicago area. Pp. 295–302 in R. Bryce-Laporte, ed., *Sourcebook on the New Immigration: Implications for the United States and the International Community.* New Brunswick, N. J.: Transaction Books.

Hurh, Won Moo, and Kim, Kwang Chung
1979a   Methodological problems in the study of Korean immigrants: Conceptual, interactional, sampling and interviewer training difficulties. Paper presented at the Annual Meeting, Midwest Sociological Society, Minneapolis, Minnesota, April 25–28.
1979b   Korean immigrants in the Los Angeles area: A sociological study. Interim Report submitted to NIMH, U. S. Department of Health, Education and Welfare (Grant No. 1 RO1 MH 30475-01), October.
1980a   The process of Korean immigrants' adaptation in the U. S.: Length of residence and life satisfaction. Paper presented at the Annual Meeting, American Sociological Association, New York, August 27–31.
1980b   Variables related to life satisfaction of Korean immigrants. Paper presented at the Annual Meeting, Society for the Study of Social Problems, New York, August 24–27.

1981 Social and psychological ambivalence of Korean immigrants in the United States. Paper presented at the Annual Meeting, Society for Applied Anthropology, Edinburgh, Scotland, April 12–17.
1982 Race relations paradigms and Korean-American research: a sociology of knowledge perspecitive. Pp. 219–245 in E. Yu, E. Phillips, and E. Yang, eds., *Koreans in Los Angeles: Prospects and Promises*. Los Angeles, California: Center for Korean-American and Korean Studies, California State University, Los Angeles.

Hyman, H., and Singer, E., eds.
1968 *Readings in Reference Group Theory*. New York: The Free Press.

Jo, Yung-Hwan, and Nahm, In Sook
1979 Korea as portrayed in American textbooks: A policy suggestion. Pp. 218–29 in Papers of the 1st International Conference on Korean Studies. Seoul, Korea: The Academy of Korean Studies.

Johnson, Colleen Leahy
1977 Interdependence, reciprocity and indebtedness: An analysis of Japanese American kinship relations. *Journal of Marriage and the Family* 39:351–63.

Joong-ang Ilbo
1980 Mikuk sokui hankukin:odie olma? (Koreans in America: How many and where?). January 1.

Kallen, Horace B.
1915 Democracy versus the melting pot. *The Nation* 100: 190–94, 217–22.
1924 *Culture and Democracy in the U.S.* New York: Liveright.
1956 *Cultural Pluralism and the American Idea*. Philadelphia: University of Pennsylvania Press.

Kang, T. S.
1971 Name change and acculturation. *Pacific Sociological Review* 14:403–412.

Keely, Charles B.
1980 Immigration policy and the new immigrants. Pp. 15–25 in R. Bryce-Laporte, ed., *Sourcebook on the New Immigration*. New Brunswick, N. J.: Transaction Books.

Kerr, Clark
1954 The Balkanization of labor market. Pp. 92–110 in E. W. Bakke, ed., *Labour Mobility and Economic Opportunity*. New York: Wiley.

Kim, Bernice Bong Hee
1934 The Koreans in Hawaii. *Social Science* 4:409–413.
1937 The Korean in Hawaii. Master's thesis, University of Hawaii.

Kim, Bok-Lim
1972 Casework with Japanese and Korean wives of Americans. *Social Casework* 53:273–79.

1977	Asian wives of U.S. servicemen: Women in shadows. *Amerasia Journal* 4:91–115.
1978a	Problems and service needs of Asian Americans in Chicago: An empirical study. *Amerasia Journal* 5:23–24.
1978b	Pioneers in intermarriage: Korean women in the United States. Pp. 59–95 In H. H. Sunoo and D. C. Kim, eds., *Korean Women*. Memphis, Tenn.: Association for Korean Christian Scholars in North America.
1978c	*The Asian Americans: Changing Patterns, Changing Needs.* (See Chapter VII. The Korean Sample). Montclair, N. J.: Association for Korean Christian Scholars in North America.

Kim, David S., and Wong, Charles C.
1977 Business development in Koreatown, Los Angeles. Pp. 229–45 in Hyung-chan Kim, ed., *The Korean Diaspora*. Santa Barbara, Calif.: ABC-Clio Press.

Kim, Dong Soo
1977 How they fared in American homes: A follow-up study of adopted Korean children. *Children Today* 6:2–6, 31.

Kim, Hae-Jong
1979 A Korean parish and the duality of its social context. Mimeographed paper. Cresskill, New Jersey.

Kim, Hei Chu; Hurh, Won Moo; and Kim, Kwang Chung
1978 Ethnic roles of the Korean church in the Chicago area. Paper presented at the Annual Meeting, Society for the Scientific Study of Religion, Hartford, Connecticut, October 27–29.

Kim, Hyung-chan
1971 Korean emigrants to the U.S.A., 1959–1969. *Korea Journal* 11:16–24, 31.
1974 Some aspects of social demography of Korean Americans. *International Migration Review* 8:23–42.

Kim, Hyung-chan, and Patterson, Wayne
1974 *The Koreans in America 1882–1974: A Chronology of Fact Book.* Dobbs Ferry, N. Y.: Oceana Publications.

Kim, Kwang Chung; Kim, Hei Chu; and Hurh, Won Moo
1978 Life of Korean Christians in the Chicago area: Their church, job and home. Paper presented at the Annual Meeting, Korean Ministerial Association of Chicago, Chicago, April 1.
1979 Division of household tasks in Korean immigrant families in the United States. *International Journal of Sociology of the Family* 9:161–75.
1981 Job information deprivation in the United States: A case study of Korean immigrants. *Ethnicity* 8:219–32.

Kim, Kwang Chung, and Hurh, Won Moo
1979 Occupational experience of Korean immigrants in the Los Angeles area. Paper presented at the Annual Meeting, Illinois Sociological Association, Springfield, Illinois, October 26–27.
1980a Ethnic confinement and job satisfaction: A case of Korean

immigrants in the Los Angeles area. Paper presented at the Annual Meeting, Midwest Sociological Society, Milwaukee, Wisconsin, April 2–5.

1980b   Occupational career of Asian immigrants: A case study of Korean immigrants in the Los Angeles area. Paper read at the Annual Meeting, North Central Sociological Association, Dayton, Ohio, May 1–3.

1980c   Social and occupational assimilation of Korean immigrants in the United States. *California Sociologist* 3:125–42.

1980d   Employment role and division of household tasks in Korean immigrant families. Paper presented at the Annual Meeting, National Council on Family Relations, Portland, Oregon, October 22–25.

1980e   Interpersonal networks and job information acquisition: The case of Korean immigrants in the Los Angeles area. Paper presented at the 4th National Conference on the Third World, Omaha, Nebraska, October 22–25.

Kim, Sil Dong
1975   Findings of national inquiries on Asian women of U.S. servicemen: Post consultation report. Paper presented at the Methodist conference, Tacoma, Washington, March 20–21. See also Sil Dong Kim's Ph. D. dissertation, University of Washington, 1979.

Kim, Won Yong (Warren)
1959   Chaemi Hanin Osimnyonsa (A Fifty-Year History of the Koreans in the United States). Reedly, Calif.: Charles Ho Kim.
1971   *Koreans in America* (English Translation of the above). Seoul: Po Chin Chai.

Kish, Leslie
1965   *Survey Sampling*. New York: John Wiley.

Kitano, Harry L.
1974   *Race Relations*. Englewood Cliffs, N. J.: Prentice-Hall.
1976   *Japanese Americans: The Evolution of a Subculture.* Englewood Cliffs, N. J.: Prentice-Hall.

The Korean Times
1979   Koreans in Russia estimated at 400,000. February 12.

Korea Week
1978   Korean religion/1977. February 28.

The Korean Directory of Southern California
1972   Los Angeles, Calif.: Keys Advertising and
1975   Printing Company.
1979

Kramer, Judith R.
1970   *The American Minority Community*. New York: Thomas Y. Crowell.

Kurokawa, Minako, ed.
1970   *Minority Responses: Comparative Views of Reactions to Subordination*. New York: Random House.

Laumann, Edward O.
1966   *Prestige and Association in an Urban Community*, Indianapolis: Bobbs-Merrill.
1973   *Bonds of Pluralism: The Form and Substance of Urban Social Networks*. New York: John Wiley.

Lawler, Edward D, III
1977   Satisfaction and behavior. Pp. 39–50 in J. R. Hackman, E. E. Lawler III and L. W. Porter, eds., *Perspectives on Behavior in Organizations*. New York: McGraw-Hill.

Lee, Changsoo
1979   Los Angeles Hanindul ui Chongchak Hyonhang (The settlement patterns of Koreans in Los Angeles). Pp. 36–43 in Eun Sik Yang et al., eds., *Mikukan ui Hanin Community* (The Korean Community in the United States). Los Angeles: The Association for Korean Studies–Korean Pioneer Press.

Lee, Changsoo, and Wagatsuma, Hiroshi
1979   The settlement patterns of Koreans in Los Angeles: A demographic survey. Paper presented at the 31st Annual Meeting, Association for Asian Studies, Los Angeles, March 3–April 1.

Lee, Sang Hyun
1980   Called to be pilgrim: Toward a theology within a Korean immigrant context. Pp. 37–74 in Byongsuh Kim and Sang H. Lee, eds., *The Korean Immigrant in America*. Montclair, N. J.: Association of Korean Christian Scholars in North America.

Levinger, George
1964   Task and social behavior in marriage. *Sociometry* 27:433–48.

Lind, Andrew William
1938   *An Island Community: Ecological Succession in Hawaii*. Chicago: University of Chicago Press.

Litwak, Eugene
1959–   The use of extended family groups in the achievement of social
60   goals. *Social Problems* 7:177–87.

Litwak, Eugene, and Szelenyi, Ivan
1969   Primary group structures and their functions: Kin, neighbors, and friends. *American Sociological Review* 34:465–81.

Lyman, Stanford M.
1974   *Chinese Amercians*. New York: Random House.
1977   *The Asian in North America*. Santa Barbara, Calif.: ABC-Clio.

Lyu, Kingsley K.
1977   Korean nationalist activities in Hawaii and the continential United States, 1900–1945, Part I: 1900–1919. *Amerasia Journal* 4:23–90.

McKennel, A. C.
1977   Attitude scale construction. Pp. 183–220 in C. A. O'Muircheartaigh and C. Payne, eds., *Exploring Data Structures*. New York: Wiley.

Merton, Robert K.
1964 *Social Theory and Social Structure.* New York: The Free Press.
1972 Insiders and outsiders: A chapter in the sociology of knowledge. *American Journal of Sociology* 78:9–47.

Merton, Robert K., and Kitt, Alice S.
1950 Contribution to the theory of reference group behavior. Pp. 40–105 in R. K. Merton and P. F. Lazarsfeld, eds., *Continuities in Social Research: Studies in the the Scope and Method of "The American Soldier.* Glencoe, Ill.: Free Press.

Miller, Delbert C., and Form, William H.
1964 *Industrial Sociology: The Sociology of Work Organizations.* 2d ed. New York: Harper & Row.

Mincer, Jacob
1970 Incomes: A survey with special reference to the human capital approach. *Journal of Economic Literature* 8:1–26.

Ministry of Health and Social Affairs
1967 *Child Welfare Statistics.* Seoul: Ministry of Health and Social Affairs, Republic of Korea.

Myrdal, Gunner
1944 *An American Dilemma: The Negro Problem and Modern Democracy.* New York: Harper & Row.

Naroll, Raoul
1970 What have we learned from cross-cultural survey? *American Anthropologist* 72:1227–88.

Newman, William M.
1973 *American Pluralism: A Study of Minority Groups and Social Theory.* New York: Harper & Row.

Newsweek
1975 The pioneers. May 26:10.

Nye, Ivan F.
1974 Emerging and declining family roles. *Journal of Marriage and the Family* 36:238–45.

Nye, Ivan F., ed.
1976 *Role Structure and Analysis of the Family.* Beverly Hills, Calif.: Sage Publications.

Packard, Vance
1972 *A Nation of Strangers.* Chicago: David McKay.

Park, Siyoung
1980 Residential mobility of Koreans in Chicago. Paper presented at the Annual Meeting of the Association of American Geographers, Louisville, Kentucky, April 13–16.

Park, Robert E., and Burgess, Ernest
1924 *Introduction to the Science of Sociology.* Chicago: University of Chicago.

Parsons, Talcott
1949 The social structure of the family. Pp. 173–201 in R. N.

Anshen, ed., *The Family: Its Functions and Destiny*. New York: Harper & Brothers.

Patterson, Wayne
1976   *The Koreans in North America*. Philadelphia: The Balch Institute. (A bibliography.)
1977   The first attempt to obtain laborers for Hawaii, 1896–1897. Pp. 9–31 in Hyung-chan Kim, ed., *The Korean Diaspora*. Santa Barbara, Calif.: ABC-Clio Press.
1979   A profile of early Korean immigrants to America. Paper presented at the 31st Annual Meeting, Association for Asian Studies, Los Angeles, March 30–April 1.

Petersen, William
1971   *Japanese Americans*. New York: Random House.

Pike, Kenneth L.
1954   Emic and etic standpoints for the description of behavior. Pp. 8–28 in K. L. Pike, ed., *Language in Relation to Unified Theory of the Structure of Human Behavior*. Glendale, Calif.: Institute of Linguistics.

Piore, Michael J.
1969   On-the-job training in the dual labor market: Public and private responsibilities in on-the-job training of disadvantaged workers. Pp. 101–32 in A. R. Weber, F. H. Cassell, and W. L. Ginsburg, eds., *Public-Private Manpower Policies*. Madison, Wis.: Industrial Research Association.

Popper, Karl R.
1965   *Conjectures and Refutations: The Growth of Scientific Knowledge*. New York: Harper Torchbooks.

Portes, Alejandro, and Bach, Robert L.
1980   Immigrant earnings: Cuban and Mexican Immigrants in the United States. *International Migration Review* 14:315–41.

Portes, Alejandro, and Wilson, Kenneth L.
1976   Black-white differences in educational attainment. *American Sociological Review* 41:414–31.

Propper, Alice Marcella
1972   The relationship of material employment to adolescent roles, activities and parental relationships. *Journal of Marriage and the Family* 34:417–21.

Rees, Albert
1966   Information networks in labour market. *American Economic Review* 56:559–66.

Reid, Graham L.
1972   Job search and the effectiveness of job-finding methods. *Industrial and Labor Relations Review* 25:479–95.

Richmond, Marie L.
1976   Beyond resource theory: Another look at factors enabling women to affect family interaction. *Journal of Marriage and the Family* 38:257–66.

Romney, A.K., and D'Andrade, R. G., eds.
1964   Transcultural Studies in cognition. *American Anthropologist* 66. Special publication.

Rosenthal, Erich
1960   Acculturation without assimilation. *American Journal of Sociology* 66:275-88.

Rosow, Irving
1967   *Social Integration of the Aged.* New York: The Free Press.

Roy, Prodipto
1961   Adolescent roles, rural-urban differentials. *Marriage and Family Living* 23:340-49.

Ryu, Jai P.
1977   Koreans in America: A demographic analysis. Pp. 205-228 in Hyung-chan Kim, ed., *The Korean Diaspora.* Santa Barbara, Calif.: ABC-Clio.

Schaefer, Richard T.
1979   *Racial and Ethnic Groups.* Boston: Little, Brown.

Schmitt, Raymond L.
1972   *The Reference Other Orientation: An Extension of the Reference Group Concept.* Carbondale, Ill.: Southern Illinois University Press.

Schütz, Alfred
1967   *The Phenomenology of the Social World.* Evanston, Illinois: Northwestern University Press.

Schultz, T. W.
1961   Investment in human capital. *American Economic Review* 51:1-17.

Sears, Robert R.
1961   Transcultural variables and conceptual equivalence. Pp. 445-55 in B. Kaplan, ed., *Studying Personality Cross-Culturally.* New York: Harper & Row.

Seligman, Edwin R. A., and Johnson, Alvin, eds.
1954   *Encyclopedia of the Social Sciences*, Vol. XV. New York: The Macmillan Co.

Sellitz, Claire; Jahoda, Marie; Deutsch, M.; and Cook, S. W.
1961   *Research Methods on Social Relations.* New York: Holt, Rinehart and Winston.

Sheppard, Harold L., and Belintsky, A. Harvey
1966   *The Job Hunt: Job-Seeking Behavior of Unemployed Workers in a Local Economy.* Baltimore, M.: The Johns Hopkins Press.

Sherman, Diana
1979   Korea town's extent, population growth daily. *Los Angeles Times*, February 25.

Shibutani, Tomatsu
1955   Reference group as perspectives. *American Journal of Sociology* 60:562-69.

1961   *Society and Personality.* Englewood Cliffs, N. J.: Prentice-Hall.

Silverman, William, and Hill, Reuben
1967   Task allocation in marriage in the United States and Belgium. *Journal of Marriage and the Family* 29:352–59.

Simpson, George E., and Yinger, J. Milton
1972   *Racial and Cultural Minorities: An Analysis of Prejudice and Discrimination.* New York: Harper & Row.

Siu, Paul C. P.
1952   The sojourner. *American Journal of Sociology* 58:34–44.

Sklare, Marshall
1955   *Conservative Judaism: An American Religious Movement.* Glencoe, Ill.: The Free Press.

Sowell, W. H., and Hauser, R. M.
1975   *Education, Occupation, and Earnings: Achievement in Early Career.* New York: Academic Press.

Spiro, Melford E.
1955   The acculturation of American ethnic groups. *American Anthropologist* 57:1240–52.

Stafford, Rebecca; Backman, Elaine; and Dibona, Pamela
1977   The division of labor among cohabiting and married couples. *Journal of Marriage and the Family* 39:43–57.

Stermole, David F.
1980   Reaggregation of an ethnic group in Toronto. Paper presented at the Annual Meeting of the Association of American Geographers, Louisville, Kentucky, April 13–16.

Sturtevant, William C.
1964   Studies in Ethnoscience. *American Anthropologist* 66:99–131.

Stone, Richard L.
1976   Emics. Pg. 142 in D. E. Hunter and P. Whitten, eds., *Encyclopedia of Anthropology.* New York: Harper & Row.

Sunoo, Harold Hakwon, and Sunoo, Sonia Shin
1977   The heritage of the first Korean women immigrants in the United States, 1903–1924. *The Korean Christian Journal* no. 2:142–71.

Sussman, Marvin B., ed.
1968   *Sourcebook in Marriage and the Family,* 3d ed. Boston, Mass.: Houghton Mifflin.

Sutcliffe, J. P., and Crabbe, B. D.
1963   Incidence and degrees of friendship in urban and rural areas. *Social Forces* 42:60–67.

Teske, R. H. C., Jr., and Nelson, B. H.
1974   Acculturation and assimilation: A classification. *American Ethnologist* 1:351–68.

Thibaut, John W., and Kelley, Harold H.
1967   *The Social Psychology of Groups.* New York: Wiley.

Thurow, Lester
1969   *Poverty and Discrimination.* Washington, D. C.: The Brookings Institution.
1975   *Generating Inequality: Mechanisms of Distribution in the U.S. Economy.* New York: Basic Books.

Thurnwald, Richard
1932   The psychology of acculturation. *American Anthropologist* 34:557–69.

Toennies, Ferdinand
1957   *Community and Society.* East Lansing, Mich.: Michigan State University Press.

Toffler, Alvin
1970   *Future Shock.* New York: Random House.

Trebilcock, Dorothy W.
1973   The individual social and cultural implications of the cross-cultural marriage: Korean wives and their American husbands in Michigan. Master's thesis, Michigan State University.

Turner, R. H.
1955   Reference groups of future-oriented man. *Social Forces* 34:130–36.

Tylor, Edward B.
1889   On the method of investigating the development of institutions: Applied to laws of marriage and descent. *Journal of the Royal Anthropological Institute* 18:245–69.

Ullman, Joseph C.
1968   Interfirm differences in the cost of search for clerical workers. *The Journal of Busness* 41:153–65.

U.S Department of Commerce (Bureau of Census)
1977   *Social Indicator 1976.* Washington, D. C.: U. S. Government Printing Office.
1977a   *Census of Population* PC (1)-D1, HC (7)-9. Washington, D. C.: U. S. Government Printing Office.
1979   *Statistical Abstract of the United States.* Washington, D. C.: U. S. Government Printing Office.
1981   *Census of Population, Supplementary Report* (PC 80-S1-3): Race of the Population by State, 1980. Washington, D. C.: U. S. Government Printing Office.

U.S. Commissioner of Immigration and Naturalization
1952–1978   *Annual Report.* Washington, D. C.: U. S. Government Printing Office.

U. S. Department of Health, Education and Welfare
1974   *A Study of Selected Socioeconomic Characteristics of Ethnic Minorities Based on the 1970 Census,* Volume II: Asian Americans. Washington, D. C.: U. S. Government Printing Office.
1977   Asian American Field Survey: Summary of Data. Washington, D. C.: U. S. Government Printing Office.

U. S. Department of Labor, Bureau of Labor Statistics
1978a   *Handbook of Labor Statistics*. Washington, D. C.: U. S. Government Printing Office.
1978b   *Long Hours and Premium Pay*, May 1978. Washington, D. C.: U. S. Government Printing Office.
1979   *Bureau of Labor Statistics News*. September 7.

Vander Zanden, James W.
1966   *American Minority Relations*. New York: Ronald Press.

Vermeulen, C. J., and de Ruijter, A.
1975   Dominant epistemological presuppositions in the use of the cross-cultural survey method. *Current Anthropology* 16:29–52.

Wagley, Charles, and Harris, Marvin
1958   *Minorities in the New World*. New York: Columbia University Press.

Warner, W. Lloyd, and Srole, Leo
1945   *The Social System of American Ethnic Groups*. New Haven,: Yale University Press.

Warriner, Charles K., and Prather, Jane E.
1965   Four types of voluntary associations. *Sociological Inquiry* 35:138–48.

Warwick, Donald P., and Osherson, S., eds.
1973   *Comparative Research Methods*. Englewood Cliffs, N. J.: Prentice-Hall.

Warwick, Donald P., and Lininger, Charles A.
1975   *The Sample Survey: Theory and Practice.* New York; McGrew-Hill.

Weber, Max
(1913)   *Soziologie, Weltgeschichtliche Analysen*, Politik.
1956   Stuttgart: Kroner.

Weber, Max
1959   *From Max Weber: Essays in Sociology*. Translated by C. W. Mills and H. H. Gerth. New York: Oxford University Press.

Weinstock, S. Alexander
1963   Role elements: A link between acculturation and occupational status. *British Journal of Sociology* 14:144–49.
1964   Some factors that retard or accelerate the rate of acculturation. *Human Relations* 17:321–40.

Wilcock, Richard C.
1957   The secondary labor force and the measurement of unemployment. Pp. 167–208 in the Measurement and Behavior of Unemployment, compiled from a conference of the Universities — National Bureau Committee for Economic Research. Princeton, N. J.: Princeton University Press.

Williams, Margaret Aasterud
1970   Reference groups: A review and commentary. *Sociological Quarterly* 11:545–54.

Winch, Robert F.
1968   Some observations on extended familism in the United States. Pp. 127–38 in Robert F. Winch and Louis W. Goodman, eds., *Selected Studies in Marriage and the Family*, 3d ed. New York: Holt, Rinehart and Winston.

Winick, Charles
1964   *Dictionary of Anthropology*. Paterson, N. J.: Littlefield, Adams.

Wirth, Louis
1938   Urbanism as a way of life. *American Journal of Sociology* 44:1–24.

Wright, Charles, and Hyman, Herbert H.
1958   Voluntary association memberships of American adults: Evidence from national sample survey. *American Sociological Review* 23:284–94.

Yancey, William L.; Ericksen, Eugene P.; and Juliani, Richard N.
1976   Emergent ethnicity: A review and reformulation. *American Sociological Review* 41:391–403.

Yu, Eui-Yong
1977   Koreans in America: An emerging ethnic minority. *Amerasia Journal* 4:117–31.
1979a   Demographic profile of Koreans in Los Angeles: Size, composition and distribution. Paper presented at the Koryo Research Institute Workshop, Los Angeles, March 10.
1979b   Occupational and work patterns of Korean immigrants in Los Angeles. Paper presented at the Koryo Research Institute Workshop, Los Angeles, March 10.
1980   Koreans in America: Social and economic adjustment. Pp. 75–98 in Byong-suh Kim and Sang Hyun Lee, eds., The Korean Immigrant in America. Montclair, N. J.: The Association of Korean Christian Scholars in North America.

Yu, Elena
1979   Dilemmas in Asian-American research. Paper presented at the Annual Meeting, the Midwest Sociological Society, Minneapolis, Minnestoa, April 25–28.

Yuan, D. Y.
1963   Voluntary segregation: A study of New York Chinatown. *Phylon* (Fall):255–65.

Yun, Yo-chun
1977   Early history of Korean immigration to America. Pp. 33–46 in Hyung-chan Kim, ed., *The Korean Diaspora*. Santa Barbara,: Calif.: ABC-Clio Press.

Znaniecki, Florian
1934   *The Method of Sociology*. New York: Holt, Rinehart and Winston.

Selected Bibliography on Korean-Americans

Adams, Romanzo
(1937) *Interracial Marriage in Hawaii.* Montclair, N. J.:
1967   Patterson Smith (see Korean interracial marriage).

Ahn, Byung Chul
1981   The determinants of the husband's household task participation in Korean immigrants families. Master's thesis, University of Iowa.

Bonacich, Edna
1978   U.S. capitalism and Korean Immigrant small business: A study in the relationship between class and ethnicity. Paper presented at the 9th World Congress of Sociology in Uppsala, Sweden, August 14–19.
1979   New immigrant small business as a form of cheap labor. Paper presented at the 145th National Meeting, the American Association for the Advancement of Science, Houston, Texas, January 3–8. (Korean small busines as an example.)

Bonacich, Edna; Light, Ivan; and Wong Charles C.
1980   Korean immigrant small business in Los Angeles. PP. 167–84 in R. Bryce-Laporte, ed., *Sourcebook on the New Immigration: Implications for the United States and International Community.* New Brunwick, N. J.: Transaction Books.

Bonacich, Edna, and Jung, Tai Hwan
1979   A portrait of Korean small business in Los Angeles, 1977. Paper presented at a meeting, "Korean Community in Los Angeles: Problems and Issues in Settlement." Koryo Research Institute, Los Angeles, March 10.

Cha, Marn J.
1975   Ethnic political orientation as function of assimilation: With reference to Koreans in Los Angeles. *Journal of Korean Affairs* 5:14–25.

Chai, Alice Yun
1957   Attitude of American-educated Korean students toward American and Americanization. Master's thesis, Ohio State University.

Chang, T. S.
1975   The self-concept of children in ethnic groups: Black-American and Korean-American. *Elementary School Journal* 76:52–58.

Chang, Won H.
1977   Communication and acculturation. Pp. 129–34 in Hyung-chan Kim, ed., *The Korean Diaspora*. Santa Barbara, Calif.: ABC-Clio Press.

Cho, Pill Jay
1979   The Korean church in America: A Dahrendorf model. Paper presented at the 1st Annual Meeting, Asian American Sociological Association, Boston, August 28.

Choi, Hyo Sup
1980   Faith and life of the immigrants in the Bible. Pp. 129–45 in Byong-suh and Sang Hyun Lee, eds., *The Korean Immigrant in America*. Montclair, N. J.: The Association of Korean Christian Scholars in North America.

Choy, Bong-youn
1979   *Koreans in America*. Chicago: Nelson Hall.

Dearman, Maria, and Shim, Steve
1979   Current religious dimensions of Korean immigrant community in Los Angeles area. Paper presented at a meeting, Koryo Research Institute, Los Angeles, March 10.

Fowler, Michael G.
1978   An analysis of the problems of Korean students in American secondary schools as perceived by Korean students and parents and the teachers in public schools. Ed. D. dissertation, University of Northern Colorado.

Gardner, Arthur L.
1970   *The Koreans in Hawaii: An Annotated Bibliography*. Honolulu: Social Science Research Institute, University of Hawaii.

Givens, Helen L.
(1939)   *The Korean Community in Los Angeles*. San Francisco:
1974   R and E Research Associates.

Gregor, Kyung Sook Cho
1963   *Korean immigrants in Gresham, Oregon: Community life and social adjustment*. Master'a thesis, University of Oregon.

Guilbault, Claude
1972   A descriptive study of the adjustment of Korean children adopted by families in Minnesota. Master's thesis, University of Wisconsin.

Han, Sang-in
1973   A study of social religious participation in relationship to occupational mobility and self-esteem among Korean immigrants in Chicago. Ph. D. dissertation, Northwestern University.

Hong, Lawrence
1979   Family profile and marital satisfaction of Koreans in the Los Angeles metropolitan area. Paper presented at a meeting, Koryo Research Institute, Los Angeles, March 10.

Houchins, Lee, and Houchins, Chang-su
1976 The Korean experience in America, 1903–1924. Pp. 129–156 in N. Hundley, Jr., ed., *The Asian American: The Historical Experience*. Santa Barbara, Calif.: ABC-Clio Press.

Hubler, William H.
1977 The acculturation of South Korean immigrants in a suburban community of a large city in Northeastern U. S. Ed. D. dissertation, Pennsylvania State University.
1978 *Koreans in Emlyn: A Community in Transition*. Elkins Park, Penn.: Philip Jaisohn Memorial Foundation.

Hurh, Won Moo
1972 Marginal children of war: An exploratory study of American-Korean children. *International Journal of Sociology of the Family* 2:10–20.
1977a *Comparative Study of Korean Immigrants in the United States: A Typological Approach*. San Francisco: R and E Research Associates.
1977b *Assimilation of the Korean Minority in the United States*. Elkins Park, Penn.: Philip Jaisohn Foundation.
1978 Hanguk Imin ui Miguk Chongchak Kwa Donghwa Kwajong (Korean Translation of the above). Translated by Heedok Bang. Elkins Park, Penn.: Philip Jaisohn Foundation.
1980 Towards a Korean-American ethnicity: Some theoretical models. *Ethnic and Racial Studies* 3:444–463.

Hurh, Won Moo; Chu Kim, Hei; and Kim, Kwang Chung
1981 Cultural and social adjustment patterns of Korean immigrants in the Chicago area. Pp. 295–302 in R. Bryce-Laporte, ed., *Sourcebook on the New Immigration: Implications for the United States and the International Community*. New Brunswick, N. J.: Transaction Books.
1979a *Assimilation Patterns of Immigrants in the United States: A Case Study of Korean Immigrants in the Chicago Area*. Washington, D. C.: University Press of America.

Hurh, Won Moo, and Kim, Kwang Chung
1980 Methodological problems in the study of Korean immigrants: Conceptual, interactional, sampling and interviewer training difficulties. Paper presented at the Annual Meeting, Midwest Sociological Society, Minneapolis, Minnesota, April 25–28.
1981 Korean immigrants in the Los Angeles area: A sociological study. Interim Report submitted to HIMH, U. S. department of Health, Education and Welfare (Grant No. 1 RO1 MH 30475-10), October.
1980a The process of Korean immigrants' adaptation in the U. S.: Length of residence and life satisfaction. Paper presented at the Annual Meeting, American Sociological Association, New York, August 27–31.
1980b Variables related to life satisfaction of Korean immigrants. Paper presented at the Annual Meeting, Society for the Study of Social Problems, New York, August 24–27.
1980c Korean immigrants in America: A structural analysis of ethnic confinement and adhesive adaptation. Final Report submitted

to National Institute of Mental Health, U. S. Department of Health and Human Services. Macomb, Ill.: Western Illinois University, December.
1981a   Social and psychological ambivalence of Korean immigrants in the United States. Paper presented at the Annual Meeting, Society for Applied Anthropology, Edinburgh, Scotland, April 12–17.
1981b   Methodlogical problems in cross-cultural research: A Korean immigrants study. *California Sociologist* 4:17–32.
1982   Race relations paradigms and Korean-American research: A sociology of knowledge perspective. Pp. 219–245 in E. Yu, E. Phillips, and E. Yang, ed., *Koreans in Los Angeles*. Los Angeles, Calif.: Center for Korean-American and Korean Studies, California State University, Los Angeles.

Jade
1975   Korean influx. *Jade Magazine* December: 22–23.

Jin, Hyung-Ki
1978   Jemi Kyopo kiopche ui kyongyong siltae josa. (*A Survey on Economic and Managerial Status on Korean Business in the Los Angeles Area*). Los Angeles: Korean Chamber of Commerce of Southern California.

Jo, Yung-Hwan
1979   Strategies of participation in American politics: A footstep into the future. Paper presented at a meeting, Koryo Research Institute, Los Angeles, March 10.

Jo, Yung-Hwan, and Nahm, In Sook
1979   Korea as portrayed in American textbooks: A policy suggestion. Pp. 218–29 in Papers of the 1st International Conference on Korean Studies. Seoule, Korea: The Academy of Korean Studies.

Jones, George Heber
1906   Koreans abroad. *Korea Review* 6:446–51.

Kim, Bernice Bong Hee
1937   The Koreans in Hawaii. Master's thesis, University of Hawaii.

Kim, Bo Kyung
1980   Attitudes, parental identification, and locus of control of Korean-Canadian, and Canadian adolescents. Pp. 219–42 in K. V. Ujimoto and G. Hirabayashi, eds., *Minorities and Multiculturalism: Asians in Canada.* Toronto: Butterworth.

Kim, Bok-Lim
1972   Casework with Japanese and Korean wives of Americans. *Social Casework* 53:242–79.
1977   Asian wives of U. S. servicemen: Women in Shadows. *Amerasia Journal* 4:91–115.
1978a   Problems and service needs of Asian Americans in Chicago: An empirical study. *Amerasia Journal* 5:23–24.
1978b   Pioneers in intermarriage: Korean women in the United States. Pp. 59–95 in H. H. Sunoo and D. C. Kim, eds., *Korean Women*. Memphis, Tenn.: Association for Korean Christian Scholars in North America.

1978c   *The Asian Americans: Changing Patterns, Changing Needs.* (See Chapter VII. The Korean Sample). Montclair, N. J.: Association for Korean Christian Scholars in North America.

1980   The Korean-American Child at school and at home. Final Project Report to the Administration for Children, Youth, and Families, U. S. Department of Health, Education and Welfare.

Kim, Byong-suh, and Lee, Sang Hyun, eds.
1980   *The Korean Immigrant in America.* Montclair, N. J.: The Association of Korean Christian Scholars in North America.

Kim, Byong-suh
1980   The functions of conflict in the construction of Korean-American communitities. Pp. 147–62 in Byong-suh Kim and sang Hyun Lee, eds., *The Korean Immigrant in America.* Montclair, N. J.: The Association of Korean Christian Scholars in North America.

Kim, Chim, and Carroll, Timothy G.
1977   Intercountry Adoption of South Korean orphans: A lawyer's guide. *Journal of Family Law* 14:223–53.

Kim, David S., and Wong, Charles C.
1977   Business development in Koreatown, Los Angeles. Pp. 229–45 in Hyung-chan Kim, ed., *The Korean Diaspora.* Santa Barbara, Calif.: ABC-Clio Press.

Kim, Dong Soo
1977   How they fared in American homes: A follow-up study of adopted Korean children. *Children Today* 6:2–6,31.

1978   Issues in transracial and transcultural adoption. *Social Casework* 59:447–86 (see Korean children).

Kim, Dong Soo, and Kim, Byong-suh, eds.
1979   *Human Rights in Minority Perspective.* Montclair, N. J.: The Association of Korean Christian Scholars in North America. (See articles by Sunoo, Kim, and Strawn, Kim, Lee and Ogle.)

Kim, Gertrude
1979   Voluntary associations among Koreans in Chicago. Paper presented at the Annual Meeting, Asian American Sociological Association, Boston, August 28.

Kim, Hei Chu; Hurh, Won Moo; and Kim, Kwang Chung
1978   Ethnic roles of the Korean church in the Chicago area. Paper presented at the Annual Meeting, Society for the Scientific Study of Religion, Hartford, Connecticut, October 27–29.

Kim, Hyun-Tae
1966   Relationship between personal characteristics of Korean students in Pennsylvania and their attitude toward Christian church in America. Ph. D. dissertation, University of Pittsburgh.

Kim, Hyung-chan
1971   Korean emigrants to the U. S. A., 1959–1969. *Korea Journal* 11:16–24,31.

1974   Some aspects of social demography of Korean Americans. *International Migration Review* 8:23–42.

1976   Ethnic enterprises among Korean emigrants in America. *Journal of Korean Affairs* 6:40–58.
1977   Korean community organizations in America: Their characteristics and problems. Pp. 65-83 in Hyung-chan Kim, ed., *The Korean Diaspora*. Santa Barbara, Calif.: ABC-Clio.
1980   Koreans. Pp. 601–6 in S. Thernstrom, ed., Harvard Encyclopedia of American Ethnic Groups. Cambridge, Mass.: Harvard University Press.

Kim, Hyung-chan, ed.
1977a   *East Across the Pacific: Historical and Sociological Studies of Korean Immigration and Assimilation*. Santa Barbara, Calif.: ABC-Clio.
1977b   *The Korean Diaspora*. Santa Barbara, Calif.: ABC-Clio.

Kim, Hyung-chan, and Patterson, Wayne
1974   The Koreans in America in 1882–1974: *A Chronology of Fact Book*. Dobbs Ferry, N. Y.: Oceana Publications.

Kim, Ilsoo
1981   *New Urban Immigrants: The Korean Community in New York*. Princeton, N. J.: Princeton University Press.

Kim, Jin Keon
1978   Communication factors in acculturation. Ph. D. dissertation, University of Iowa.

Kim, Kenneth; Lee, Kapson; and Kim, Tai-Yul
1981   *Korean-Americans in Los Angeles: Their Concerns and Language Maintenance*. Los Angeles: National Center for Bilingual Research.

Kim, Kwang Chung
1978   Intra-and inter-ethnic group conflicts: The case of Korean small business in the United States. Pp. 201–32 in H. H. Sunoo and D. S. Kim, eds., *Korean Women in a Struggle for Humanization*. Memphis, Tenn.: Association for Korean Christian Scholars in North America.

Kim, Kwang Chung, and Hurh, Woo Moo
1979   Occupational experience of Korean immigrants in the Los Angeles area. Paper presented at the Annual Meeting, Illinois Sociological Association, Springfield, Illinois, October 26–27.
1980a   Ethnic confinement and job satisfaction: A case of Korean immigrants in the Los Angeles area. Paper presented at the Annual Meeting, Midwest Sociological Society, Milwaukee, Wisconsin, April 2–5.
1980b   Occupational career of Asian immigrants: A case study of Korean immigrants in the Los Angeles area. Paper read at the Annual Meeting, North Central Sociological Association, Dayton, Ohio, May 1–3.
1980c   Social and occupational assimilation of Korean immigrants in the United States. *California Sociologist* 3:125–42.
1980d   Employment role and division of household tasks in Korean immigrant families. Paper presented at the Annual Meeting, National Council on Family Relations, Portland, Oregon, October 22–25.

1980e   Interpersonal networks and job information acquisition: The case of Korean immigrants in the Los Angeles area. Paper presented at the 4th National Conference on the Third World, Omaha, Nebraska, October 22-25.
1981a   Labor force participation of Korean immigrant wives. Paper presented at the Annual Meeting, National Council on Family Relations. Milwaukee, Wisconsin, October 13-17.
1981b   Ethnicity of the major work colleagues and customers of Korean immigrant workers in the Los Angeles area. Paper presented at the Annual Meeting, Illinois Sociological Association. Chicago, Illinois, October 23-24.

Kim, Kwang Chung; Kim, Hei Chu; and Hurh, Won Moo
1978   Life of Korean Christians in the Chicago area: Their church, job and home. Paper presented at the Annual Meeting, Korean Ministerial Association of Chicago, Chicago, April 1.
1979   Division of household tasks in Korean immigrant families in the United States. *International Journal of Sociology of the Family* 9:161-75.
1981   Job information deprivation in the United States: A case study of Korean immigrants. *Ethnicity* 8:219-32.

Kim, Peter
1980   Behavior symptoms of three transracially adopted Asian children: Diagnosis dilemma. *Child Welfare* 59:213-24.

Kim, Sangho J.
1975   *A Study of a Korean Church and Her People in Chicago, Illinois*. San Francisco: R and E Research Associates.

Kim, Sang-mo
1979   A process of Growth in Christian experience: Through small group sharing and searching: For constituent members in a Korean-American congregation. D. Min. dissertation, Drew University.

Kim, Sil Dong
1975   Findings of national inquiries on Asian women of U. S. servicemen: Post consultation report. Paper presented at the Methodist conference. Tacoma, Washington: March 20-21. See also Sil Dong Kim's Ph. D. dissertation, University of Washington, 1979.
1979   Interracially married Korean Women immigrants: A study in marginality. Ph. D. dissertation, University of Washington.

Kim, Won Yong (Warren)
1959   *Chaemi Hanin Osimnyonsa* (A Fifty-Year History of the Koreans in the United States). Reedly, Calif.: Charles Ho Kim.
1971   *Koreans in America* (English translation of the above). Seoul: Po Chin Chai.

Kim, Yong Tae
1976   *Komerican ui natkwa bam* (Day and Night of "The Komerican"). Seoul: Hanjin Choolpansa.

Kim, Yong Yun
1976   Communication patterns of foreign immigrants in the process

of acculturation: A survey among the Korean population in Chicago. Ph. D. dissertation, Northwestern University, Evanston, Illinois.

1977   Inter-ethnic and intra-ethnic communication: A study of Korean immigrants in Chicago. in N. C. Jain ed., *International and Intercultural Communication Annual*. Falls Church, Virginia: Speech Communication Association.

Koh, Kwang-lim, and Koh, Hesung C., eds.
1974   Koreans and Korean-Americans in the United States: A Summary of Three Conference Proceedings. New Haven, Conn.: East Rock Press.

Koo, Hagen, and Yu, Eui-Yiung
1981   *Korean Immigration to the United States: Demographic Pattern and Social Implication for Both Societies*. Papers of the East-West Center Population Institute (No. 74). Honolulu: East-West Center.

Kwon, Peter
1972   Report on the needs of Korean Community and churches in the United States. Paper presented at Asian American Presbyterian Caucus in Southern California, July 27.

Lee, Changsoo, and Wagatsuma, Hiroshi
1979   The settlement patterns of Koreans in Los Angeles: A demographic survey. Paper presented at the 31st Annual Meeting, Association for Asian Studies, Los Angeles, March 30–April 1.

Lee, Chang Soon
1975   The U. S. immigration policy and the settlement of Koreans in America. *Korean Observer* 4:412-51.
1979   *Growth Ministry in Korean Immigrant Churches*. Los Angeles: The New Korea Printing Co. (D. Min. dissertation, School of Theology at Claremont, California.)

Lee, David Y.
1974   Organization activities of Korean community. Master's thesis, University of California at Los Angeles.

Lee, Dong Chang
1975   *Acculturation of Korean residents in Georgia*. San Francisco: R and E Research Associates.
1977a   Korean families in America. *Migration Today* 5:13-15.
1977b   A study of social networks within two Korean communities in America. Pp. 135-54 in Hyung-chan Kim, ed., *The Korean Diaspora*. Santa Barbara, Calif.: ABC-Clio Press.

Lee, Hwa Soo
1979   A study of Korean American voluntary organizations in Los Angeles: Structure, function, and leadership. Paper presented at a meeting, Koryo Research Institute, Los Angeles, March 10.

Lee, Kyung
1969   Settlement patterns of Los Angeles Koreans. Master's thesis, University of California, Los Angeles.

Lee, Ok Ro
1977   Early bilingual reading us an aid to bilingual and bicultural adjustment for a second generation Korean child in the U. S. Ph. D. dissertation, Georgetown University.

Lee, Sang Hyun
1980   Called to be pilgrim: Toward a theology within a Korean immigrant context. Pp. 37–74 in Byong-suh Kim and Sang Hyun Lee, eds., *The Korean Immigrant in America*. Montclair, N. J.: The Association of Korean Christian Scholars in North America.

Leon, Joseph
1975   Sex-ethnic marriage in Hawaii: A nonmetric multidimensional analysis. *Journal of Marriage and the Family* 37:775–81. (See Korean intermarriages.)

Luhmann, Hi Chung
1979   The correlation of the frequency of social interaction and level of life satisfaction among older Korean immigrants. Paper presented at the 13th Annual Meeting, Association of Korean Christian Scholars in North America, Boston, May 31–June 2, 1979.

Lyu, Kingsley K.
1977   Korean nationalist activities in Hawaii and the continental United States, 1900–1945, Part I: 1900–1919. *Amerasia Journal* 4:23–90. (No. 1).
1977   Korean nationalist activities in Hawaii and the continential United States, 1900–1945. Part II: 1919–1945. *Amerasia Journal* 4:53–100. (No. 2).

Melendy, H. Brett
1977   *Asians in America: Filipinos, Koreans, and East Indians*. Botson: G. K. Hall.

Moon, Hyung June
1976   The Korean immigrants in America: The quest for identity in the formative years, 1903–1918. Ph. D. dissertation, University of Nevada, Reno.

Nandi, Proshanta K.
1980   *The Quality of Life of Asian Americans: An Exploratory Study in a Middle-Size Community*. Chicago: Pacific/Asian American Mental Health Research Center. (See study results on a Korean sample.)

Noh, Chae-Yon
1951   *Chaemi Hanin Saryak (A Short History of Koreans in America)*. Los Angeles: American Publishing Co.

Park, Jang Kyun
1979   A study of the growth of the Korean church in Southern California. D. Min. dissertation, School of Theology at Claremont.

Park, Jong Sam
1975   A three generational study: Traditional Korean value systems and psychological adjustment of Korean immigrants in Los

Angeles. DSW dissertation, University of Southern California, Los Angeles.

Park, Peter
1978 Needs Assessment of the Korean Community in Massachusetts. Chicago: Asian American Mental Health Research Center SIR Research Report no. 4.
1979 Methodological critique on ethnic research. Paper presented at a meeting, Koryo Research Institute, Los Angeles, March 10.

Park, Philip Kyung Sik
1977 Koreans in North America. *Bridge: An Asian American Perspective* 5:13–17.

Park, Siyoung
1980 Residential mobility of Koreans in Chicago. Paper presented at the Annual Meeting of Association of American Geographers. Louisville, Kentucky, April 13–16.

Parkman, Margaret, and Sawyer, Jack
1967 Dimensions of ethnic intermarriage in Hawaii. (See Korean intermarriage.) *American Sociological Review* 32:593–606.

Patterson, Wayne
1976 *The Koreans in North America*. Philadelphia: The Balch Institute. (A bibliography).
1977 The first attempt to obtain laborers for Hawaii, 1896–1897. Pp. 9–31 in Hyung-chan Kim, ed., *The Korean Diaspora*. Santa Barbara, Calif.: ABC-Clio Press.
1979a A profile of early Korean immigrants to America. Paper presented at the 31st Annual Meeting, Association for Asian Studies, Los Angeles, March 30–April 1.
1979b Sugar-coated diplomacy: Horace Allen and Korean immigration to Hawaii, 1902–1906. *Diplomatic History* 3:29–38.

Ryu, Jai P.
1977 The mass media and the assimilation process: A study of media use by Korean immigrants. Ph. D. dissertation, University of Oregon.

Ryu, Jung Shig
1977 The mass media and the assimilation process: A study of media use by Korean immigrants. Ph. D. dissertation University of Oregon.

Shim, Steve
1977 *Korean Immigrant Churches Today in Southern California. San Francisco*: R and E Research Associates.

Shin-Kim, Hyunsoon
1980 Bilingual/bicultural education and the development of self-concept for Korean immigrant children. Pp. 99–146 in Byongsuh Kim and Sang Hyun Lee, eds., *The Korean Immigrant in America*. Montclair, N. J.: The Association of Korean Christian Scholars in North America.

Shin, Linda
1971 Koreans in America, 19-3-1945. Pp. 201–206 in A. Tachiki et

al., eds., *Roots: An Asian American Reader.* Los Angeles: The Regents of the University of California.

Shin, Tae Kyu
1979   The elderly Korean immigrants in New York City. Paper presented at the 13th Annual Meeting, Association of Korean Christian Scholars in North America, Boston, May 31–June 2.

So, Kwang-Woon
1973   Miju Hanin Chilsipnyun-Sa *(A Seventy-Year History of Koreans in America).* Seoul: Haewai Kyopo Munjae Yonku-sa.

Song, John D.
1979   Educational problems of Korean students. Paper presented at a meeting, Koryo Research Institute, Los Angeles, March 10.

Song, Seok Choong
1977   Bilingualism and immigrant children. *The Korean Christian Journal* 2 (Spring): 126–41.

Sunoo, Hakwon, ed.
1980   Koreans in America. *The Korean Christian Journal* No. 2. Memphis Tenn.: Association of the Korean Christian Scholars in North America.

Sunoo, Hakwon, and Kim, Dong Soo, eds.
1980   *Korean Women in a Struggle for Humanization.* Memphis, Tenn.: Association of Korean Christian Scholars in North America, Inc.

Sunoo, Harold Hakwon, and Sunoo, Sonia Shin
1977   The heritage of the first Korean women immigrants in the United States, 1903–1924. *The Korean Christian Journal* No. 2 (Spring): 142–71.

Sunoo, Sonia
1978   Koran women pioneers of the Pacific Northwest. *Oregon Historical Quarterly* 79:51–64.

Trebilcock, Dorothy W.
1973   The individual social and cultural implications of the cross-cultural marriage: Korean wives and their American husbands in Michigan. Master's thesis, Michigan State University.

U. S. Department of Health, Education and Welfare
1977   Asian American Field Survey: Summary of Data. (See the Korean sample.) Washington, D. C.: U. S. Government Printing Office.

Whang, Minsum Sung
1976   An exploratory descriptive study of inter-country adoption of Korean children with Korean parents. Master's thesis, University of Hawaii.

Won, Woo-Hyun
1977   Values and mass media preferences of Korean immigrants Ph. D. dissertation, Boston University.

Yang, Eun Sik
1979   Korean community, 19-3-1970s: Identity versus economic

prosperity. Paper presented at a meeting, Koryo Research Institute, Los Angeles, March 10.

Yang, Eun Sik et al., eds.
1979 Mikukanui Hanin Community. *(The Korean Community in the United States).* Los Angeles: The Association for Korean Studies–Korean Pioneer Press.

Yim, Sun Bin
1974 Mate selection and Marriage as perceived by native Americans and immigrant Koreans. Master's thesis, University of California, Santa Barbara.
1978 Korean battered wives: A sociological and psychological analysis of conjugal violence in Korean immigrant families. Pp. 171–99 in H. H. Sunoo and D. S. Kim, eds., *Korean Women*. Memphis, Tenn.: Association of Korean Christian Scholars in North America.

(Yoo, Jay Kun)
1979 *The Koreans in Seattle*. Elkins Park, Penn.: Philip Jaisohn Foundation.

Yu, Chae-kun
1977a Personality adjustment of Korean children in the United States. Pp. 177–190 in Hyung-chan Kim, ed., *The Korean Diaspora*. Santa Barbara, Calif.: ABC-Clio Press.
1977b The correlates of cultural assimilation of Korean immigrants in the United States. Pp. 167–76 in Hyung-chan Kim, ed., *The Korean Diaspora*. Santa Barbara, Calif.: ABC-Clio Press.

Yu, Eui-Young
1977 Koreans in America: An emerging ethnic minority. *Amerasia Journal* 4:117–31.
1979a Demographic profile of Koreans in Los Angeles: Size, composition and distribution. Paper presented at a meeting, Koryo Research Institute, Los Angeles, March 10.
1979b Occupational and work patterns of Korean immigrants in Los Angeles. Paper presented at a meeting, Koryo Research Institute, Los Angeles, March 10.
1979c Korean bilingual education in sociological perspective. Paper presented at the Conference on Korean Bilingual Teacher Training in the United States at Seton Hall University, South Orange, New Jersey, April 20–21.
1980 Koreans in America: Social and economic adjustment. Pp. 75–98 in Byong-suh Kim and Sang Hyun Lee, eds., *The Korean Immigrant in America*. Montclair, N. J.: The Association of Korean Christian Scholars in North America.
1981 Koreans in America: struggling for cultural adjustments. *Korean Culture* 1:18–23.
Koreantown, Los Angeles. *Korean Culture* 1:24.

Yu, Eui-Young; Phillips, Earl H.; and Yang, Eun Sik, eds.
1982 *Koreans in Los Angeles: Prospects and Promises*. Los Angeles, Calif.: Center for Korean-American and Korean Studies, California State University, Los Angeles.

Yu, Jin H.
1980   *The Korean Merchants in the Black Community*. Elkins Park, Penn.: Philip Jaisohn Foundation.

Yun, H.
1976   The Korean personality and treatment considerations. *Social Casework* 57:173–78.

Yun, Yo-chun
1977   Early history of Korean immigration to America. Pp. 33–46 in Hyung-chan Kim, ed., *The Korean Diaspora*. Santa Barbara, Calif.: ABC-Clio Press.

Name Index

Abrams, Franklin, 60
Adams, Bert N., 88
Adams, J. S., 120
Adams, Romanzo, 43, 46, 47, 134
Andrews, F., 144, 148, 155

Babchuk, Nicholas, 95, 100
Bach, Robert L., 117
Backman, Elaine, 122, 123
Barnett, Milton L., 88
Becker, Tamar, 139
Belintosky, A. Harvey, 104
Berry, Brewton, 40, 41, 75
Blau, Francine, 101, 117
Blood, T. O., 186
Bogardus, Emory S., 22, 26, 86, 167, 168, 188
Bonacich, Edna, 66, 102, 116, 117, 168
Bowman, Mary Jean, 101
Brown, David G., 104
Bruce, J. M., 88
Brunnner, G. A., 191
Burgess, Ernest, 25

Campbell, A., 138, 139, 148, 153, 155
Caroll, S. J., 191
Cha, Marn J., 139, 142
Chakerian, Charles G., 50
Choy, Bong-youn, 39, 41, 42, 43, 44, 45, 46, 48, 49, 134
Cohen, Yehdi A., 35
Converse, P. E., 138, 139, 148, 153, 155
Cook, S. W., 193
Crabbe, B. D., 87
Crain, Robert L., 104, 118
Cutler, Stephen J., 87

D'Andrade, R. G., 185
de Ruijter, A., 186
Deutsch, M., 193
Dibona, Pamela, 122, 123

Doeringer, Peter, 25, 102, 103, 199
Dohrenwend, Bruce, 85
Durkheim, E., 87

Edwards, John N., 95
Eisenstadt, S. N., 25, 29, 35, 74, 138, 148, 178
Ericksen, Eugene P., 25
Ericksen, Julia A., 25
Everitt, John C., 62

Festinger, L., 177
Form, William H., 110, 147
Francis, E. K., 133
Frazier, E. Franklin, 186
Freedman, Jonathan L., 148
Freedman, Marcia, 102, 103, 117, 118

Gallup, George H., 137
Gardner, Arthur L., 47
Geschwender, James H., 110, 147
Gillin, John, 74
Glazer, Nathan, 25, 85, 86, 139
Goldscheider, Calvin, 169
Goldstein, Sidney, 169
Goode, William J., 184
Gorden, Raymond L., 75, 175, 189, 191, 192, 193, 194, 196
Gordon, Milton M., 25, 73, 74, 85, 89
Granovetter, Mark S., 104
Greeley, Andrew M., 25, 89, 133
Greenstone, J. David, 35, 78

Hansen, Marcus L., 168
Harris, Keith D., 67
Harris, Marvin, 29
Hatt, Paul K., 184
Hays, William C., 88
Hendrix, Lewelly, 88
Herberg, Will, 144, 136
Homans, George C., 87, 120

Name Index

Honigmann, John J., 35
Hosokawa, Bill, 168
Hsu, Francis L. K., 186
Hu, Hsien Chin, 194
Hunter, David E., 185
Hurh, Won Moo, 22, 23, 25, 26, 30, 56, 75, 76, 89, 97, 129, 131, 139, 144, 155, 160, 167, 168, 175, 184, 188, 197
Hyman, H., 139, 143, 147

Jahoda, Marie, 193
Jo, Yung-Hwan, 22
Johnson, Alvin, 89
Juliani, Richard N., 25
Jung, Tae Hwan, 117
Jusenius, Carol L., 101

Kallen, Horace B., 86, 167
Kang, T. S., 77
Katz, D., 177
Keely, Charles B., 52, 54, 60
Kelly, Harold, H., 120
Kerr, Clark, 102
Kim, Bernice Bong Hee, 41, 42
Kim, Bok-Lim, 25, 50, 57, 129, 137, 169
Kim, David S., 66
Kim, Dong Soo, 51
Kim, Hae-Jong, 134, 135
Kim, Hei Chu, 23, 26, 30, 56, 75, 129, 144, 184, 197
Kim, Hyung-chan, 40, 41, 44, 45
Kim, Kwang Chung, 23, 26, 30, 56, 75, 76, 89, 97, 129, 131, 144, 160, 175, 184, 197
Kim, Sil Dong, 50
Kim, Won Yong (Warren), 39, 40, 43, 45, 47, 48, 49, 134
Kish, Leslie, 32, 199
Kitano, Harry L., 25, 28, 168
Kitt, Alice S., 147
Kramer, Judith R. 74, 85
Kurokawa, Minako, 27

Lawler, Edwin D., 120
Lee, Changsoo, 35, 60
Lee, Sang Hyun, 134
Light, Ivan, 66, 168
Lind, Andrew W., 46
Lininger, Charles A., 185
Litwak, Eugene, 94
Lyman, Stanford M., 15–17, 23, 25, 41, 60, 168
Lyu, Kingsley K., 45, 48

McKennel, A. C., 144
Merton, Robert K., 25, 29, 30, 147, 177, 181, 182, 186, 200
Miller, Delbert C., 110
Mincer, Jacob, 101
Mindel, Charles H.. 88
Moynihan, Daniel P., 25, 85, 86

Nahm, In Sook, 22
Naroll, Raoul, 185
Nelson, B. H., 25, 74
Newman, William M., 25, 86, 167

Osherson, S., 185

Packard, Vance, 197
Park, Robert E., 25, 27
Park, Siyoung, 61–71, 65
Parsons, Talcott, 87
Patterson, Wayne, 40, 41, 42, 44, 45, 46, 52
Petersen, William, 25, 60, 168
Pike, Kenneth L., 185
Piore, Michael J., 25, 102, 103, 199
Popper, Karl R., 200
Portes, Alejandro, 117

Raimy, Victor, 74
Rees, Albert, 104
Reid, Graham L., 104
Rodgers, W. L., 138, 139, 148, 153, 155
Romney, A. K., 185
Rosenthal, Erich, 25
Rosow, Irving, 89, 94
Ryu, Jai P., 50

Schaefer, Richard T., 75
Schmitt, Raymond L., 143, 146
Schultz, T. W., 101
Schütz, Alfred, 133
Sears, Robert R., 184
Seligman, Edwin R. A., 89
Selitz, Claire, 193
Sheppard, Harold, 104
Sherman, Diana, 65
Shibutani, Tomatsu, 146, 148
Simpson, George E., 26, 41
Singer, E., 139, 143, 147
Siu, Paul C. P., 48
Sklare, Marschall, 89, 133, 136
Smith, Robert J., 85
Spiro, Melford E., 25

Name Index

Srole, Leo, 74
Stafford, Rebecca, 122, 123
Stermole, David F., 62
Stone, Richard L., 185
Sturtevant, William C., 185
Sunoo, Harold Hakwon, 45
Sunoo, Sonia Shin, 45
Sussman, Marvin B., 88
Sutcliffe, J. P., 87
Szelenyi, Ivan, 94

Teske, R. H. C., 25, 74
Thibaut, John W., 120
Thompson, Ralph V., 95
Thurnwald, Richard, 74
Thurow, Lester, 101
Tischler, Henry L., 40, 41, 75
Toennies, Ferdinand, 87
Toffler, Alvin, 197
Trebilcock, Dorothy W., 50
Turner, R. H., 146, 148
Tylor, Edward B., 35

Ullman, Joseph C., 104

Vander Zanden, James W., 75

Vermeulen, C. J., 186

Wagatsuma, Hiroshi, 35
Wagley, Charles, 29
Warner, W. Lloyd, 74
Warwick, Donald P., 185
Weber, Max, 200
Weinstock, S. Alexander, 26, 74
Whitten, Philip, 119
Williams, Margaret A., 146, 148
Winch, Robert F., 88
Winick, Charles, 35
Wirth, Louis, 87
Withey, S., 144, 148, 155
Wolfe, W., 186
Wong, Charles C., 66, 169

Yancey, William L., 25
Yinger, Milton J., 26, 41
Yu, Elena, 185
Yu, Eui-Yong, 21, 35, 40, 43, 54, 55, 60, 63, 198, 199
Yuan, D. Y., 27
Yun, Yo-chun, 40, 41

Znaniecki, Florian, 182

Subject Index

Acculturation (cultural assimilation): conceptual problems of, 74; "controlled," 74; of Korean immigrants, 73-86; and social assimilation, 25-27, 73; and structural variables, 83-86
Adaptation: definition of, 35 n.4; modes of, 27; "successful," 138; variables of, 29
Adhesion, 15, 35 n.5
Adhesive adaptation: and cognitive ambivalence, 166-67; cultural, 85-96; definition of, 35 n.5; as a general theory, 162; of Korean immigrants, 27; practical implications of, 167-69; in residential mobility, 68; social, 99; structural roots of, 161-69; theoretical propositions on, 171-72
Anglo-conformity, 27

Chinese immigrants. See East Asian immigrants in U. S.

Division of household tasks, 124-27

East Asian immigrants in U. S., 53-54
Ethnic attachment: definition of, 35 n.3; and detachment, 27; variables related to, 78-79
Ethnic confinement, 26, 86-100, 120

Family relations, 122-28
Filipino immigrants. See East Asian immigrants in U. S.

"Hermit Kingdom," 15, 39
Human capital theory, 101-5

Intermarriage: attitudes toward, 79-80; of Koreans in Hawaii, 47; between Korean women and American servicemen, 49
Interview: difficulties, 189-97; refusal rates, 191-92; schedule, 32, 186-87, 201-8
Interviewers: age and sex of, 195; comments from, 175-83

Japanese immigrants. See East Asian immigrants in U. S.
Job information transmission, 107-9

"Kim sample technique," 198-99
Korean-American Treaty, 22, 39
Korean Buddhists in Los Angeles, 65, 129
Korean Directory of Southern California, The, 31-33, 35 n.7, 61, 199
Korean ethnic church: attendance at, 96, 130; functions of, 133-37; geographic distribution of, 64-65; motives for attending, 130-32; number of, 129
Korean immigrants: early (1903-05), 21-22, 39-49; in Hawaii, 46-48; interim (1951-64), 49-52; in Mexico, 40; new (1965-), demographic characteristics of, 21, 53-60; recent empirical studies on, 23
Korean immigrants in Los Angeles: acculturation of, 73-86; adaptation problems of, 160-61; demographic characteristics of, 56-58; employment segregation of, 116-21; family role adjustment of, 122-28; job information acquisition of, 107-9; job satisfaction of, 113-16; length of residence of, 57-58; life satisfaction of, 138-55; occupational category of, 121 n.1; occupational mobility of,

277

105–7; religious participation of, 129–37; residential mobility of, 61–71; social assimilation of, 87–100; socioeconomic characteristics of, 58–59; suburbanization of, 64; work conditions of, 110–13
Korean immigrant small business: extent of, 106; geographic distribution of, 65–67; types of, 121; work conditions of, 110–13, 116
Korean students in U. S., 48–49, 51–52
"Korean-war brides," 49–50
Korean-war orphans, 50–51
Koreatown, 21, 62–63

Labor market segmentation theory, 101–5
Length of residence in U. S.: and acculturation, 83–85; of Koreans in Los Angeles, 57–58; and life satisfaction, 139–42, 144–48; and religious participation, 132; and small business, 105–6; and social assimilation, 92–93
Life satisfaction: adhesive reference group and, 148–49; of Koreans in Los Angeles, 138–55; reference group shifting and, 146; scale of, 144; social marginality and, 142; variables related to, 149–52

Methodological problems in cross-cultural study, 184–200

Occupational assimilation, 101–21. *See also under* Korean immigrants in Los Angeles

"Picture brides," 41, 42–43
Pluralism: "accommodative," 27; ethnic, 85, 86 n.3, 167; ideal type of, 27, 167; "limited," 162
Psychological adaptation, a hypothetical model of, 139–42

Race factor, 26, 168
Religious participation, 129–37
Return migration, attitude toward, 80

Sampling in Los Angeles and Chicago, 30–31, 197–99; problems of, 35 n.7
Second-generation Koreans, 168
Segregation: ethnic 27, 87–100; occupational, 116; social (structural), 26; voluntary and involuntary, 27; workplace, 116
Separatism. *See* Segregation
Sex ratio: of early Chinese and Japanese immigrants, 60; of early Korean immigrants, 42–43, 60; of interim Korean immigrants, 151; of new Korean immigrants, 155–56
Social distance, 26, 168
Socialization-ideology, 124, 128
Social (structural) assimilation: and acculturation, 25–27, 73, 88–89; of Korean immigrants in Los Angeles, 87–100; perception of, 97–98
Split or dual labor market theory, 102–5

Time-availability hypothesis, 123, 128

U. S. immigration law: of 1924, 40; of 1965, 21, 53, 59–60 n.1, 60 n.2

Voluntary association: definition of, 89; Korean immigrants' participation in, 89–90, 96–97

Zero-sum model of assimilation, 27